Handbook
of
Major Appliance
Troubleshooting
and Repair

Handbook
of
Major Appliance
Troubleshooting
and Repair

David L. Heiserman

PRENTICE-HALL, INC., Englewood Cliffs, New Jersey

Library of Congress Cataloging in Publication Data

HEISERMAN, DAVID L (date)
    Handbook of major appliance troubleshooting
and repair.

    Includes index.
    1.–Household appliances, Electric—Maintenance
and repair.   I.–Title.
TK7018.H42   683'.83'028   76–10684
ISBN   0–13–380295–7

Printed in the United States of America
10 9 8 7 6 5 4 3 2 1

PRENTICE-HALL INTERNATIONAL, INC., *London*
PRENTICE-HALL OF AUSTRALIA PTY. LIMITED, *Sydney*
PRENTICE-HALL OF CANADA, LTD., *Toronto*
PRENTICE-HALL OF INDIA PRIVATE LIMITED, *New Delhi*
PRENTICE-HALL OF JAPAN, INC., *Tokyo*
PRENTICE-HALL OF SOUTHEAST ASIA PTE. LTD., *Singapore*

1933662

Contents

3   Principles of Electric Heating   *33*

4   Thermostats and Electric Heat Controls   *49*

5   Electric Motors and Motor Controls   *73*

6   Principles of Refrigeration   *90*

7   Garbage Disposers   *103*

8   Trash Compactors   *113*

Preface

The narrow profit margin in today's appliance servicing industry has created a great demand for appliance servicemen who can adequately deal with nonroutine, "tough-dog" troubles in any appliance, regardless of its make and model. A single tough-dog trouble that is not handled properly can wipe out the profit from several days' routine work.

Of course there is no substitute for training and experience in the appliance servicing trade, but the key to real success is a well-founded troubleshooting technique that goes beyond the troubleshooting charts normally found in service bulletins and books on appliance repair.

The main purpose of this book is to give the reader a positive approach toward troubleshooting any kind of electrrical trouble in any kind of major electrical appliance. It is not easy to live up to this purpose because the basic principles of troubleshooting—truly effective troubleshooting—cannot be spelled out in a few words or even in a few pages of words. This entire book is about troubleshooting, and although it is organized according to certain electrical principles and specific kinds of major electrical appliances, a sound troubelshooting technique gradually emerges one step at a time from the first page to the last.

The first six chapters deal with general principles of troubleshooting, and electrical heating and cooling as they apply to modern major appliances. The procedure in almost every instance is to present the theory of a circuit followed immediately by some appropriate troubleshooting hints.

Chapters 7 through 14 deal with specific electrical major appliances. It is important to understand from the outset that very few of the circuit diagrams and related information apply to any one particular appliance on the market today. The diagrams are actually composites of several makes and models, each one emphasizing one or two important features.

This book cannot possibly take the place of a complete and up-to-date file of manufacturers' service bulletins. Anyone working in the appliance industry, however, will find this book to be a valuable addition to a file of service bulletins because it pulls together theories and procedures that are otherwise hopelessly scattered.

DAVID L. HEISERMAN

Columbus, Ohio

Handbook
of
Major Appliance
Troubleshooting
and Repair

1

Standard Electrical
Test Equipment

As most major appliance service work is carried out in customers' homes, a serviceman is forced to tote around whatever test instruments he might need. Unfortunately, it is impossible to know exactly what instruments are needed until coming face to face with the troubled appliance, and that means carefully selecting a few essential test instruments that are highly portable, reliable, rugged, and useful under many different troubleshooting and servicing situations.

This chapter describes popular test instruments that are suitable for servicing and troubleshooting the electrical portions of any major appliance. Some of the instruments are simple and inexpensive; others are more elaborate and costly. In the long run, it is up to the serviceman to select the test equipment that best suits his own good working habits and conditions.

1-1 CONTINUITY TESTERS

Most electrical troubles in major appliances are caused, in one way or another, by an unwanted open- or short-circuit condition. An open circuit

1

is one that totally lacks electrical continuity, and a short circuit is one that displays the characteristics of good circuit continuity.

It is possible to pinpoint most open- and short-circuit faults by running the proper kinds of continuity tests. Ideally, a continuity tester is any kind of device that responds in some very definite way to a circuit having good electrical continuity and in an entirely different way to a circuit that lacks continuity. Continuity test equipment used in the appliance servicing industry is not quite ideal, but it does the job rather well in the hands of a knowledgeable troubleshooter.

The basic idea behind a continuity tester is to apply a voltage to a circuit from an outside source and somehow monitor the current flow, if any, that results. A circuit that has good electrical continuity responds to the outside power source by carrying some electrical current that can turn on a lamp. A circuit having no electrical continuity cannot conduct current from the external voltage source, and the lamp or meter movement does not register any change from its normal "resting" condition.

It is important to note that a continuity tester contains its own power source, such as a battery, which provides the test voltage and current. And because continuity testers supply their own test currents, electrical power supplied by any other sources are bound to upset the continuity test results and, perhaps, seriously damage the test equipment. This fact leads to the most rigid rule for using any kind of continuity tester: *All continuity tests must be performed on circuits that are completely shut down* and, preferably, unplugged from their power source as well.

1-1.1   A Simple Lamp-Type Continuity Tester

Figure 1-1 shows a common lamp-type tester and its electrical schematic. The tester uses a pair of 1.5 V batteries connected in series to produce a total output of about 3 V. A 2.7 V flashlight lamp is connected in series with the battery supply and a pair of test probes. Whenever the test probes are touched together or applied directly to a circuit having almost zero resistance, the lamp burns brightly. The lamp glows brightly under these conditions because the low resistance between the test probes completes a series path for current flow between the battery terminals. Separating the tips of the test probes or connecting them to an open circuit breaks open the path for current flow, and the lamp cannot light.

The lamp in this type of continuity tester thus lights up to full brilliance whenever it is applied to a circuit having zero resistance or a short circuit. The lamp does not go on whenever the probes are applied to an open circuit or one having very high resistance.

The only real disadvantage of a simple lamp-type tester is that it cannot reliably distinguish an open circuit from a circuit that normally has high

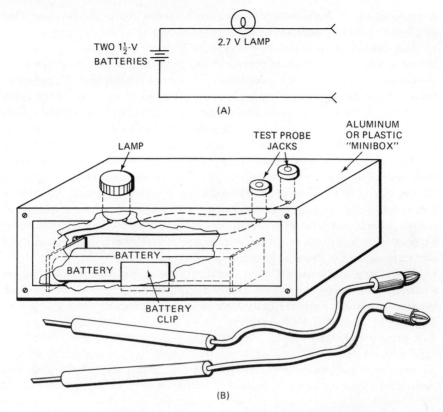

TWO 1½-V
BATTERIES

2.7 V LAMP

(A)

LAMP

TEST PROBE
JACKS

ALUMINUM
OR PLASTIC
"MINIBOX"

BATTERY

BATTERY

BATTERY
CLIP

(B)

Fig. 1-1 A simple lamp-type continuity tester. (A) Schematic diagram, (B) Pictorial drawing.

electrical resistance to current flow. A complete, but high-resistance, circuit
limits the amount of current that can flow through the lamp. The lamp thus
burns very dimly or not at all, giving the unwary troubleshooter the impression that he has found an open circuit condition.

Suppose a serviceman wants to check the continuity of the coil in a solenoid valve. Such coils can have a relatively high electrical resistance under
normal conditions, and a lamp-type tester applied to the two ends of the coil
normally shows no response. That is, the lamp glows with very little light or
does not go on at all. A troubleshooter not fully acquainted with the limitations of lamp-type continuity testers might interpret this result as an indication that the solenoid coil is open.

Lamp-type testers are most reliable and useful for testing the continuity
of switches, connectors, and wiring—circuit elements that can only be
completely open or completely shorted. Testing the continuity between the
two ends of a long section of wire, for instance, should make the lamp burn at

full brightness. If the wire is broken open, however, the lamp does not light at all, and the troubleshooter can be quite certain that he has uncovered an open circuit trouble.

Of course the batteries in this kind of continuity tester run down after prolonged use, so that it is a good idea to check the condition of the batteries before beginning a set of continuity tests. To check the batteries, touch together the test probes. The batteries are in good order if the lamp burns brightly. If the lamp does not burn brightly, it is time to replace the batteries. A prudent serviceman, by the way, always carries a spare set of fresh batteries so that he is never caught with a "dead" continuity tester while on the road.

Lamp-type testers can be purchased ready-made from appliance parts dealers. These devices are not very expensive, and it is normally cheaper to buy one than it is to build it from all new parts. Of course the least expensive lamp-type continuity tester is one assembled in the shop from spare parts.

Several other types of simple continuity testers appear in the author's book, *Handbook of Small Appliance Troubleshooting and Repair*, (Englewood Cliffs, N.J.: Prentice-Hall, Inc., 1974). Other simple continuity testers generally lack the portability of the 3 V lamp tester described here, and are thus more suitable for bench-top work on small appliances.

1-1.2   Ohmmeter Testers

For just about every shortcoming inherent in one kind of test instrument, there is another available to make up for it. In this instance, it turns out that an ohmmeter makes up for the limitations of lamp-type continuity testers described in the previous section.

An ohmmeter, like a simple lamp-type tester, supplies a small test voltage to the circuit being checked out. Instead of counting on the test current to turn on a lamp, however, an ohmmeter actually meters the amount of test current that flows.

Figure 1-2 shows an ohmmeter and a schematic diagram to illustrate its principle of operation. The 1.5 V battery built into the ohmmeter unit supplies the continuity test voltage, and whenever the test leads are shorted together (or placed across a circuit having zero resistance) they complete a path for current flow through the meter movement.

The meter movement in an ohmmeter is actually an ammeter-type movement—a sensitive meter designed to respond to current flowing through it. The circuit is designed and calibrated so that this meter movement shows a full-scale deflection whenever the meter leads are shorted together.

Whenever the meter leads are separated or connected across a circuit having infinite resistance, current cannot flow through the meter movement and it shows no response.

The meter movement inside an ohmmeter thus shows full scale deflection

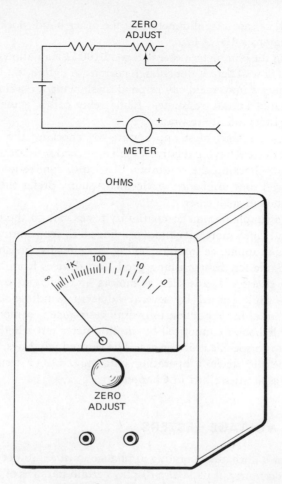

Fig. 1-2   A simple ohmmeter.

in response to a zero-resistance condition between the test leads, and it shows no deflection at all under open-circuit conditions. This feature makes an ohmmeter a fine instrument for testing for open circuits or short circuits, but the discussion to this point does not demonstrate any special advantages over a simpler and cheaper lamp-type tester.

   The real advantages of ohmmeter testers come into play when testing the continuity of circuits that normally have something other than zero or infinite resistance. A relay coil, for example, might have a normal resistance of 100 Ω. Whenever there is some reason to believe the windings might be open, it is a good idea to check them by means of the appropriate kind of continuity test. A simple lamp-type tester, however, cannot distinguish an open-circuit fault from a normal 100 Ω load resistance—the lamp does not light up in either case. An ohmmeter, on the other hand, does respond in a meaningful way to a 100 Ω load.

Connecting the ohmmeter tester to a good 100 Ω load allows a little bit of test current to flow. There is not enough current to light a test lamp, but the sensitive ohmmeter movement can respond by showing a reading somewhere between zero and infinite resistance. If the relay coil is actually open, the ohmmeter registers infinite resistance.

Ohmmeters are thus most appropriate for checking the continuity of electrical load devices having relatively high electrical resistance. Ohmmeters can be used for checking the continuity of wiring, connections, and switch contacts, as well, but appliance servicemen usually prefer the simplicity of lamp-type testers in such cases.

Although a simple ohmmeter continuity tester can do the job of a lamp-type tester (and much more), it cannot provide all the continuity testing needs of modern major appliance troubleshooting. Specifically, ohmmeters are not absolutely reliable for distinguishing good load devices from those that are only partially shorted. Loads such as motors and solenoid coils sometimes suffer from a fault caused by several adjacent windings being shorted together. The resulting reduction in overall resistance is sometimes so small that the troubleshooter cannot tell by an ohmmeter test whether the motor resistance is up to specifications or not. The shorted windings, however, can greatly reduce the device's operating efficiency. Other tests for shorted motor windings are described in Chapter 5.

1-2   VOLTAGE TESTERS

Just as a normally operating appliance must exhibit certain patterns of electrical continuity, it must also display certain patterns of voltage drops. Some elements of an appliance operate properly only when voltage is applied to them, and other elements take on a voltage only when there is something wrong with the circuit.

It is thus possible to pinpoint many different kinds of troubles by measuring the voltages in a faulty section of an appliance and comparing the results with the voltages found whenever the appliance is working properly. Of course it is up to the troubleshooter to determine what the voltages should be, either by consulting the manufacturer's service notes or by analyzing a schematic diagram.

Many of the troubles that can be detected by means of voltage measurements can also be found by running continuity tests. Voltage testing procedures, however, call for working with a "live" circuit, and that can be a significant advantage when facing troubles that appear only when the appliance is running. Recall that continuity tests can be run only on circuits that are completely shut down.

The main purpose of this chapter is to describe voltage test instruments and procedures from a very general point of view. More detailed voltage testing procedures appear in subsequent chapters dealing with specific appliances and their common troubles.

The basic idea behind any voltage test is to determine whether or not a certain component or group of components have any voltage dropped across them. A certain amount of voltage should be present under some conditions and completely lacking in others. In any event, a set of voltage tests can give the troubleshooter a very good idea of what is going on inside a troubled appliance.

There are two basic kinds of voltage testing devices suitable for major appliance servicing work: *simple neon lamp voltage testers* and *voltmeters*. Lamp-type voltage testers can tell the user whether one of the two basic voltage levels, 120 V and 240 V, is present at some part of a circuit. These simple and inexpensive testers, however, cannot respond to lower voltages such as the 12 V or 24 V sometimes found in certain sections of some major appliances.

A voltmeter tester, on the other hand, can accurately inform the user of any voltage level from 0–240 V or more. The only disadvantage of voltmeters is that they are rather expensive compared to a lamp-type tester.

The following two sections describe the features and applications of neon lamp voltage testers and voltmeters in detail.

1-2.1 Neon Lamp Voltage Testers

Figure 1-3 shows a common lamp-type voltage tester and its electrical schematic. The tester uses a 120 V neon lamp cartridge connected in series with a set of test probes. It is very difficult to suggest a circuit that is any simpler than this one.

Since neon lamps are actually rated at about 70 V, however, the lamp cartridge must have a fixed resistor wired in series with one terminal of the neon lamp. This resistor, rated at about 22,000 Ω, lowers the 120 V test voltages to about 70 V for properly operating the lamp.

Whenever the voltage tester's probes are placed across (in parallel with) a circuit or component having 120 V across it, the lamp lights up. If the circuit under test has about 100 V or less across it, the lamp does not light at all. Figure 1-4 illustrates the way a simple neon lamp voltage tester responds to a circuit that is being turned off and on.

Of course a neon lamp voltage tester rated at 120 V cannot be used for voltage testing 240 V appliances. Applying 240 V to these lamps would burn them out within a few seconds. There is, however, a need for a simple and reliable voltage tester for 240 V circuits.

Neon lamp cartridges rated at 240 V are available commercially from industrial electronics supply houses. These higher voltage versions cost very little more than their 120 V counterparts.

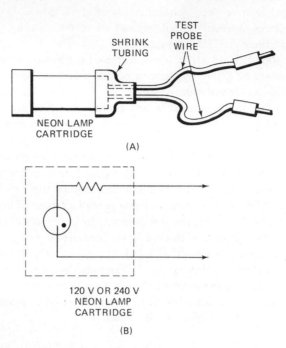

Fig. 1-3   A neon lamp voltage tester. (A) Pictorial drawing, (B) Schematic diagram.ˑ

1-2.2   Voltmeter Testers

Whereas a neon lamp voltage tester cannot respond to voltages more than about 10 percent below its rated operating level, a voltmeter can respond reliably to voltages anywhere between zero and its full-scale voltage reading. Voltmeters are more expensive than the simple neon testers, but there is no substitute for a voltmeter when it comes to checking out voltages that are not close to 120 V or 240 V.

Figure 1-5 shows a home-made voltmeter that is wholly suitable for all major appliance voltage tests. The meter movement is rated at 300 Vac—it can, in other words, indicate voltages anywhere from 0–300 Vac. A pair of banana plugs accept the jacks on a pair of long test leads.

Ready-made voltmeters suitable for major appliance servicing are available from appliance parts distributors and electronics supply houses.

Voltmeters are specified according to their maximum, or full-scale, voltage readings. A voltmeter rated at 150 Vac, for instance, is capable of indicating voltages anywhere between 0 and 150 Vac. This particular meter is good for checking voltages found in 120 V appliances. Checking voltages in

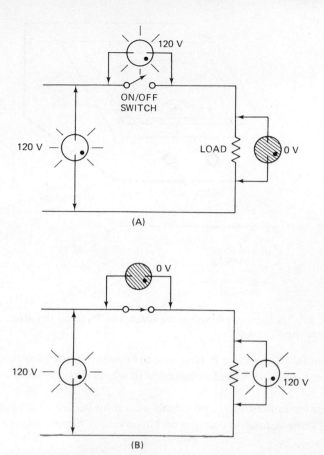

Fig. 1-4 Response of a neon lamp voltage tester. (A) A normal circuit that is turned off, (B) A normal circuit that is turned on.

a 240 V appliance, however, requires a voltmeter capable of registering 240 V
or more. A standard voltmeter for 240 V work is rated at 300 Vac.

Of course a 300 V voltmeter can be used for checking voltages in both 120
V and 240 V appliances. The only problem with a 300 V meter is that very
low voltages—on the order of about 6 V—do not cause very much meter
deflection. Major appliance servicemen seldom encounter voltages less than
12 V, however; therefore a 300 Vac meter is the better all-around choice.
Some voltmeters, by the way, have a range switch on them that lets the
troubleshooter set the full-scale reading to either 150 V or 300 V. The advantage of using the lower scale is that readings in the 10 V region are more
accurate.

Voltmeters are also specified as ac or dc types. Major appliance servicemen seldom encounter dc voltages in their work, so that an ac voltmeter is

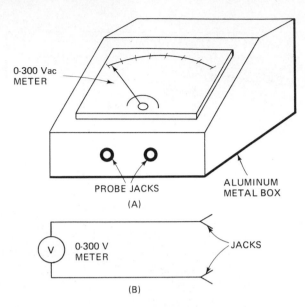

Fig. 1-5   A home-made voltmeter tester. (A) Pictorial drawing, (B) Schematic diagram.

the most useful of the two. If circumstances permit, it is nice to carry a dc voltmeter to take care of the few instances in which it is necessary to check dc voltages.

The last section of this chapter deals with a multimeter that is capable of registering both ac and dc voltages on about four different voltage ranges.

1-3 CURRENT TESTERS

Technically speaking, a current tester is any kind of instrument that is capable of detecting and registering the amount of current flowing through an electrical conductor. There are only two basic kinds of current testers used in the major appliance servicing industry today: direct-reading ac ammeters and clamp-on ammeters. The essential difference between the two is in the way they detect the amount of current flowing through a circuit. They both register the current flow on a meter scaled in ampere units.

Figure 1-6 shows a direct-reading ac ammeter and its schematic drawing. There isn't much to the circuit: only a meter movement and a set of test probes.

A direct-reading ac ammeter must be inserted in series with the circuit to be monitored (see Fig. 1-7). This means that the serviceman has to physically break open the electrical path to the circuit, usually by disconnecting one end of the wire and completing the circuit again through the meter.

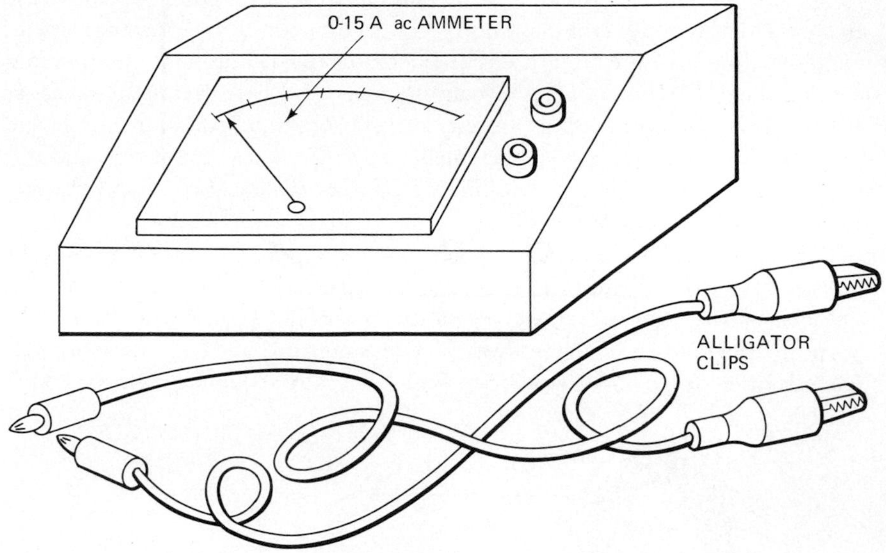

0-15 A ac AMMETER

ALLIGATOR
CLIPS

Fig. 1-6   A direct-reading ammeter for appliance troubleshooting.

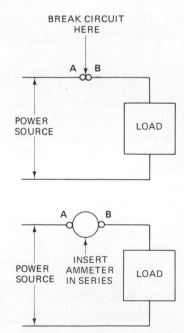

BREAK CIRCUIT
HERE

A   B

POWER
SOURCE

LOAD

A   B

POWER
SOURCE

INSERT
AMMETER
IN SERIES

LOAD

Fig. 1-7 Proper series connections for direct-reading ammeters.

The fact that a direct-reading ammeter has to be inserted in series with the circuit makes it quite troublesome to use. Why should a serviceman spend valuable time disconnecting a circuit, hooking in an ammeter, then reconnecting the circuit again when he can use quick-and-easy voltage tests just as effectively? Sometimes the cumbersome process of disconnecting and reconnecting wires actually causes further troubles in the appliance, and it is little wonder that most major appliance servicemen consider direct-reading ammeters a real nuisance.

There is a second kind of ammeter, however, which does not have to be physically connected into the circuit to be tested. This instrument, called a *clamp-on* or *tong* ammeter, uses transformer action to obtain power from a current carrying conductor indirectly. The meter has a clamp assembly that fits around a single conductor. (See Fig. 1-8). Any current flowing through

Fig. 1-8 This clamp-on ammeter has been attached to a small, hand-held multimeter. (Courtesy of Triplett Corporation)

the conductor induces a secondary current flow in the clamp, and it is this secondary current that operates a meter movement. The connection between the meter movement and the circuit under test is made by way of external magnetic fields rather than by a direct electrical connection.

Clamp-on ammeters *must* be connected around only one conductor to obtain reliable results. The reason for this rule is that the meter depends on transformer action, which, in turn, relies upon a magnetic field generated by the current carrying conductor. Anything that disturbs the magnetic field from the conductor is bound to upset the readings, and one good way to upset the field is by mixing it with a field from a second conductor.

The fact that a clamp-on meter must be attached around only one conductor at a time does not pose any serious problems for an experienced user. Wires in major appliances are sometimes bundled together in a way that makes it rather troublesome to sort out one of them for taking a current reading. Even so, the time spent unravelling one wire far enough to fit a clamp around it is less than the time spent disconnecting the wire to make a direct-meter reading.

It would be nice if a troubleshooter could get a total current reading for an appliance by simply placing the clamp-on meter around the main power cord. The trouble is that appliance power cords contain three separate conductors bonded tightly together, making it impossible to place the clamp around just one of them. Total current readings, however, are made at the appliance end of the power cord—at the point where the three conductors separate and attach to the main power terminals on the appliance.

The only insurmountable problem inherent in clamp-on ammeters is that they cannot respond to conductors carrying dc power. The transformer action that makes these meters work calls for an alternating magnetic field; and since the magnetic fields from dc circuits are unchanging, there can be no voltage current induced into the clamp-on meter. It is fortunate that dc circuits appear in very few major appliances, because the troubleshooter's only recourse in such instance is either measuring the current with a direct-reading dc ammeter or calculating the current after measuring the dc voltage across a known resistance in the circuit. (The current can be calculated by Ohm's law, which states that current is equal to voltage divided by resistance.)

A troubleshooter using a clamp-on ammeter can run into a couple of other kinds of difficulties, but neither of them is insurmountable. One such instance arises when the conductor in question is too short to accommodate the clamp, and a similar problem arises when the conductor is tucked away in a space that is too small for the clamp assembly. In both instances, an experienced troubleshooter learns to look for an alternate conductor that, with luck, carries the same current and is more accessible.

Summarizing the important applications procedures for clamp-on ammeters: (1) the clamp must be fastened only to the conductor to be tested, and (2) the meter cannot be used to measure dc.

1-4   WATTMETERS

Determining the overall power consumption of a faulty major appliance can add some valuable information to a list of symptoms. An appliance that is in some way faulty nearly always consumes an abnormal amount of power. In some instances the power consumption is above normal and in other cases, it can be below normal. Of course there are instances where the trouble causes only a slight change from normal power consumption. In any case, a *wattmeter*—an instrument capable of accurately registering total power consumption—can be an asset to a busy major appliance serviceman.

Electrical power is a combination of current and voltage. A wattmeter senses both current and voltage and combines them to produce a reading that represents the circuit's power consumption. Figure 1-9 shows how a typical

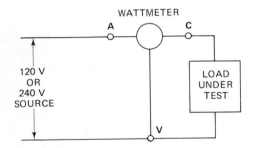

Fig. 1-9   Proper connections for a wattmeter.

wattmeter is connected into a circuit. Note that the meter has three connections: one for voltage (**V**), one for current (**A**), and one common to the other two (**C**). The current connections, **A** and **C**, have to be connected in series with the circuit being monitored, and the voltage connections, **V** and **C**, have to be connected in parallel with the circuit.

Wattmeters, like voltmeters and ammeters, are specified according to their maximum readings. A 1000 W wattmeter, for instance, is capable of monitoring power levels from 0–1000 W. Some wattmeters available for major appliance servicing have a selector switch that lets the troubleshooter set the meter's sensitivity to any one of two or three different levels.

The primary disadvantage of a wattmeter is that it is difficult to connect it into most circuits. It is fairly easy to make the voltage connection, but making the current connection calls for breaking open the circuit. Because of this difficulty, wattmeters are used almost exclusively for monitoring overall power consumption rather than the power consumption of selected portions of a circuit. Monitoring overall power consumption is a matter for inserting the wattmeter between the power outlet and the appliance plug. Wattmeters equipped with a feed-through connection as shown in Fig. 1-10 can be conveniently attached to any appliance that uses a plug-type power connection.

Many major appliance servicemen consider wattmeters a low-priority item on their inventory of test equipment. The reason for this is that a current test can usually provide information that is equally meaningful. A trouble that causes an appliance to consume an abnormal amount of power also draws an abnormal amount of current from the lines. And as described in the previous section, clamp-on meters are very easy to use.

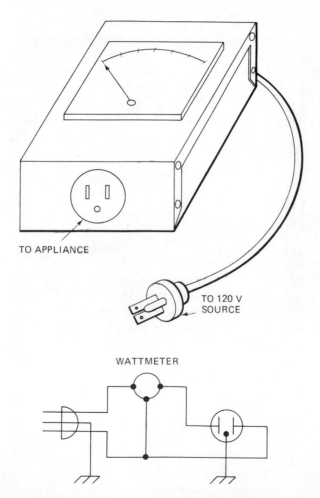

TO APPLIANCE

TO 120 V SOURCE

WATTMETER

Fig. 1-10 A convenient in-line wattmeter.

1-5 MULTIMETERS

As the name implies, a *multimeter* is a multiple-purpose test instrument. Commercially available multimeters normally have provisions for measuring ac and dc voltages, dc current, and resistance on the same meter face. A multimeter is, in other words, several different test instruments in one; and its special advantage is that it reduces the quantity of equipment that a major appliance serviceman has to carry around with him.

Most multimeters have a function selector switch that lets the user set up the instrument to act as a dc voltmeter, ammeter, ohmmeter, and so on. As shown in Fig. 1-11, the meter also has a range selector switch that sets the instrument's sensitivity to an appropriate level.

Fig. 1-11 A multimeter that includes special functions that are especially useful for appliance servicing. (Courtesy of Triplett Corporation)

There are a number of different multimeters on the market today. Considering the kinds of circuits a major appliance serviceman faces every day, the best all-around choice for a multimeter is a VOM—a volt-ohm-milliammeter. VOMs are rugged, reliable and do not require an external power source. The only real shortcoming inherent in most VOMs is that they cannot measure ac currents. Adaptors for measuring ac currents, however, are available for some of the better models.

1-6 QUESTIONS

1. It is always a good idea to test the operation of a lamp-type continuity tester before using it to check a questionable appliance circuit. Describe a simple and reliable technique for testing the operation of this kind of tester.

2. In what way is an ohmmeter a better continuity test instrument than a simple lamp-type tester?

3. Is a voltage tester connected in series or in parallel with the circuit or circuit device being tested?

4. What is the main difference between a direct-reading ammeter and a clamp-on meter?

5. What is the primary advantage of carrying a VOM to every job site?

2

Systematic
Circuit Troubleshooting

Chapter 1 describes the essential features of common electrical test equipment for major appliance troubleshooting. The finest test equipment in the world is practically useless, however, if the serviceman doesn't have a good understanding of how it can be used best in tough troubleshooting situations.

There are many occasions for instance, where voltage tests are far more useful than any other kind of tests. Then again, continuity or ohmmeter tests are sometimes better. Knowing which instrument to use is an important part of a serviceman's training; and the examples that follow can provide some valuable insight into the advantages and problems associated with common test instruments in several basic kinds of circuits.

2-1 CONTINUITY TEST TECHNIQUES

An experienced troubleshooter can use continuity tests to track down a major share of all the troubles he ever encounters in major appliances.

Continuity tests are also used in conjunction with other kinds of tests to confirm or doublecheck a conclusion.

Figure 2-1 shows a schematic diagram of a simple appliance such as a garbage disposer or trash compactor. The essential feature of the circuit is that all of its components are connected in series. Current flowing from the

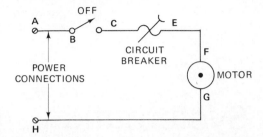

Fig. 2-1 A simple appliance with series-connected components.

power source thus flows through all the components; and an open- or short-circuit fault in any of the components affects the operation of all the others. Before analyzing the continuity of this circuit under some fault conditions, however, it might be constructive to study the circuit continuity under normal conditions.

The first step in any continuity testing procedure is to remove all power to the appliance. In the case of the circuit in Fig. 2-1, completely removing the power is a matter of disconnecting the power connections at points **A** and **H**.

With the on/off switch open (appliance turned off), attaching the test leads of a continuity tester between the power terminals (between points **A** and **H**) should show an open circuit condition or infinite resistance. An open-circuit indication is normal in this instance because the open switch effectively interrupts the only path for current flow.

Closing the switch (turning on the appliance) completes the path for current flow through the circuit, and the resistance between the input terminals (points **A** and **H**) should drop to some value that is lower than infinity, but greater than zero. A greater-than-zero resistance appears at the input terminals because the motor windings act as a load to limit current flow somewhat. It is difficult to say exactly what the resistance should be without consulting the manufacturer's servicing notes.

Flipping the switch on and off should make an ohmmeter tester connected between points **A** and **H** show alternate readings of infinity and some lower resistance. Unfortunately, a simple lamp-type tester might not respond to the complete circuit condition at all. The lamp, in other words, might remain dark in spite of the fact that the circuit is indeed complete when the power switch is closed. This particular test is thus better carried out using an ohmmeter tester.

The continuity across the switch (between points **B** and **C**) should show either good continuity or a total lack of it, depending upon whether the switch is open or closed. If the switch is closed (appliance turned on), the switch acts as a straight piece of wire, and it should display a good continuity or zero resistance. Whenever the switch is opened, however, it should show a total lack of continuity or infinite resistance.

As far as continuity tests are concerned, the built-in circuit breaker produces the same effects as the on/off switch. Whenever the circuit breaker is properly set, its continuity (as measured between points **D** and **E**) should be very good. If the circuit breaker is open for any reason, it will show a complete lack of continuity or infinite resistance. Its effect upon the overall circuit condition, as monitored with a continuity tester between points **A** and **H**, is the same as that of the on/off switch.

Testing the continuity of the conductor between the power connection at point **A** and the on/off switch at point **B** should show good continuity or zero resistance, regardless of the state of the on/off switch. This particular segment of wire is often a rather long one, and an electrical continuity test is appropriate because it is rather troublesome to visually trace the wire searching for possible broken sections.

Other sections of wiring, such as the one stretching from the motor to a power terminal (between points **G** and **H**) should show good continuity.

Continuity tests across the motor (between points **F** and **G**) should not vary according to the state of either the on/off switch or the circuit breaker. The electrical resistance of the motor itself can be determined from the manufacturer's servicing bulletins for that particular appliance. In any event, the electrical continuity as tested across the motor should be the same as that observed when making a continuity test between points **A** and **H** with the on/off switch closed and the circuit breaker properly set.

The following troubleshooting guide applies to the series appliance circuit shown in Fig. 2-1. In some instances, continuity tests might not be the easiest or most appropriate; but since the objective of this discussion is to illustrate continuity troubleshooting procedures, they are the only ones considered here.

Appliance does not run when the switch is turned on

The appliance is probably suffering from an open-circuit fault. To confirm the trouble, disconnect the power source from the appliance, close the on/off switch, and make certain that the circuit breaker is set closed. Connect the test leads of a continuity tester across the entire circuit (between points **A** and **H**). The appliance is indeed suffering from an open-circuit fault if the test shows a total lack of continuity or infinite resistance.

The open-circuit problem can be in the on/off switch, the circuit breaker, the motor, or in any section of the wiring. Tracking down the exact location of the open circuit is a matter of systematically checking the continuity of every part of the circuit.

Select a starting point for the test, say point **A**. Place both tester leads on that point, and observe that the tester shows good continuity. (If the tester does not show good continuity in this condition, there is something wrong with the tester itself.)

Leaving one of the test leads attached to point **A**, move the other to the switch end of the wire, point **B**. An indication of good continuity confirms that the wiring and all electrical connections between points **A** and **B** are good. Move the test lead from point **B** across the switch contacts to point **C**. As long as the switch is turned on, the continuity tester should show good continuity. If the test between points **A** and **C** show a lack of continuity, the switch is either turned off or it contains a set of broken contacts.

Assuming that the switch showed good continuity, the next step is to move the test probe off point **C** and over to point **D**. The continuity tester is now checking the circuit between the line and circuit breaker. The test shows good continuity if all the wiring and switch contacts between those two points are in good order.

Continue moving the one test probe along the series circuit from one point to the next. Each test checks a larger portion of the circuit; and as soon as one of the tests fails to show good continuity, the troubleshooter knows the open-circuit fault is between the present test point and the previous one. Suppose, for instance, that the tests all showed good continuity up to the point where the probes are placed between points **A** and **F**. That means the open-circuit problem is between points **E** and **F**.

A good troubleshooter does not stop at the point where he finds an open-circuit condition. Unless he can see the actual break in the wire or one of its contacts, he doublechecks the conclusion by connecting a jumper wire across the suspected break and checking the overall circuit continuity once again. In this example, he would connect the jumper wire between points **E** and **F**. If the break is indeed between those two points, the jumper completes the circuit and makes any subsequent tests between the input terminals (points **A** and **H**) show normal continuity.

Appliance circuit breaker continually trips open

The trouble might be due to a faulty circuit breaker, but it is more likely caused by a short-circuit condition. The short circuit has to be somewhere between the motor side of the circuit breaker and the line side of the motor (between points **E** and **G**). The reasoning behind this conclusion follows:

1. The trouble cannot be anywhere between points **A** and **D**. If that were the case, it would be a service line fuse, and not the appliance's circuit breaker, which would trip.

2. The trouble cannot be anywhere between the line side of the motor and the line connection, itself (between points **G** and **H**). The reason for this conclusion is that a short circuit between points **G** and **H** would not significantly alter the normal operation of the appliance.

The inevitable conclusion is that the short circuit has to be between points **D** and **G**.

If the short is outside the motor (between points **E** and **G**), current from the ac supply completely bypasses the motor; and since the motor is the only device in the entire appliance that limits current flow, the circuit breaker will trip every time the appliance is turned on.

To see whether or not the short is actually between points **E** and **G**, disconnect one of the power leads going to the motor—at point **F**, for instance. This maneuver removes the motor from the circuit. If the short-circuit condition is actually outside the motor, a continuity tester applied between points **A** and **H** will show good continuity, even with the motor disconnected. The serviceman would then have to visually inspect the circuit for the cause of a short between points **E** and **G**.

Now suppose that the test for a short between points **E** and **G** showed there was no short-circuit condition with the motor disconnected. The trouble in this instance has to be in the motor circuit itself. Troubleshooting hints in Chapter 5 describe the procedures for testing a motor for shorts.

There is always an outside chance that the motor is in good condition and that there is no short circuit between points **E** and **G**. The process of elimination described in the first part of this short-circuit analysis allows for a possible trouble between points **D** and **E**—at the circuit breaker.

Circuit breakers do not "burn out" on their own accord. Circuit breaker troubles are usually a secondary effect of some more serious trouble in the past. If all continuity tests show that there are no short circuits when the motor is disconnected, and if the motor tests show that it is in good working order, the trouble has to be in the circuit breaker itself. The serviceman's only alternative is to replace the breaker and final-test the appliance.

Appliance blows service line fuse when turned on

This particular symptom always points to a serious short-circuit condition in the appliance. The fact that the appliance blows fuses only when it is turned on places the short somewhere on the motor side of the on/off switch. If the short happens to be on the line side of the fuse (across points **B** and **H**, for example) the appliance would blow fuses whether it was turned on or not.

The fact that the appliance circuit breaker between points **D** and **E** does not open is a fairly good indication that the trouble is on the line side of the circuit breaker. By the process of elimination, then, the short circuit has to be between the line connecting points **C** and **D** and the line between points **G** and **H**.

To confirm that this kind of short really exists, disconnect all power connections to the appliance (at points **A** and **H**), close the on/off switch, make certain that the appliance circuit breaker is properly set, and check the overall circuit continuity between points **A** and **H**. The basic nature of the suspected trouble is confirmed if the test shows good continuity or zero resistance. Opening the on/off switch will make the continuity test show a complete lack of continuity or infinite resistance.

It is important to note that a simple lamp-type continuity tester responds in the same fashion whether the suspected short circuit is present or not. The problem is that lamp testers cannot tell the difference between the normal low resistance provided by the motor circuit and a dead short elsewhere in the appliance. An ohmmeter tester, on the other hand, shows zero resistance whenever a short circuit exists, and shows from $1-10 \Omega$ resistance (the resistance of the normal motor winding) if there are no short circuits in the appliance.

The procedures for running continuity tests on parallel circuits are, in principle, exactly the same as the tests on series circuits. The idea, basically, is to remove all power from the appliance and systematically check the continuity of the overall circuit and each of its parallel branches. The procedures for running continuity tests on one branch of a parallel circuit, however, calls for some additional steps aimed at eliminating the effects that other branches exert upon the circuit continuity.

Figure 2-2 is a schematic that represents a typical appliance circuit having three parallel branches. One of the branches contains a motor, another branch is made up of a heating element, and the third branch contains a 120 V indicator lamp.

Whenever switch S1 is open as shown in the diagram, current cannot flow anywhere in the circuit. S1 is a series-connected switch that stands between the main ac power source and the rest of the circuit. Closing S1 completes a

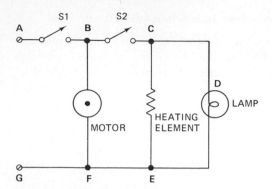

Fig. 2-2 A circuit having parallel-connected components.

path for current flow between the ac connections and the motor, making the motor run. If switch S2 is open at the time, the heating element and lamp remain disconnected from the power source. It is only the motor circuit that is complete when S1 is closed and S2 is open.

Closing both S1 and S2 completes the separate paths for current flow through the heating element and lamp. The heating element thus gets hot and the lamp burns at its full brilliance. The motor is of course running at the time, too. In fact it is impossible to operate the heating element and lamp when the motor is turned off by opening S1.

An analysis of the continuity characteristics of this circuit should begin with the ac power completely disconnected from the terminals at points **A** and **G**, and both switches in their open (off) conditions. With both switches open, a continuity test across the ac terminals (between points **A** and **G**) should show a total lack of continuity or infinite resistance.

Closing S1 makes the continuity tester connected across the ac power connections (between points **A** and **G**) show a sudden change from no continuity to good continuity. The reason for this change is that the motor is not connected across the power source; and an ohmmeter reading at the power terminals should show a resistance of about 2 or 3 Ω—the dc resistance of the motor windings.

Once S1 is closed, closing S2 does not cause any further change in continuity. At least the change is so small that a typical continuity tester cannot detect it. The reason for the small change is that the motor windings pull the overall circuit resistance down to only a few ohms; and unless components connected in parallel with the motor happen to have a resistance that is lower still, the resistance of the motor dominates the overall readings.

The continuity of the circuit branches containing the heating element and lamp must be tested separately. As long as the motor is part of the circuit under test, the troubleshooter has no way of telling whether the heating element and lamp branches have normal continuity or are broken open. Either way, a test across the ac power terminals shows only a few ohms.

A convenient way to test the continuity of the heating element and lamp circuits—without interference from the motor—is by opening S2 and placing the test probes of the continuity tester across the heating element itself (between points **C** and **E**). Opening S2 thus isolates the motor from the other two parallel branches; and under these test conditions, the continuity tester responds to the combined continuity of the heating element and lamp.

Heating elements normally have a rather low resistance when they are at room temperature. This resistance is somewhat higher than that of an ac motor winding, but less than a hundred ohms or so. The resistance of lamp filaments is also rather low when they are not burning, so that a continuity test between points **C** and **E**—with S2 open—should show good continuity or a rather low resistance on the order of 20 Ω.

The troubleshooter now faces the problem of separating the continuity of the heating element from that of the lamp. Suppose there is good reason to believe the heating element is broken open. As long as the lamp is connected in parallel with the heater, the lamp provides a continuous path for current flow, and any continuity test across the heater will show good continuity—whether it is broken open or not.

Just as the motor had to be electrically isolated from the circuit before meaningful continuity tests could be carried out on the heater and lamp, the heater and lamp have to be isolated from one another before either one of them can be tested separately.

Isolating the heater and lamp in this instance is a simple matter of removing the lamp from its socket. That maneuver breaks open the parallel path through the lamp circuit, leaving the heater connected alone between points **C** and **E**. A continuity test between those two points thus indicates the actual continuity of the heating element. If the element is indeed broken open, the test will show a complete lack of continuity or infinite resistance.

Getting reliable continuity test results from a parallel combination of components requires isolating all branches from the one under test. Sometimes the procedure is as simple as opening the right combination of switches or removing a lamp from its socket. Other times, however, components have to be disconnected by some less convenient means.

2-2 VOLTAGE TESTING TECHNIQUES

A trained troubleshooter can use voltage tests to track down almost every electrical trouble he encounters in major appliances. One of the real advantages of using voltmeter testers is that they can often do the job of a continuity tester as well. The only situation that makes it impossible to use a voltage tester is one in which a short-circuit condition makes it impossible to apply power to the appliance.

Figure 2-1 shows a schematic of a simple appliance that has all the components connected in series with one another. The essential feature of this circuit, as far as the voltage distribution is concerned, is that the 120 V source voltage appears at only one place in the circuit: either across the load or across any part of the circuit that acts as an open circuit.

The first step in any voltage testing sequence is to apply full power to the appliance. In the case of the circuit in Fig. 2-1, the 120 V is permanently connected to the appliance by means of a set of screw-type connections.

With the on/off switch open (appliance turned off), a voltage tester applied to the power terminals (between points **A** and **H**) should indicate the presence of 120 V power. This test shows that the source is supplying voltage to the circuit, and the next part of the analysis is to determine where that applied voltage might be found in the appliance.

As long as the appliance is connected to its 120 V lines and the off/on switch is open, full line voltage should appear across the switch terminals (between points **B** and **C**). A voltage tester should show no voltage across the load (between points **F** and **G**).

Closing the on/off switch contacts transfers the circuit voltage from the switch to the load; and the motor will run if the circuit is operating properly.

Now suppose the motor does not run when the on/off switch is closed. Assuming that the 120 V power is properly connected to the power connections, the appliance must be suffering from an open-circuit fault. The following paragraphs describe the procedure for locating the open circuit using a voltmeter tester. (Section 2-1 describes the technique for analyzing the same trouble with a continuity tester.)

Connect the voltage tester across the power terminals (between points **A** and **H**) to confirm that 120 V power is being applied to the circuit. After doing that, fix one of the probes securely to one of the power terminals, say at point **A**, and use the other probe to "explore" the circuit for voltage drops.

Touch the "exploring" probe to point **B**, for instance. Since the wiring between points **A** and **B** has virtually no electrical resistance, there should be no voltage dropped between those points. If indeed there is no voltage indication, move the "exploring" probe to point **C**. The probes are then testing the circuit between points **A** and the load side of the on/off switch. There should be no voltage indication as long as the switch is in its ON position. If the switch *is* ON and the test shows 120 V across it, there is a very good chance that the switch is suffering from an open-circuit fault—a set of broken contacts, for instance.

Assuming that the voltage test between points **A** and **C** shows that part of the circuit is in good condition—that there is, in other words, no voltage across the closed switch contacts—move the exploring probe to point **D** and then to **E**. If the test still shows no voltage, the circuit is good up to point **E**.

Suppose now that the next test, fixing the voltage test probes between points **A** and **F**, shows 120 V. This tells the troubleshooter that the open-circuit fault is somewhere between the power connector at point **A** and the circuit breaker side of the motor. Furthermore, previous voltage tests have showed that the open-circuit condition is *not* anywhere between the power connector and point **E**. By the logical process of elimination, then, the open-circuit trouble has to be in the line running between points **E** and **F**.

A close visual inspection of that part of the circuit is usually adequate for determining the exact cause of the open-circuit condition. If the open-circuit fault is not readily visible upon making the visual inspection, it is a good idea to doublecheck the conclusion by connecting a jumper wire across the suspected portion of the wiring (between points **E** and **F**). With the jumper in place, the voltage detected between points **E** and **F** should shift to the load where it belongs. The motor should then operate normally, confirming the fact that the wiring between points **E** and **F** has to be replaced.

Summarizing the basic idea behind troubleshooting series circuits with a voltage tester: Only the load device should have line voltage developed across it when all switches are closed and the appliance is operating normally. An open-circuit fault steals the line voltage from the load device, and the troubleshooter finds line voltage where it should not be.

It is important to note that successful voltage troubleshooting procedures have to be very systematic. Of course it is possible to uncover an open circuit by simply checking for 120 V potentials here and there, but a systematic approach—starting at the beginning of the circuit and working to the end point by point—gets the job done faster and far more effectively.

A parallel circuit is defined as one having more than one complete path for current flow. And concerning the distribution of voltages in a parallel circuit: Every parallel branch has exactly the same voltage across it. These two important points are illustrated in Fig. 2-3.

Referring to Fig. 2-3, part of the current from the 120 V source flows through the heater and back to the source, whereas the rest of the current

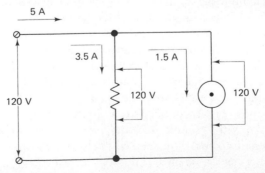

Fig. 2-3 Voltage and current distribution in a typical parallel circuit.

from the source flows through the motor circuit. If the heater burns open, current can still flow through the motor. What is more important for this discussion, however, is the fact that the voltage across the two parallel-connected branches—the heater and the motor—both have the full 120 V source voltage dropped across them. Even if one of the parallel circuits burned open, the 120 V would still appear across both of them.

It is thus very difficult to make any certain judgments about the condition of a parallel circuit on the basis of voltage tests alone. Voltage tests *can* be used to confirm the presence of line voltage at a parallel component, but other tests and observations are necessary for drawing any sound conclusions about the real nature of the trouble. These other tests include continuity tests of the type described in the previous section and visual inspections of the wiring and troubled component.

Few major appliance circuits are purely parallel circuits, and few are made up wholly of series-connected components. Instead, most major appliances use combinations of series and parallel circuits. This means that a troubleshooter must understand the basic characteristics of both kinds of circuits and be able to apply his understanding to more complicated combinations of the two.

Figure 2-2 illustrates one kind of series/parallel appliance circuit. In this instance, the motor, heating element, and lamp make up separate parallel branches. That is, these three load devices each complete a separate path for current flow from the source. The switch contacts, S1 and S2, on the other hand, are connected in a series arrangement. Every bit of the current that flows through this circuit must flow through S1. Opening S1, for instance, cuts off current to all the load devices. The contacts for S2 carry all the current fed to the heater and lamp. Turning off S2 cuts off current flow to the heater and lamp, but it has no influence upon the operation of the motor.

An analysis of the voltage drops in the series/parallel circuit in Fig. 2-2 should begin with both of the switches in their off condition. A voltage check across the power terminals (between points **A** and **G**) should show that 120 V line power is reaching the appliance. Voltage tests across the motor (points **B** and **F**), heating element (points **C** and **E**), and the lamp (points **D** and **E**) should show no voltage at all because the open switches interrupt the application of line voltage to the circuit components. The full line voltage, however, should appear across the contacts of S1 (between points **A** and **B**).

Closing S1 completely changes the distribution of voltages in the circuit: the 120 V that had been only across the open contacts of S1 shifts over to the motor and the open contacts of S2. This action completes a path for current flow between the 120 V source and the motor, and of course the motor responds by starting to run. The open contacts of S2 prevent the line voltage from reaching the heating element and lamp, however.

The final step in this analysis is to turn on S2. Turning on S2 shifts the

120 V previously dropped across its contacts to the lamp and heating element, and the closed contacts thus complete two more paths for current flow from the source. In this instance, one path is through the heating element and the other is through the lamp.

A voltage analysis of the circuit in Fig. 2-2 with both switch contacts closed shows 120 V power across all three load elements. Since the switches are closed, they should have no voltage across them. The circuit, in other words, is now in full operation. The motor is running, the heating element is operating at its rated power, and the lamp is burning at its full brightness.

A complete analysis of likely troubles that could occur in the circuit in Fig. 2-2 can be based on the fact that most troubles are caused by open or shorted loads, switches, or wiring. Opening and shorting each of the circuit elements one at a time thus provides an overall view of possible troubles in the circuit; and an analysis of the resulting symptoms, in the light of the theories of parallel and series circuits, provides a valuable exercise in trouble-shooting.

To put the trouble analysis on a practical footing, however, it is necessary to realize that certain kinds of troubles are better analyzed by techniques other than a voltage analysis. In some instances a continuity test is more appropriate, and in other cases it is better to diagnose the trouble by merely observing the behavior of the circuit.

Suppose, for example, that the contacts in S1 are broken open. Under this fault condition, none of the load devices can receive 120 V power from the source. In fact, the circuit appears to be turned off completely, regardless of the position of S1. This symptom is a good indication of the trouble, but it is a good idea to confirm the conclusion with a voltage or continuity test. A voltage test is more desirable in this case because it does not require disconnecting the power terminals from the main 120 V source.

To confirm a diagnosis of open contacts in S1, connect a voltage tester across the switch's contacts (between points **A** and **B**). Flip the switch on and off several times, noting the response of the voltage tester. If the switch contacts are broken open, the voltage tester will show 120 V at all times. If, on the other hand, the diagnosis is incorrect—or, in other words, there is nothing wrong with the switch—the voltage test will show 120 V whenever the switch is in its off position and no voltage when it is turned on.

Continuing this on-paper trouble analysis of the circuit in Fig. 2-2, consider the symptoms that would appear if the contacts of S1 happen to be shorted together. The symptom in this case would be that the motor would run at all times, regardless of the switch setting. There can be little doubt that the switch is at fault, but there is always a possibility that a short-circuit condition outside the switch is causing the switch to *appear* shorted.

It so happens that voltage tests on the switch and motor are not very meaningful in this instance. As long as the motor is running, there can be absolutely no doubt that a voltage check across it (between points **B** and **F**) will show 120 V. By the same token, there will be no voltage across the switch contacts (between points **A** and **B**), regardless of the switch setting.

Confirming the diagnosis of a shorted switch thus calls for some action other than a voltage test. The most appropriate doublechecking procedure is to shut off the main power supply to the appliance, disconnect all the wires connected to one terminal on the switch, and reapply the main power. The response of the motor under these test conditions can determine whether or not the diagnosis is correct.

If the diagnosis of shorted switch contacts is correct, the motor does not run when 120 V power is applied to the appliance while S1 is removed. If, on the other hand, the motor runs when the switch is disconnected from the circuit, it means that the tentative diagnosis is incorrect and that the 120 V power is reaching the motor through a short-circuit fault outside the switch. A careful visual inspection of the wiring and electrical connections around the switch, motor, and power terminals is generally adequate for pinpointing the exact cause of this short.

Turning to possible troubles in the motor, rather than S1, consider symptoms that would appear if the motor is opened or shorted. If the motor circuit is somehow opened the motor cannot run, regardless of the setting of S1. A voltage test across the motor (between points **B** and **F**) normally shows 120 V when the switch is closed. And if 120 V is present across the motor and it is not running there can be little doubt that the motor circuit is suffering from an open-circuit fault. To confirm this diagnosis temporarily remove 120 V power from the appliance disconnect all wires connected to one terminal of the motor, and check the continuity of the motor. The diagnosis of an open motor winding is confirmed if the continuity test shows a complete lack of continuity.

Symptoms that occur when the motor is completely shorted are much more distinct. Whenever the contacts for S1 are closed, an inrush of current through the shorted motor is so great that it soon blows a fuse in the service line. Voltage tests are not appropriate at all in such a case because they require the application of full line voltage.

To confirm the diagnosis of a badly shorted motor remove the 120 V power from the appliance and disconnect the motor from the circuit. If the motor is indeed shorted the appliance no longer blows a fuse when power is applied and S1 is turned on.

2-3 CURRENT AND POWER TEST PROCEDURES

Whereas voltage and continuity tests are indispensable to successful troubleshooting techniques, current and power tests are not normally used for routine troubleshooting purposes. Current- and power-measuring instruments do have their place in the major appliance repair industry; and whenever their application is appropriate they can save the troubleshooter a great deal of time and guesswork.

A certain amount of current flows through an appliance as long as it is in operation. By the same token, all appliances consume a certain amount of power. By knowing how much current or power the appliance is supposed to be using, a serviceman can compare ammeter or wattmeter readings with the appliance's specifications to check on the condition of the circuitry.

Major appliances carry a nameplate that has, among other things, current and power ratings stamped on it. One of the primary purposes of the nameplate current rating is to give an appliance owner or its installer some idea about the fusing requirements. If an all-electric clothes dryer has a nameplate current rating of 25 A, for example, the installer knows he has to outfit the service line with a 25 A fuse or circuit breaker.

Troubleshooters can take advantage of the listed current and power ratings, too. An appliance's nameplate rating is very close to the maximum current and power the circuit is ever expected to use from the lines. And whenever there is some question about the condition of the appliance, comparing an actual reading against the nameplate rating can provide some useful troubleshooting information.

It is important to bear in mind that the appliance's nameplate current and power ratings reflect the highest expected current drain or power consumption. Many complex appliances, especially those having automatically timed operating cycles, draw varying amounts of current, depending upon the portion of the cycle that is in effect at the time. Using the example of an all-electric clothes dryer again, it might draw 25 A from the lines when its main drive motor and heating elements are both turned on. Whenever the heat control thermostat cuts off the heaters, however, the motor might pull only 5 A from the lines.

2-4 QUESTIONS

1. Suppose that the coil in the diagram in Fig. 2-4 is suspected of being open. Describe a simple continuity test procedure for confirming the trouble if the 120 V source cannot be disconnected.

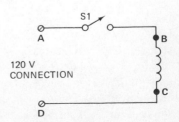

Fig. 2-4 A series- connected appliance circuit.

2. Suppose that the coil in the diagram in Fig. 2-4 is suspected of being open. Describe a simple voltage test for confirming the trouble if the coil operates a hot water valve.

3. Describe the theory of operation of the circuit shown in Fig. 2-5. (This circuit does not necessarily have a practical application.) Also list all possible component troubles and describe the outward symptoms that would result.

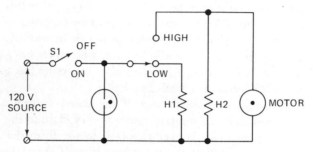

Fig. 2-5 A parallel-connected appliance circuit.

3

Principles
of Electric Heating

Some kinds of major appliances, for example, ranges and clothes dryers, require a source of heat energy to do their jobs. Most major appliances used in the United States and Europe use either electricity or fuel gas as sources of heat energy. A few appliances are designed to burn other fuels such as oil, kerosene, or alcohol, but their application is restricted to regions where reliable sources of electricity and gas are not available.

This chapter emphasizes the principles of converting electrical energy into useful heat—electrical energy, *per se*, is totally useless. Chapter 4 takes up the subject of controlling electrically generated heat.

There are a number of ways that useless electrical energy can be converted into useful and controllable heat energy. A principle known as *resistance heating*, however, is the simplest and most common electricity-to-heat conversion process used today. A second kind of process, *microwave heating*, is beginning to make itself known to the American appliance industry. There are still a relatively small number of microwave heating appliances in use today, and since the troubleshooting and servicing procedures for these special appliances require extensive training in electronics and specialized test equipment, this book does not deal directly with microwave heating.

3-1 RESISTANCE HEATING

Heat is always a by-product of current flowing through an electrical resistance. Even the best kinds of electrical conductors, namely copper and silver wire, generate some heat whenever a sufficient amount of current flows through them. This resistance heating effect is often considered a nuisance, and appliance engineers always have to minimize the resistance of conductors that are meant to carry large amounts of current.

Resistance heating can be used to great advantage, however, whenever it is necessary to convert electrical power into heat. In such instances, a voltage is applied to a wire that is especially selected to have a high electrical resistance. Current forced to flow through the resistance wire generates a controllable amount of heat that is proportional to both the resistance of the wire and the amount of current forced through it.

3-1.1 Heat versus Current, Voltage, and Power

Electrical power is a combination of voltage and current. Current or voltage alone cannot make a circuit consume or dissipate power. Electrical power is in fact equal to voltage multiplied by current in resistance heating circuits. If either term is equal to zero, the product is, also.

It turns out that the amount of current that flows through an electrical resistance is closely related to the applied voltage: in general, the higher the applied voltage, the greater the amount of current flow. The combination of voltage and current cause a circuit to consume electrical power; and that power has to be dissipated in some way. In the case of resistance heating, the power is dissipated as heat.

One example of a device that relies upon resistance heating is an ordinary fuse. There are a number of different kinds of fuses, but the one that is important to this illustration is the kind that has a thin band of lead alloy running between two terminals. Such fuses are designed to burn open whenever the current flowing through them exceeds their rated current values. A 10 A fuse, for example, is supposed to burn open whenever 10 A of current flows through it. The whole idea is to protect appliances from excessive current flow by burning open the fuse and thereby completely interrupting the flow of excessive current through the circuit.

Resistance heating is essential to the operation of this kind of fuse because the *fuse element*—the thin band of lead alloy—is designed to melt open at a certain temperature. The lead element has a small amount of electrical resistance. The resistance is very low, and it is virtually impossible to read anything but zero ohms across a good fuse element. Some resistance is present, however, and it is enough resistance to produce a little bit of heat whenever current flows through the element. The resistance heating effect becomes significant whenever the current through the fuse element reaches the fuse's amperage rating. And if the current level exceeds the rated value for a sufficient period of time, the heat generated in the small resistance rises to a point where the fuse element melts in two.

The main point of this fuse illustration is to show that a resistance, even a comparatively small one, can generate high temperatures if a sufficient amount of current is forced through it. The important practical implication is that the amount of heating can be controlled by varying the amount of current flow. **1933662**

As an example of how voltage influences the amount of heat produced in a resistance heating situation, consider how an ordinary incandescent light bulb responds to different levels of applied voltage. An incandescent light bulb works on the principle that a resistance material heated to a high temperature emits light energy as well as heat. A 120 V light bulb burns at its proper brightness only when 120 V is applied to it. Applying only 30 or 40 V makes it burn with a very dim light. Of course the resistance element in the bulb can destroy itself if more than about 150 V is applied to it.

The performance of an incandescent light bulb thus depends upon the amount of voltage applied to it. The principle, however, is not different from that of a fuse. It is possible to make this statement because the voltage applied to a light bulb determines the amount of current that flows through it; and just like a fuse, it is the amount of current that is primarily responsible for the resistance heating effect.

Carrying the example of a common light bulb a bit further, note that these little appliances are rated according to their wattage or lower consumption. This is no accident. Resistance heating relies upon current flowing through a resistive material; and the amount of current flow is, in turn, proportional to the applied voltage. Current and voltage together account for circuit power consumption. And a careful analysis of these facts leads to the conclusion that the amount of heat produced in a resistance heating situation is proportional to the amount of power the circuit consumes.

Summarizing the main technical points of this section:

1. Heat produced by resistance heating is proportional to the amount of current flowing through the resistive material: the greater the amount of current flow, the greater the heating effect.

2. The amount of current flowing through any kind of circuit is proportional to the amount of applied voltage. Voltage, then, can be said to be an important factor in determining the amount of heating in a resistance heating process.

3.   Voltage and current both influence the amount of heating in the same
     way; and since electrical power is the product of voltage times current
     in a resistive circuit, it can be said that the heating effect is propor-
     tional to the circuit's power consumption.

3-1.2   Heat versus Resistance

Once a resistance heating element is manufactured, the amount of
heat it generates depends primarily on the amount of current flowing through
it. The amount of current is determined, in turn, by the amount of applied
voltage. When planning or designing a resistance heating device, however,
appliance engineers must consider another important factor: the resistance of
the element.

It might seem that the resistance characteristics of a resistance heating
element is of no real concern to a practicing appliance serviceman. How can
something that is fixed at the time of manufacture have any importance to
work-a-day troubleshooting? It is true that a serviceman has no control over
the resistance characteristics of such devices, but it turns out that the theory
behind the resistance effects has some practical consequences.

One of the main features of a resistance heating element is that its resistance increases with its operating temperature. The filament in a 100 W light
bulb, for example, has a resistance of about 7 Ω when no power is applied to
it. When the same bulb is operating at full power, however, the resistance is
about 140 Ω. All heating elements in a resistance heating system work the
same way.

The fact that the resistance of a heating element is much lower at room
temperature than it is at its full operating temperature accounts for a surge-
current effect. An electric heating appliance, such as an all-electric range,
draws a great deal of current from the service lines when a heating element is
first turned on. In fact, it is quite likely that a user could blow a service line
circuit breaker by turning on all four electric surface units at the same
instant.

A sudden inrush of current is thus a normal part of warming up any kind
of resistance heating element, and it is rather simple to demonstrate this
effect by connecting an ac ammeter in series with a 120 V light bulb circuit.
The circuit will draw up to 20 times its normal current for the first one or two
seconds power is applied to it. The current flow settles down to its normal
operating level after the initial surge is over.

Anyone familiar with the basic mathematics of electricity might be troubled by some of his observations if he is unaware of the temperature-versus-
resistance relationship in resistance heating elements. A power formula that
applies to resistive circuits, for example, says that a 100 W light bulb should
draw about 0.8 A from the line and have a resistance of 144 Ω. Measuring the

resistance of the bulb with an ohmmeter, however, the experimenter finds a resistance that is closer to 10 Ω. With a resistance of 10 Ω, Ohm's law says the bulb should draw 12 A from the line—15 times as much current as it actually does.

The reason for the discrepancy lies in the fact that the ohmmeter check shows the cold resistance of the filament, while the operating conditions assume a hot filament. The bulb does indeed draw 12 A from the lines, but only for a tiny fraction of a second when it is first turned on. The current quickly decreases to the normal 0.8 A level as the temperature and resistance rise. Line fuses, by the way, are designed to withstand normal surge currents of short duration. Although a 100 W light bulb draws up to 12 A from the lines, the surge current flows for such a short time that a typical 10 A fuse has no trouble handling the excess current.

All resistance heating elements exhibit this surge-current effect when they are first turned on. The surge currents may be fifteen to twenty times the normal operating current levels, but that should not concern a serviceman unless the current level fails to settle down for some reason.

3-1.3   Resistance Heating Wire

In theory at least, any kind of wire could serve as a heating wire because any conductor gets warm if enough current is passed through it. The problem is that high currents are difficult to handle, so that it is better to select a resistance heating wire that produces a lot of heat with the smallest possible amount of current drain.

A good wire for resistance heating has the following characteristics:

1. High electrical resistance.
2. High melting point.
3. High resistance to corrosion.

Copper wire loses out on all three counts. Its resistance is rather low—about 0.01 Ω for a 1 ft section of No. 20 wire. Copper melts at temperatures required for most appliance heating operations, and it takes on a thick layer of black or red corrosion as it cools down from a high temperature.

The appliance industry obviously has to use something other than copper wire for resistance heating elements, and the overwhelming choice is a special alloy of nickel and chromium, commonly called *nichrome*. Nichrome can be drawn into wire of any diameter and it fits all three basic requirements for a good resistance heating wire. The resistance of nichrome wire, for instance, is about 0.66 Ω per foot—66 times greater than copper wire of the same size. The melting point of nichrome is well above the temperatures needed for any appliance application, and it resists corrosion of all kinds.

Like most other conductors, nichrome undergoes a dramatic increase in resistance as it heats up. A foot of nichrome might have 0.66 Ω resistance at room temperature, but close to 15 Ω at a moderately high operating temperature. Carrying the analysis a bit further, the power dissipation of this wire will be 960 W when 8 A of current flows through it. To get the same heating power from a piece of copper wire having the same size, 65 A of current would have to be forced through it.

Copper wire thus heats up very little while carrying enough current to make a section of nichrome wire burn at red-hot temperatures. This vast difference in the heating capabilities of copper and nichrome make it possible to carry current through copper wire to nichrome heating wires in an appliance. The copper wire dissipates no significant amount of heat, while the nichrome connected to it grows quite hot. The only "hot spot" in the copper is at the points where the two kinds of wire come together. The copper does get hot at that one point because it picks up heat from the nichrome, and not because it generates its own heat.

Because the copper gets quite hot at the heater connections, most appliances have a short brass or steel connector running between the copper supply wire and the nichrome heating wire. The connector carries the current quite well, but tends to cut off the flow of heat from the heater to the copper wire. The only alternative is using copper wire that has an asbestos insulation—vinyl insulation would quickly burn away at a copper-to-nichrome heater junction.

3-2 HEATING ELEMENTS

Nearly all electrical heating appliances use resistance heating (microwave ovens are the only exceptions), and all heating appliances that use resistance heating employ nichrome heating elements in one form or another. Heating elements used in major appliances throughout North America and Europe take on one of three basic forms: coiled wire, tubular, and flat-surface units. Each type has its own advantages and disadvantages, and an understanding of their basic characteristics makes the troubleshooting and servicing procedures more effective. This section outlines the essential features of three common kinds of heating elements and describes the appropriate troubleshooting and servicing procedures.

3-2.1 Types of Resistance Heating Elements

As shown in Fig. 3-1, a coiled heater is made up of a long section of nichrome wire that is wound up into spiral form. The spiral is supported and isolated from surrounding sections of the appliance by means of porcelain stand-offs.

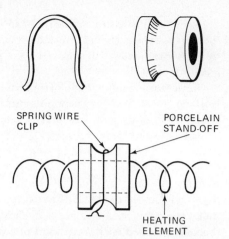

Fig. 3-1 Supporting heater wires with porcelain stand-offs.

Coiled heating elements are used today mainly in places where there is little chance that anyone will accidentally touch them—behind the grill work of a space heater or inside an all-electric clothes dryer, for example. Small electric hot plates once used coiled heating elements for cooking purposes, but they have been replaced with the safer tubular elements.

Figure 3-2 shows a cut-away section of a typical tubular heating element. The principle of operation is the same as that of a coiled heater. In fact, the heat is derived from a coiled heating element. The main difference is that the coil is run through the middle of a stainless steel or nickel alloy tube. The tube is then filled with powdered magnesium oxide and fired to fuse the oxide into a porcelain-like substance. Fused magnesium oxide is a very good heat conductor but a poor electrical conductor. Heat from the nichrome wire is thus transferred to the jacket quite efficiently, but the jacket is completely isolated from the electrical circuit.

Because tubular heating elements, often called *calrod* units, are electrically safe, they are commonly used in electrical cooking appliances.

Flat-surface heating elements, like tubular elements, use nichrome wire

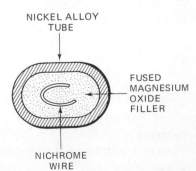

Fig. 3-2 Cut-away view of a tubular (calrod) heating element.

as their primary source of heat. In the case of flat-surface units, however, the heaters warm a cooking surface that closely resembles that of a grill in a restaurant. The user has the option of placing pots and pans on the surface or cooking on it directly.

Flat-surface units made of nichrome coils cemented into cast iron cooking surfaces have been more popular in Europe for many years. Similar units using a ceramic base, instead of metal, are now beginning to make a good showing in the United States.

3-2.2 Troubleshooting and Servicing Heating Elements

The list of things that can go wrong with a basic heating element is not very long: it can burn open, short out either completely or partially, or become covered with some kind of baked-on foreign material. Of course the list of things that can cause these few troubles is almost endless, but most of them can be reduced to user abuse, misuse, or improper installation. Heating elements rarely go bad on their own accord with normal use. A good service-man recognizes the reliability of heating elements and always searches for the reason why an element failed before considering that a repair job is finished.

An open heating element is relatively easy to detect. Even with full line voltage applied to it, an open heating element neither draws current from the lines nor generates heat. Confirming the diagnosis of a heating element is almost as easy: check the element's continuity with an ohmmeter or continuity tester. If the element shows infinite resistance or a complete lack of electrical continuity—regardless of how "good" it looks—it is indeed suffering from an open-circuit trouble.

Diagnosing and doublechecking an open-circuit trouble in a heating-element can be a rather straightforward task, but repairing it is seldom easy. In fact, it is virtually impossible to repair tubular heating elements because the nichrome wire that actually produces the heat is sealed away inside a tough alloy jacket and several ounces of fused magnesium oxide. The open-air coiled elements of the kind normally found in clothes dryers, however, can be repaired in some instances.

If the break in a coiled heating element happens to be within an inch or so of a screw-type electrical terminal, the serviceman can use the "stretch-and-tie" technique for making a quick repair. The idea is to remove the short piece of broken-off heating wire from the terminal and stretch the end of the good section to fasten it to the terminal. This procedure reduced the efficiency of the heater and makes it draw greater-than-normal current; but it is a quick and easy repair in emergencies and in cases where replacement elements are not readily available.

A more suitable way to mend a broken heater wire, especially if the break is nowhere near a screw-down connection, is with the help of a mending sleeve and crimp splice. A mending sleeve is a short section of thin metal tubing that is normally made of nichrome. The broken ends of the nichrome heater wire can be slipped into the ends of the mending sleeve and crimped firmly into place with either a crimping tool or a pair of diagonal pliers.

Mending sleeves for heater wire should be made of nichrome, but other kinds are available for the same purpose. One of the primary advantages of using nichrome mending sleeves is that they expand and contract at the same rate as the heater wire. Other materials expand and contract at slightly different rates, thus placing a strain on the connection as the temperature changes.

A simple "welding" process for mending broken heater wire uses a special material called heating element flux. This material has a relatively low melting temperature the first time it is heated. After the initial heating, however, its chemical properties change drastically, and its melting point thereafter is well above the operating temperature of most heater wires.

The idea is to stretch the broken sections of the heater wire so that the ends overlap a little bit and make a reasonably good electrical connection. Apply some of the flux to this joint and turn on the heater power. The heat at the joint fuses the flux, making it change into a conductive solid material that forms both a good electrical and mechanical connection. Specific directions for using heating element flux are normally included with the package.

One note of caution: never use porcelain wire nuts to splice a broken heater wire. Porcelain wire nuts are intended for making copper-to-copper splices in oven compartments and other places where the surrounding air temperature is high enough to melt the usual kinds of plastic wire nuts. Nichrome wire is not as flexible as copper wire, and a simple wire-nut connection on nichrome wire is bound to loosen when a normal amount of electric heat makes the joint expand and contract a few times.

Short-circuit troubles in heating elements are usually more difficult to diagnose electrically than open-circuit troubles are. Part of the trouble is that heating elements often have a low electrical resistance under normal, nonheated conditions. This means that a serviceman should always consult the manufacturer's specifications to determine the normal resistance at room temperature before condemning a heater that happens to show an unexpectedly low amount of electrical resistance. Another difficulty associated with diagnosing shorted heaters is the fact that they are sometimes only partially shorted—the entire heating element is not directly involved. Again, the manufacturer's specifications for the appliance can clear up any question about what the element's overall resistance should be.

Fortunately, short-circuit troubles rarely occur in the heating elements of major appliances. Tubular heating elements are virtually short-circuit proof. Nothing short of beating them with a hammer can make the internal nichrome wiring short itself or the metallic jacket. It is relatively easy to short out the coiled heating elements in appliances such as all-electric clothes dryers, but these elements are not exposed to normal wear and tear. When shorts do occur in coiled heating elements, they are the result of a major mechanical trouble, a disastrous accident or tampering by an unskilled repairman.

Tubular heating elements cannot be repaired. Whether they are open, completely shorted, or partially shorted, they must be replaced. Coiled heaters are easier to repair. In fact, repairing a shorted coil-type heater is normally a simple matter of locating the point of the short circuit and clearing it by adjusting the position of the heater wire or moving a metallic object that should not be touching the exposed wiring.

3-3 BASIC HEATER CIRCUITS

Most major heating appliances can be operated at two or more temperature levels. All-electric clothes dryers, for instance, often have a two-level heat selector switch that lets the user choose a NORMAL heating level or a LOW level for delicate fabrics. The most complex heat selector switches are found in the surface unit controls for electric ranges. It is not unusual to find ranges that let the user select any one of five or six heating ranges for each of the surface units.

The following sections describe the essential operating features and troubleshooting procedures for basic heater circuits. These circuits are common to many of the heating appliances described in other chapters of this book. The principles also hold for thermostatically controlled heating units of the type discussed in Chapter 6.

3-3.1 Parallel Heater Circuits

One of the simplest and most clear-cut ways to control the amount of heat an appliance generates is by switching parallel-connected heaters in and out of the circuit. Figure 3-3 illustrates a basic two-element heating circuit. The heating elements are rated at 1200 W and 3000 W. When the 1200 W element is connected directly across the 120 V line, it consumes about 1200 W of electrical power and generates an equivalent amount of heat. Adding the 3000 W element in parallel by closing the heat selector switch adds another 3000 W of power, bringing the total power rating of the appliance to 4200 W.

For troubleshooting purposes, a heating element can be considered in good operating condition if it consumes power within 10 percent of the nameplate of its rated value. The 1200 W heater in Fig. 3-3, for example,

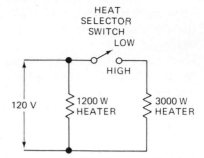

Fig. 3-3   A parallel-connected heat selector circuit.

might consume 120 W above or below that amount under normal circumstances—between 1080 W and 1320 W. Throwing the switch that adds the 3000 W element into the circuit increases the rated power consumption to 4200 W, but the actual power consumption can be anywhere from 3880–4620 W.

Looking at the continuity characteristics of this circuit, a serviceman finds that the overall circuit shows a lower resistance when the control switch is closed than he does when it is open. That fact reflects one of the essential features of a parallel circuit: *the total resistance of a parallel circuit is always less than the resistance of any of the individual components.*

It is difficult to determine exactly what the element resistance should be without consulting the manufacturer's specifications for the appliance. The problem is that the resistance of any heater wire depends on its diameter and length as well as its temperature, and these design factors vary from one appliance make and model to another. Identical heating appliances have the same heater designs, however, and it is possible to check out the resistance of a heating appliance by comparing its resistance with that of an identical appliance that is known to be in good working order.

The voltage characteristics of the circuit in Fig. 3-3 are relatively easy to determine. Whenever the heat control switch is open, the full line voltage appears across the 1200 W heating element—it is the only element connected to the line. There is no voltage across the 3000 W element when the switch is open because the switch, itself, acts as an open circuit that takes up the full line voltage. Closing the control switch contacts applies the line voltage to the 3000 W element, leaving the circuit in a condition whereby the line voltage appears across both elements. And this situation reflects a unique condition for parallel circuits: *the voltage across parallel circuits is the same across all branches.*

Like the resistance and voltage characteristics, the current distribution in this parallel circuit is wholly determined by the setting of the heat control switch. Whenever the heat control switch is open, current flows through the only complete path available—through the 1200 W heater. The heat control switch has the ability to interrupt current flow through the 3000 W element.

Closing the control switch completes the second path for current flow, however, and creates a situation whereby current flows through both paths at the same time.

The nameplates on major heating appliances show the maximum current drain as well as the peak power consumption of the device. These printed figures represent the overall current and power figures, and the serviceman is often faced with the task of determining what the normal current flow through individual elements should be. The job is not a very difficult one, however.

Determining the amount of current a given heating element should draw from the lines is a matter of dividing its power rating by the amount of voltage applied to it. The 1200 W element in Fig. 3-3, for instance, normally draws 1200/120 or 10 A from the line. After making this calculation, a serviceman can measure the element's actual current drain with an ammeter. If the measured current level is within 10 percent of the calculated value, he can be reasonably certain the heater is working properly.

Using the same calculation for finding current, the 3000 W element should draw 25 A from a 120 V line. The combined power rating is equal to 4200 W, and applying the calculation again shows the overall current drain to be 35 A. Notice that the overall current drain as calculated with the power/voltage formula is the same as the sum of the individual currents. That is, 4200 W/120 V is the same as 10 A plus 30 A. These calculations demonstrate a third important feature of parallel-connected heater circuits: *the overall current drain of a parallel circuit is equal to the sum of the current flowing through the individual branches.*

The same calculation for determining the current drain of a heater applies equally well to 240 V circuits. A heater rated at 3000 W at 240 V, for example, draws 3000/240 or 12.5 A from the lines.

Whenever something goes wrong with a circuit of the type shown in Fig. 3-3 (or the serviceman has reason to suspect something is wrong with it), he is armed with a variety of possible techniques for confirming the trouble and pinning down an exact diagnosis. As stated many times throughout this book, a careful serviceman does not make a major repair on the basis of hunches—he must know exactly what is wrong before he can be absolutely sure that his diagnosis and servicing procedures are right.

If one of the heating elements in this parallel circuit should break open, the serviceman can track down the trouble with any kind of test that is especially sensitive to open-circuit troubles; namely any test that checks the continuity of the circuit. A continuity or resistance check across an open heating element, for example, shows a complete lack of continuity or infinite resistance. Of course the element not being tested must be removed from the circuit somehow, either by disconnecting it or, in the case of the circuit in Fig. 3-3, opening the heat control switch.

Current tests for open heating elements are appropriate, too. A heater that is working properly should draw a certain amount of current from the lines. If it is open, it doesn't draw any current at all.

Voltage tests are less reliable in the case of open heating elements because the full line voltage can appear across them whether they are open or not. A serviceman can make a tentative diagnosis of an open heater, however, if he sees that it is not working and measures full line voltage across it. This voltage test should be backed up with a continuity test.

There are not many test procedures that are appropriate for trouble-shooting heater circuits that contain a dead short. In such instances, the appliance blows a line fuse the instant power is applied, making it impossible to run power-on tests such as voltage, current, and power tests. That fact leaves only continuity or resistance tests as reliable ways to pinpoint a shorted heater. And since a simple continuity test cannot distinguish a normal low resistance from a short-circuit trouble, the field of possible instrument tests is finally reduced to a resistance check. A normal heater has a resistance on the order of 10 Ω or more, while a completely shorted heater has a resistance of 0 Ω.

In the case of a parallel heater circuit of the kind illustrated in Fig. 3-3, a troubleshooter can diagnose a completely shorted element without resorting to a resistance check. The trick is to disconnect the suspected heater from the circuit and apply full line power to the appliance. If the appliance no longer blows fuses, he can be reasonably certain that the element he disconnected is shorted out. He can back up the conclusion by looking for physical signs of a dead short (burned components and wiring) and running a resistance test on the suspected element.

It is relatively easy to diagnose a partially shorted heating element in a parallel circuit once the serviceman understands the electrical characteristics of such circuits. An element that is partially shorted has less electrical resistance to current flow than the same element does when it is in good working order. The lower resistance makes it consume above-normal power and draw more than the normal amount of current from the lines. A partially shorted heater, by the way, tends to produce more heat than it normally does.

A serviceman can diagnose a partially shorted heater by comparing its resistance with the manufacturer's specifications or the resistance of the same element in another appliance that is know to be in good working condition. Current and power tests are good for diagnosing partially shorted heating elements. If the appliance consumes more than its rated power when the suspected element is turned on, chances are quite good that element is partially shorted. And by the same token, the element consumes above-normal current from the supply lines.

Voltage tests are altogether inappropriate for checking on partially shorted heating elements that are connected in parallel. The problem is that the voltage across a parallel-connected element is equal to the line voltage, whether or not it is partially shorted.

3-3.2   Series Heater Circuits

Figure 3-4 shows a common type of series-connected heater circuit. The operating level in this instance is controlled by a switch connected in parallel with one of the heating elements. Whenever the switch is closed, full line voltage appears across the remaining element, making it generate its full 120 V heat. Opening the switch, however, forces the line voltage to be divided between the two elements, allowing the element with the highest resistance to take on a proportionally larger share of the voltage.

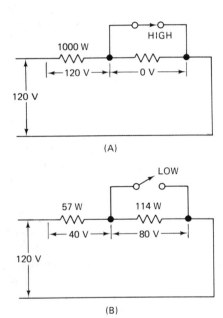

Fig. 3-4   A series-connected heat selector circuit. (A) High heat setting, (B) Low heat setting.

The consequences of adding a heater in series with another can be confusing to anyone just learning his way around the world of electricity. Contrary to what might seem like common sense at first, adding a heating element in series with a constant-voltage circuit lowers the overall power dissipation of the circuit, regardless of the relative resistances or power ratings of the heaters involved.

In Fig. 3-4(A), for instance, the lone heating element dissipates 1000 W when it has 120 V impressed across it. Throwing the other element in series as shown in Fig. 3-4(B) lowers the voltage across the 1000 W element to 40 V and thereby decreases its power dissipation to about 57 W. The switched element takes on the remaining 80 V of supply voltage and dissipates about 114 W. The total power dissipation of the circuit is thus 171 W when the elements are connected in series and a full 1000 W when the common element is operating alone.

A troubleshooter's analysis of this circuit can begin with consideration of the effects of an open heating element. *The current flow through a series circuit is the same through every component of the circuit*; and anything that changes the amount of current flowing through one of the components causes a corresponding change in the current flowing through all the others. If the 1000 W heating element should burn open, for example, its current flow goes to zero; and by the same token, the current flow through the other element or switch (depending on whether the switch is open or closed) drops to zero.

If the switched element should open, however, the trouble will appear only when the switch is open. Whenever the switch is closed, the circuit current bypasses the switched element anyway. Opening the switch interrupts that path, forcing current to flow through the 114 W element. But if that element is open, current ceases altogether.

A current test is thus appropriate for diagnosing an open heating element in a series heater circuit. If full line power is applied and no current flows, one of the elements is open. Opening and closing the heat control switch while watching the circuit's current drain can pinpoint the open element: If it is the 1000 W element, current does not flow, regardless of the switch setting. If it is the 114 W element that is open, current flows when the switch is closed but stops altogether when the switch is open.

Voltage tests for open circuits in a series heater string are reliable and rather easy to run. The full line voltage will always appear across an open element whenever there is more than one element in the circuit. If the 1000 W element is open, 120 V appears across it whether the switch is open or closed. Compare that result with the normal voltage distributions shown in Fig. 3-4(A) and (B). If the 114 W element is open, the serviceman will read the full 120 V line potential across that element when the heat control switch is opened. There can be no voltage across the 114 W element when the switch is closed, no matter whether the element is open, shorted, or in good condition. A convenient way to run a continuity test for open elements in a series circuit is by disconnecting the appliance from its power source, opening all the switches, and monitoring the continuity as measured from the power input terminals. If an open-circuit condition is present, the circuit's overall resistance is infinity. Running a jumper wire across the elements one at a time can uncover the open element because the overall resistance suddenly drops to some low value the instant the jumper is placed across the open element.

3-4 QUESTIONS

1. How much power is a heating element consuming if it draws 15 A from a 120 V source?

2. How much current will flow through a 1200 W heating element when 120 V is applied to it?

3. Does the resistance of a typical heating element (a) increase, (b) decrease, or (c) remain unchanged as its temperature increases?

4. If a 1 ft section of nichrome wire has a resistance of 0.66 Ω, how much resistance will a 10 ft section have?

5. If a 1 ft section of nichrome wire has a resistance of 0.5 Ω, how much wire is required to obtain a resistance of 10 Ω?

6. The total resistance of a parallel heater circuit is (a) greater than, (b) less than, or (c) equal to the smallest resistance in the circuit.

7. The total power dissipation of a parallel heater circuit is (a) equal to the sum of the individual power ratings, (b) equal to the average power ratings, or (c) less than the smallest heating element power rating.

8. The voltage across the elements in a parallel circuit are (a) equal or (b) unequal.

9. The total resistance of a series heater circuit is (a) greater than, (b) less than, or (c) equal to the smallest resistance in the circuit.

10. The total power dissipation of a parallel heater circuit is (a) equal to the sum of the individual power ratings, (b) equal to the average power ratings, or (c) less than the power rating of the largest heating element.

11. Shorting out one heating element in a series heater circuit causes the total power dissipation to (a) increase, (b) decrease, or (c) remain unchanged.

4

Thermostats and Electric Heat Controls

All major electrical heating appliances use heat control switching circuits of one kind or another. The last part of Chapter 3 takes up the subject of manually operated heat controls, and this chapter considers automatic heat controls and their associated circuits—circuits that use thermostats to control or limit the operating temperature of an appliance.

4-1 PRINCIPLES OF THERMOSTATS

Technically speaking, a thermostat is any device that transforms a change in temperature into a switching action for the purpose of controlling temperature levels. This is a very general definition of a thermostat because it applies to thermostats of all kinds, including those used in heating or cooling appliances, electrical, or gas-operated appliances.

The purpose of this chapter is to outline the essential features of three main classes of thermostats used in the heat control sections of all-electric heating appliances: bimetal, diaphragm, and resistance-type thermostats.

All three types do the same kinds of jobs, but their principles of operation are different. This chapter also deals with troubleshooting and servicing hints for basic thermostats and thermostat control circuits.

4-1.1 Bimetal Thermostats

It is a well-known fact that most metals expand when they are heated and contract when cooled. Furthermore, some metals expand more than others do when they are both heated to the same temperature; and it so happens that the metals that expand the most when heated also contract the most whenever they are cooled.

The percentage of change in the length of a bar of metal that is heated or cooled is not very great, however. It is almost impossible to notice the increase in length of a short strip of copper when it is heated from a freezing cold to a red-hot temperature. If two unlike strips of metal are tightly welded together lengthwise, however, it is easy to see the effects of their unequal rates of expansion and contraction—their small changes in length show up as a noticeable warping or bending. This is the basic principle behind bimetal thermostats.

As the name implies, a *bi*metal thermostat is made up of *two* unlike metals. The metals are tightly bonded or welded together lengthwise, and the assembly responds to changes in temperature by bending in one direction or the other. When the bimetal is heated, for instance, the metal that expands the most winds up on the outside surface of the bend; and when the metals are cooled, the metal that expanded the most also contracts the most, placing it on the inside surface of the bend. See Fig. 4-1.

If one end of the bimetal assembly is fixed so that it cannot move, the opposite end bends in response to temperature changes with enough force to

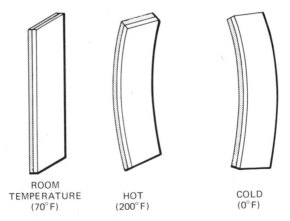

ROOM
TEMPERATURE
(70°F)

HOT
(200°F)

COLD
(0°F)

Fig. 4-1 Response of a bimetal strip to changes in temperature.

operate a set of switch contacts. Most bimetal elements have a small piece of porcelain or ceramic material attached to the movable end. This piece of tough, nonconductive material activates the electrical switch contacts while insulating the bimetal assembly from the electrically "hot" switch.

Figure 4-2 illustrates a complete thermostat assembly. This assembly includes a bimetal element and a set of electrical switch contacts that are closed at normal room temperature. As the surrounding temperature rises, the bimetal assembly begins bending in a direction that tends to open the switch contacts; and when the temperature reached a preset level, the bimetal forces the switch contacts open.

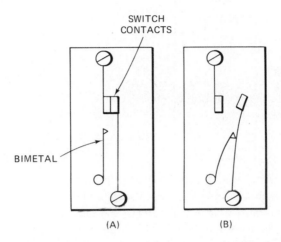

Fig. 4-2 Operation of a basic bimetal thermostat assembly. (A) Below trip-point temperature, (B) Above trip-point temperature.

A thermostat assembly of this type can be used in heating appliances as an overheat safety switch. Suppose that the operating temperature of an oven should never exceed 750°F. The thermostat could be factory calibrated to open the switch contacts at about 750°F. The normal operating temperature of the oven is well below that temperature, so that the thermostat contacts remain closed under normal conditions. If the normal oven controls should ever fail in a way that lets the oven temperature skyrocket upward, the safety thermostat contacts pop open to interrupt all current flow to the oven's heating elements. The oven is thus effectively turned off, and it remains turned off until the temperature falls to a level that allows the bimetal to close the contacts once again.

Basic bimetal thermostat controls of the type illustrated in Fig. 4-2 are simple, reliable, and inexpensive. Their operating temperature is set at the time of manufacture, however, and a serviceman should never make any attempt to change the trip-point of the contacts. For all practical purposes, then, these simple thermostat controls are not adjustable. They are used either in single-temperature heater circuits or in circuits designed to shut down an appliance in the event of a serious overheating condition.

Figure 4-3 shows the principles behind an adjustable bimetal thermostat assembly. The only real difference between this thermostat and one designed for fixed-temperature operations is that the adjustable version has a screw-type adjustment that varies the distance the bimetal element has to bend. The farther the bimetal bends, the higher the temperature required to open the electrical contacts rises.

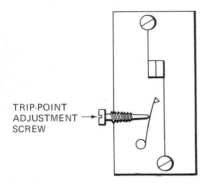

TRIP-POINT
ADJUSTMENT →
SCREW

Fig. 4-3 A bimetal thermostat equipped with an adjustable trip-point.

The general operating range of an adjustable thermostat is set at the time of manufacture. Some thermostats are to be operated in the 50°–90°F range, for example, whereas others using the same basic construction are to operate in the 100°–500°F range. This basic operating range is preset, but the user can turn the screw adjustment to obtain any desired temperature control level within that range.

The fixed and adjustable bimetal thermostats described thus far must directly sense the temperature being controlled. Such thermostats can control the operating temperature of a clothes dryer, for instance, if they are situated directly in the hot air stream or on the side of the clothes hamper. The bimetal contacts for a freezer, by the same token, must be located inside the freezer compartment.

The fact that these simple thermostat controls must be located in the temperature-controlled space poses no real problems for fixed-temperature controls. But wherever the user must be able to adjust the operating temperature, it is often inconvenient to place the thermostat adjustment and the bimetal in the same place. Who would want to readjust the operating temperature of an oven, for example, by reaching inside the heating space to find the control knob?

It is thus desirable in many instances to have the bimetal located in one place and the control knob and switch contacts in another. This poses something of a problem as far as simple bimetal thermostat designs are concerned. The main trouble is finding a reliable mechanical linkage that lets the user turn a knob on a control panel and cause a corresponding change in the thermostat setting some several feet away (and perhaps around several sharp corners). Appliance engineers have overcome this problem with several different heat-sensing temperature control schemes: *biased bimetal, hydraulic diaphragm,* and *resistance-sensing controls.* The remainder of this section deals with the principles of biased bimetal thermostat controls. The other controls are described in the two sections that follow.

A biased thermostat control senses the appliance's operating temperature indirectly. All the usual thermostat components; the bimetal strip, electrical contacts, and user's heat control adjustment, are located inside the same compact assembly. Furthermore, the control assembly can be located far from the appliance's main heating coils.

The key component in a biased thermostat control is a small auxiliary heating element, or *warp heater.* As shown in Fig. 4-4, the warp heater is connected across the power source so that it is turned on whenever power is applied to the main heating element. The warp heater effectively mimics the heating conditions of the main heating element—the hotter the main element becomes, the hotter the little warp heater gets. And whenever the warp heater reaches a temperature that is sufficiently high to make the bimetal thermostat contacts pop open, the switch cuts off the supply of current to both the warp heater and main heating element. The thermostat bimetal actually responds to the heat of the warp heater, but it ultimately controls the appliance's actual operating temperature.

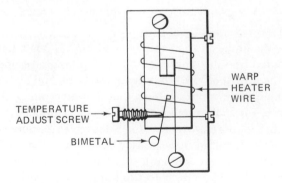

Fig. 4-4 A biased bimetal thermostat. Note the internal warp (bias) heating element.

4-1.2 The Robertshaw Hydraulic Diaphragm Thermostat Control

A hydraulic thermostat control, commonly called a Robertshaw heat control, performs the same heat controlling operations that bimetal thermostats do. The essential difference between the two kinds of thermostats is that a Robertshaw control takes advantage of the expansion and contraction characteristics of liquids instead of metals.

Most liquids expand when they are heated and contract when they are cooled. (Ordinary water is a notable exception.) Heating a long, narrow tube filled to the top with an oily fluid makes the fluid ooze out the end. If the tube is sealed, it might even rupture under the force of expansion.

Diaphragm thermostats take advantage of this force of expansion to operate a set of switch contacts. As illustrated in Fig. 4-5, a Robertshaw thermostat assembly is comprised of a long tube, or capillary, which is sealed at one end with a bulb-type reservoir and an accordion-like brass diaphragm at the other. The bulb, capillary, and diaphragm are filled with a liquid that has freezing and boiling temperatures well beyond the normal operating temperatures of the appliance.

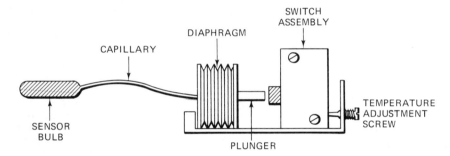

Fig. 4-5   A simplified Robertshaw hydraulic diaphragm thermostat control.

Whenever the liquid in the capillary and bulb is heated, it expands and forces more liquid into the diaphragm. The diaphragm responds by stretching. Cooling the liquid, on the other hand, forces the fluid in the assembly to contract, making more room for fluid that is drawn out of the diaphragm. In this instance, the diaphragm responds by shortening.

It is thus the diaphragm that changes length in response to changes in the temperature of the fluid in the sensor bulb. The expansion and contraction of the diaphragm can operate a set of switch contacts which, in turn, remove or apply electrical power to the appliance's heating elements. The trip-point temperature of this thermostat assembly is adjusted by changing the distance that the diaphragm must expand and contract to activate the switch. For example, turning a set screw that moves the diaphragm farther away from its switch assembly effectively increases the trip-point temperature because the diaphragm has to expand a greater amount to activate the switch.

The sensor bulb in a Robertshaw thermostat assembly must be situated in the space where the temperature is to be controlled, but using a long capillary tube makes it possible to locate the diaphragm and control adjustment at any other convenient place on the appliance—normally on the user's control panel.

The main advantage of a diaphragm control is that it allows the user to adjust the heating level of an appliance at a place that can be far removed from the actual heating space. A Robertshaw thermostat system is also more accurate and reliable than a warp heater bimetal thermostat because the diaphragm assembly responds to the actual appliance operating temperature rather than a simulated version of it.

4-1.3 The King Seeley Resistance Temperature Control

A King Seeley temperature control uses a resistance sensing circuit such as the one illustrated in Fig. 4-6. Instead of operating according to changes in fluid pressure, a resistive sensing element is made up of a solid material that changes its electrical resistance to current flow in response to changes in applied temperature.

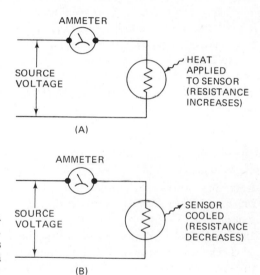

Fig. 4-6 Current response of a circuit using a resistive heat sensor. (A) Low current when sensor is heated, (B) Higher current when sensor is allowed to cool.

The resistance of the sensing element increases with temperature; and as shown in Fig. 4-6(A), the current through the circuit responds by decreasing. As the temperature around the sensor decreases, the resistance is lowered and the current flow through the circuit increases. (Note Fig. 4-6(B).)

Figure 4-7 shows a simple demonstration circuit made up of an ordinary variable resistor R1, a resistance heat sensor and an ordinary light bulb. The total current through the circuit (and the brightness of the bulb) is determined by the combined resistances of R1 and the resistance sensor.

There are two ways to change the brightness of the bulb: by changing

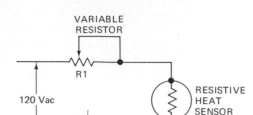

Fig. 4-7 A simple circuit for demonstrating the action of a King Seeley heat sensor control.

the setting of the variable resistor and by changing the temperature surrounding the sensor. The bulb can be made brighter, for example, by either decreasing the resistance of R1 or by lowering the temperature around the sensing element. In either case the current through the circuit increases and the bulb burns more brightly. Of course the bulb can be dimmed by either increasing the resistance value of R1 or by heating the space around the sensor. The higher combined resistances in this part of the demonstration causes the current to decrease and the bulb to burn with less light.

A King Seeley resistance thermostat circuit is normally used in conjunction with a *differential thermostat* control. It is important to have a complete understanding of these differential thermostats before it is possible to have a real appreciation of the value of King Seeley temperature controls.

Figure 4-8 illustrates the operation of a differential thermostat. The thermostat actually has two separate warp heaters and a single bimetal strip. The two heaters and bimetal are arranged so that the thermostat contacts remain closed as long as the temperature of the two heaters is the same. It does not make any difference what the temperature might be—it could be 100°F or 500°F. As long as the temperatures are equal, the contacts remain closed.

Now consider what might happen whenever the two warp heaters generate different temperatures. Differential thermostats can be designed in many different ways, but most of them are assembled so that the bimetal always attempts to bend toward the hotter warp heater. Suppose the assembly in Fig. 4-8 is operating with warp heater H2 hotter than H1. Under this particular differential heating condition, the bimetal tends to bend toward H2. And whenever H1 happens to be hotter than H2, the bimetal tends to bend in the opposite direction—toward H1.

One important modification has to be built into this basic differential thermostat before it can work as desired in a King Seeley temperature control unit. The contact assembly has to be mechanically designed so that the contacts do not separate whenever the bimetal bends toward H1. Since the contacts are normally closed whenever the warp heater temperatures are

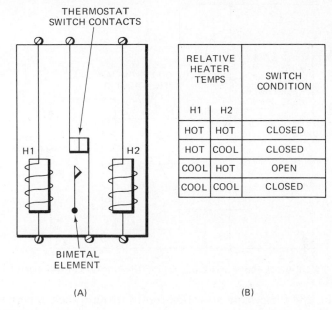

(A)   (B)

Fig. 4-8 A differential thermostat. (A) Simplified drawing of electrical and mechanical parts, (B) Table of responses.

equal, the only way to open the contacts in this modified assembly is by making H2 hotter than H1.

The table in Fig. 4-8 summarizes the operation of a differential thermostat as it is used in conjunction with a King Seeley temperature control system.

The differential thermostat and King Seeley sensor are combined in Fig. 4-9. The moment voltage is applied to this circuit, current flows through H1 and H2. As long as both warp heaters have about the same temperature (as they normally do at the beginning of a heating cycle), the thermostat contacts remain closed.

Now suppose that the heat sensor "feels" an increase in temperature from a main heating element. The sensor responds by showing an increase in resistance, which, in turn, decreases the amount of current flowing through H1. With less current flowing through H1, the temperature of that warp heater decreases.

In the meantime, the temperature of H2 remains unchanged, setting up the conditions necessary for opening the relay contacts—a condition where H1 is cooler than H2.

When the thermostat contacts finally open, they interrupt current flow through H2, letting that warp heater cool. Eventually the temperature of H2 falls to a point where it equals the temperature of H1, and the thermostat contacts close again. If the temperature of H1 is still falling, the contacts soon

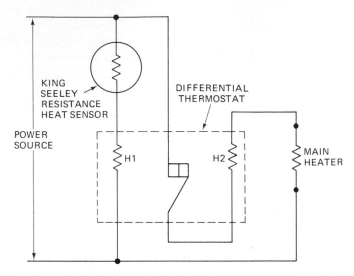

Fig. 4-9   A simplified King Seeley thermostat control circuit.

open again, and the cycling operation continues until the temperature of H1 stops changing.

The thermostat contacts in this circuit respond directly to a difference in temperature between the two warp heaters. Ultimately, however, this King Seeley system responds directly to the temperature of the main heating element. This feature makes the King Seeley system quite different from a simple warp heater thermostat control described in Sec. 4-1.1. The simpler scheme responds to a simulated, and less reliable, version of the appliance's operating temperature.

4-2   TROUBLES IN THERMOSTATS

Thermostats are relatively delicate mechanical devices that can be the cause of many different kinds of appliance troubles. The following list summarizes some of the more common thermostat problems.

THERMOSTAT CONTACTS FAIL TO CLOSE.   This trouble is often due to a mechanical failure of the connections between the heat sensing element and the thermostat switch contacts. The same kind of trouble, however, can appear in instances where the electrical contacts become covered with corrosion or a film of household grime.

THERMOSTAT CONTACTS FAIL TO OPEN.   Thermostat contacts are sometimes welded closed by a serious short-circuit condition elsewhere in the appliance. In such cases, the repairman must locate the cause of the short before replacing the defective thermostat. (There is no point in running the risk of burning out a new thermostat.) A badly misaligned thermostat control can create the same symptom.

THERMOSTAT REGULATES AT THE WRONG TEMPERATURE. A minor production flaw can sometimes cause this trouble, but it is more often due to user abuse or some tinkering on the part of an unskilled repairman. A thermostat is normally considered to be in good calibration if it maintains an operating temperature within 5 percent of the reading on the control knob.

THERMOSTAT ALLOWS TOO MUCH TEMPERATURE DIFFERENTIAL. No thermostat holds an operating temperature at exactly one point. The thermostat contacts might open at a particular temperature, but the temperature has to drop several degrees before the contacts close again. This difference between the turn-on and turn-off temperatures is called the *temperature differential*. A temperature differential of 5 percent is not unusually great. If the heat in an oven has to drop 10 or 15 percent before the heat goes on again, however, the temperature differential is indeed too wide. This kind of trouble can be caused by minor production flaws that show up only after the appliance has been in use for several years. And, as with thermostats that operate at the wrong temperature, the temperature differential can be thrown out of alignment by user abuse or tampering.

4-2.1 Servicing Thermostats

It is very difficult to service many thermostats used in modern major appliances. The main problem is that they are often sealed in a way that makes it practically impossible to open them without doing some permanent damage. The general opinion among experienced major appliance servicemen is that it is cheaper in the long run to replace a defective thermostat than it is to attempt any kind of surgery on it. Of course this replacement policy places a special burden of responsibility upon the repairman: he must make certain that the thermostat is actually the cause of the trouble he is trying to remedy.

In instances where the thermostat contacts can be exposed for servicing, the contacts can be scraped clean with fine emery paper or crocus cloth. The contacts should also be wiped with a cotton swab that has been lightly wetted with ordinary rubbing alcohol.

A set of electrical contacts that have been welded closed can sometimes be opened by gently prying them with a pointed wooden stick. The thermostat should be replaced if it turns out that the contacts are badly roughed up by the weld. Otherwise they can be smoothed and cleaned as described in the previous paragraph.

It is normally impractical to repair or replace small parts within a thermostat control, even when the working elements are readily accessible. It is a good idea to confirm a diagnosis of a faulty thermostat by making a visual inspection of the assembly; but as a serviceman, you can save yourself a great deal of tedious work and save the customer money by replacing a thermostat that is mechanically defective.

4-2.2   Calibrating Thermostats

The number one rule for calibrating major appliance thermostats is rather easy to remember: do not do it unless you can prove that it is absolutely necessary. Some well-meaning servicemen make a habit of "touching up" the thermostat on just about any job requiring work on the heat controls. This sounds good to the customer because he thinks he is getting a bonus service. The problem is that changing the service adjustments on a thermostat can create more problems that it cures.

The first rule of thermostat calibration really says that it is necessary to check out the temperature control characteristics of the heating appliance before attempting any kind of calibration procedures. It is not enough to accept the customer's word that cookies do not bake as fast or as evenly as they once did. Testing the temperature characteristics of a major heating appliance calls for careful temperature readings and other precise observations described in connection with specific appliances elsewhere in this book.

The second rule for calibrating thermostats is to use the manufacturer's specifications and servicing notes whenever possible. Many thermostats have screw adjustments that look like they should be calibration controls. It is embarrasing to adjust a screw, only to find a part of the thermostat falling off in your hand because you "adjusted" a mounting screw. The manufacturer's servicing notes describe exactly which screw to turn.

Furthermore, the manufacturer's notes describe which way to turn the screw. It is bad enough to turn the wrong screw, but turning the right screw the wrong way only compounds the problems that already exist.

Every now and then, a serviceman finds himself in the awkward position of having to make a thermostat calibration without the help of a service manual. If a quick call to the shop does not provide the right kind of information, there are only three things that can be done: leave the job undone, replace the thermostat, or attempt a trial-and-error calibration.

Fortunately, there are some techniques for resetting the calibration of a heat control without touching the thermostat itself. Such procedures are not always appropriate, but the instances in which they do work are described in connection with specific heating appliances elsewhere in this book.

It is not a good idea to leave the job undone if the system is very far out of calibration, and replacing the thermostat should be considered a final resort. Some thermostats can be opened for easy access and visual inspection, and it is these thermostats that can be calibrated without too much difficulty.

The trip-point temperature of a thermostat control is always set with an adjustment that changes the distance that the bimetal or diaphragm has to travel in order to open the switch contacts. After locating the calibration screw, note the ways the adjustment has to be turned in order to shorten and lengthen the distance of travel. If the operating temperature of the appliance has to be increased, as determined by careful preliminary testing, the adjustment has to be turned in the direction that increases its distance of travel. If the operating temperature has to be lowered, the distance of travel must be shortened.

The next problem is to determine how far to turn the trip-point adjustment. The basic idea is to monitor the appliance's operating temperature and adjust the thermostat to trip at the desired temperature level. The best way to do this is to temporarily adjust the trip-point calibration screw in a direction that increases the operating temperature (increase the distance of travel to the switch contacts). Start the heating operation and watch the temperature rise until it is about 10 percent below the desired calibration point. Quickly, but carefully, adjust the trip-point screw so that the thermostat contacts just barely trip open. Observe the operating temperature for several on-off cycles, "tweaking" the calibration screw one-quarter turn or less to compensate for any small discrepancies.

4-3 BASIC THERMOSTAT CONTROL CIRCUITS

Thermostats and the heating elements that they control often produce similar outward symptoms when one or the other goes bad. Thermostats and heating elements are both rather expensive, and they are both troublesome to replace. A wise serviceman does his best, therefore, to make an accurate diagnosis of the trouble before considering replacing a thermostat or heating element.

This section deals with the theory of operation and troubleshooting procedures for some of the most common kinds of thermostat heat control circuits. Later chapters dealing with specific kinds of major heating appliances outline the same kind of information for special heater circuits.

4-3.1 A Simple Series Heater Control

Figure 4-10 illustrates the simplest possible kind of thermostat heat control circuit. The thermostat contacts are connected in series with the heating element that they control, and while the contacts are closed, the heater generates its full rated power. Whenever the operating temperature rises sufficiently high to make the contacts pop open, all power is removed from the circuit.

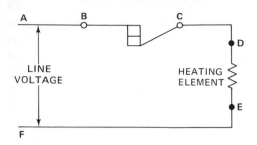

Fig. 4-10   A series-connected thermostat circuit.

The thermostat assembly in this circuit can be either a simple bimetal thermostat or a diaphragm-type control. In either case, the switch contacts open whenever the operating temperature reaches a preselected point, and they close again when the temperature drops off several degrees. The contacts thus cycle open and closed to maintain a fairly constant temperature.

The following troubleshooting guide applies to all heat control circuits that work on the principles described above in connection with Fig. 4-10. Note the care taken to distinguish thermostat troubles from troubles in the heating element.

No heat

1.   Line voltage not reaching the circuit—apply full power to the circuit, and check the voltage across the power input terminals (between points **A** and **F**). The trouble is confirmed if the test shows no voltage at the terminals.

2.   Heating element open—apply full power to the appliance, and measure the voltage across the heating element (between points **D** and **E**). The trouble is confirmed if full line voltage appears across the heater, but it is not getting hot. If the full line voltage *does not* appear across the heater, the trouble has to be elsewhere in the circuit.

   Doublecheck the diagnosis of an open heating element by disconnecting the wiring to one of the heater connections (either at point **D** or **E**) and running a continuity or resistance check on the heater. The diagnosis is doubly confirmed if the resistance between points **D** and **E** is infinite, or if a continuity test across those points shows a complete lack of continuity.

3.   Thermostat contacts broken open or dirty—apply full power to the appliance, and measure the voltage across the thermostat contacts (between points **B** and **C**). The thermostat contacts are indeed open if this test shows that full line voltage is dropped across the contacts.

To doublecheck the diagnosis, temporarily remove power from the appliance and connect a jumper wire across the thermostat contacts. Reapply full power to the appliance and note the heater's response. If the heater begins operating at full temperature, there can be no doubt that the trouble is in the thermostat.

There is little profit in attempting to repair a set of open thermostat contacts. The best all-around servicing procedure is to replace the entire thermostat assembly with a new one. Of course the replacement thermostat must have the same current rating, voltage rating and operating temperature as the original.

High heat, regardless of thermostat setting

1. Heat control badly out of adjustment—set the heat control knob to the lowest temperature range, and apply full power to the appliance. Monitor the operating temperature in a manner appropriate to the appliance (see the chapters dealing with specific appliances). If the thermostat does not cycle off when the temperature rises about 20 percent above the control setting, turn the thermostat calibration screw in a direction that lowers the operating temperature. If the thermostat then cuts off the power to the element, the thermostat can be calibrated as described in Sec. 4-2.2.

2. Thermostat contacts stuck closed—perform the test sequence described under Trouble 1. If the thermostat does not cut off power to the heater when the calibration screw is adjusted to lower the trip-point, the trouble is fairly well confirmed. If the thermostat cannot be serviced as described in Sec. 4-2.1, it should be replaced.

Heat too high or too low

1. Thermostat out of calibration—monitor the appliance's operating temperature in a manner that is most appropriate (see Chapters 7–14, which deal with specific heating appliances), and calibrate the control as described in Sec. 4-2.2.

2. Thermostat contacts sticking—if attempts to calibrate the thermostat fail to cure the trouble, the only alternative is to replace the thermostat assembly.

Appliance draws excessive current

The most likely trouble is a shorted heater. See the appropriate troubleshooting procedures in Sec. 3-2.2.

4-3.2   A Biased Heater Control Circuit

Figure 4-11 shows a circuit that uses a bias-controlled thermostat. When power is first applied to the appliance, the closed thermostat contacts allow full line voltage to appear across the thermostat bias heater and the main heating element. The temperatures of both the warp heater and main element begin to rise, and the thermostat's bimetal bends in a direction that tends to open the switch contacts. In a biased thermostat control, the contacts actually respond to the temperature of the warp heater, rather than the heating element temperature.

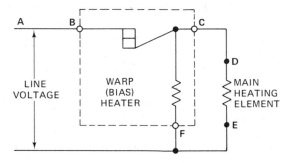

Fig. 4-11   A thermostat circuit employing a warp heater thermostat assembly.

Whenever the thermostat contacts trip open, they remove all power from the warp heater and main heating element. Both heaters thus begin to cool, and when the temperature of the warp heater drops sufficiently far, the bimetal allows the switch contacts to close again.

The following troubleshooting guide applies to heat control circuits of the type illustrated in Fig. 4-11.

No heat

1. Line voltage not reaching the circuit—apply full power to the circuit, and check the voltage across the power input terminals (between points **A** and **G**). The trouble is confirmed if this test shows no voltage.

2. Main heating element open—apply full power to the appliance, and measure the voltage across the heating element (between

points **D** and **E**). The trouble is confirmed if full line voltage appears across the heating element, but it is not getting hot. Doublecheck the diagnosis of an open heating element by disconnecting the wiring to one of the main heater terminals (either at point **D** or point **E**), and run a continuity or resistance check on the heater. The diagnosis is confirmed if the resistance is infinite or the continuity is lacking altogether.

3. Thermostat switch contacts broken or dirty—apply full power to the appliance and measure the voltage across the thermostat contacts (between points **B** and **C**). The thermostat contacts are electrically open if this test shows the presence of full line voltage. Doublecheck the diagnosis by connecting a temporary jumper wire across the thermostat switch terminals (between points **B** and **D**). The trouble is doubly confirmed if the main heating element gets hot.

High heat, regardless of thermostat setting

1. Bias heater open—remove all power to the appliance, and disconnect the wiring to the common terminal on the thermostat control (at point **C**). Check the resistance of the bias heater by connecting an ohmmeter across it (between points **C** and **F**). The trouble is confirmed if the test shows infinite resistance.

   It might be difficult to figure out which thermostat terminal is common to the switch contacts and the bias heater. In such instances, completely remove the thermostat control from the appliance, and run resistance checks on all combinations of the three thermostat connections. The trouble is confirmed if any pair of contacts show infinite resistance.

2. Heat control badly out of adjustment—attempt to calibrate the thermostat control as described in Sec. 6-2.2 or the manufacturer's specifications. The trouble is confirmed if the calibration procedure cures the problem.

3. Thermostat contacts stuck closed—this trouble is diagnosed by the process of elimination: if the steps in troubles 1 and 2 fail to cure the problem, there is little doubt that the contacts are stuck. If possible, confirm the diagnosis by visually inspecting the mechanical workings before replacing the thermostat.

Heat too high or too low

1. Thermostat out of calibration—monitor the appliance's operating temperature, and calibrate the thermostat control according

to the manufacturer's instructions. If the control does not respond to the calibration procedures, the trouble is elsewhere in the thermostat assembly.

2.   Improper heating from the bias heater—consult the manufacturer's specifications for the normal room-temperature resistance of the bias heater connections (between points **C** and **F**). If the heater resistance is more that 10 percent out of tolerance, the entire thermostat assembly must be replaced.

　　　 If the manufacturer's specification for the proper bias resistance is not available, compare the resistance to that of a similar control that is known to be in good working order.

3.   Thermostat contacts sticking—if attempts to calibrate the thermostat fail to cure the trouble, and if the resistance check on the bias heater shows it is in good order, the logical process of elimination leaves a set of sticking contacts as a strong possibility. If the sticking contacts cannot be freed as described in Sec. 4-2.1, the entire control assembly should be replaced.

4-3.3   A King Seeley Heat Control Circuit

　　　 Figure 4-12 shows a typical King Seeley heat control circuit for a 240 V heating element. For safety reasons, the control portion of this circuit is isolated from the 240 V service lines by means of a power transformer that steps the operating voltage down from 240 V to 12 V. And as described in Sec. 4-1.3, this King Seeley resistance heat sensor is used in conjunction with a differential thermostat assembly TH1.

　　　 A second thermostat assembly, TH2, is commonly known as a *hot-wire relay*. It is actually a thermostat of the bimetal variety, but the normally open contacts respond almost immediately to normal current flow through its warp heater H3. The assembly works like a relay, however, in that the thermostat contacts are pulled closed whenever current flows through its warp heater and the contacts pop open very soon after current through the warp heater is cut off.

　　　 The moment the power switch S1 is closed, the S1-A section connects one side of the main heating element to L1 and it connects the primary winding of the power transformer across the 240 V source. Closing S1 also applies 12 V to the control circuit through S1-B; applying power to the control circuit completes a path for current flow through H3, H2, and the closed contacts of TH1. The current flowing through H3 makes this warp heater generate enough heat to pull closed the contacts of TH2. Closing these contacts completes the 240 V circuit to the main heating element that now begins to warm up.

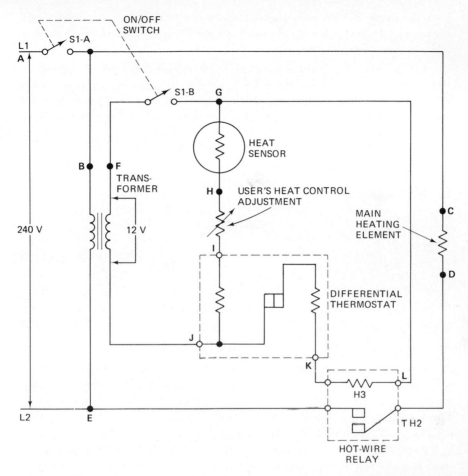

Fig. 4-12 A complete King Seeley temperature control circuit.

In the meantime, current is also flowing through the control circuit made up of the heat sensor, variable resistor (user's temperature selector) and the warp heater H1 in TH1. As long as the temperature of H1 is greater than that of H2, the thermostat contacts in TH1 remain closed. The only way to open the contacts in TH1 while the circuit is turned on is by decreasing the running temperature of H1.

The heat sensor is always located in the space being heated by the main heating element; and as described in Sec. 4-1.3, the resistance of the heat sensor increases with increased applied temperature. As the temperature of the heated space rises toward its selected level, the resistance of the heat sensor rises accordingly. Now increasing the resistance of the heat sensor in this manner causes the current through that leg of the control circuit to decrease. And as the current through the sensor branch of the control circuit decreases, the heat generated by warp heater H1 decreases by a corresponding amount.

The temperature of the main heating element and H1 always change in opposite directions. As the temperature of the main heating element rises, for example, the temperature of H1 falls. While the heating space is warming up, then, the running temperature of H1 is falling, and the temperature of that warp heater eventually becomes lower than that of H2—creating the conditions necessary for opening the contacts in the differential thermostat, TH1.

Whenever the contacts in TH1 open, current stops flowing through the heating element in the hot-wire relay, and the contacts in TH2 respond by popping open. Opening the contacts in TH2 removes 240 V power from the main heating element, thus completing the initial warm-up phase of the heating cycle.

As the temperature around the main heating element and heat sensor drops off, the heat sensor allows more current to flow through H1. This warp heater then grows hotter, and its temperature soon rises above that of H2—setting up the conditions for closing the contacts in TH1 once again. And when those contacts do close, current flows through H3 in the hot-wire relay, 240 V power is again applied to the main heating element, and another heating phase begins.

This system continues cycling the hot-wire relay on and off to maintain a fairly even operating temperature in the appliance. The operating temperature of the appliance is normally set by means of the user's temperature selector knob. This knob controls the resistance of the variable resistor connected in series with the heat sensor. Setting the variable resistor to a high resistance level means that the heat sensor's temperature does not have to rise very much before the contacts in TH1 pop open. A high resistance setting on the variable resistor thus corresponds to a relatively low temperature setting. Adjusting the variable resistor for a low resistance, on the other hand, increases the appliance's operating temperature because the heat sensor's resistance has to increase a much greater amount before the contacts in TH1 are opened.

The following troubleshooting guide applies to the King Seeley heat control circuit shown in Fig. 4-12.

No heat

1. Main line voltage not reaching the appliance—connect a voltmeter or 240 V voltage tester across the 240 V terminals. If the test shows no voltage or low voltage, the trouble is confirmed.

2. 12 V power not getting to the control circuit—connect a voltmeter across the secondary terminals on the power transformer

(between points **F** and **J**). Turn on the power switch S1 and note the voltage. The problem is confirmed if no voltage appears on the meter.

To narrow down the causes of this particular symptom, check the voltage across the transformer primary (between points **B** and **E**). If the voltage—240 V in this case—is *not* present, the trouble lies in the wiring between the 240 V power lines and the transformer primary.

If full line voltage appears across the transformer primary, however, the transformer is most likely the faulty component. *To test a transformer:* (1) Remove it from the circuit and test the continuity of the primary and secondary windings. Infinite resistance on either winding indicates an open-circuit fault in the transformer. (2) Apply full line voltage to the primary winding, but leave the secondary winding completely disconnected. The transformer has a shorted winding if it draws excessive current or grows too hot to touch under these test conditions. A defective transformer must be replaced—it cannot be repaired.

3.   Main heating element open—remove the main heating element from the appliance and check its continuity with an ohmmeter. The trouble is confirmed if this test shows infinite resistance.

4.   Heat sensor open—connect a voltmeter across the heat sensor's terminals (between points **G** and **H**), set the temperature control for a moderately high heat range, and turn on the circuit. The trouble is at least tentatively confirmed if the full control-circuit voltage appears on the meter. Doublecheck the diagnosis by removing the heat sensor assembly from the appliance and checking its resistance with an ohmmeter. The trouble is definitely confirmed if its resistance is infinity.

5.   Variable resistor open—repeat the test for an open heat sensor, using points **H** and **I** as test points.

6.   H1 warp heater open—repeat the test for an open heat sensor, using points **I** and **J** as test points.

7.   H1 warp heater shorted—turn off power to the appliance, and connect a jumper wire across the heat sensor element (between points **G** and **H**). Connect a voltmeter across H1 (between points **I** and **J**), set the heat control knob for a medium heating range, and reapply power to the circuit. A steady voltage reading that is less than 3–4 V tentatively confirms the trouble. Doublecheck this diagnosis by removing TH1 from the appli-

ance and comparing the resistance of H1 (measured between points **I** and **J**) with the manufacturer's specifications. Of course a resistance of 1 Ω or less indicates a shorted heater.

8. TH1 contacts or warp heater H2 open—it is difficult to distinguish these two troubles when the components are sealed inside a thermostat housing. The entire thermostat assembly has to be replaced if either component is defective, however; therefore, the distinction between the two troubles is purely academic, anyway.

    To confirm either of these troubles, turn off the appliance, connect a jumper wire across the two components (between points **J** and **K**), and turn on the appliance. The trouble is confirmed if the main heating element immediately rises to full heat. CAUTION: Do not leave this jumper connected longer than it is necessary to note the main heater's response. Leaving this jumper in place can destroy warp heater H3.

9. H3 open or shorted—disconnect the wiring to H3 in TH2 (wires connected to points **K** and **L**), and measure the resistance of that warp heater. An infinite resistance indicates an open heater, and a resistance less than 1 Ω indicates a shorted heater. Compare any other resistance reading with the manufacturer's specifications.

    Replace the entire thermostat assembly if H2 is open, shorted, or badly out of specification.

10. TH2 contacts broken or stuck open—connect a heavy-gauge jumper wire across the contacts of TH2 (between points **E** and **D**), set the temperature control knob for a moderately high heating range, and turn on the appliance. The trouble is confirmed if (a) the main heating element goes on at full heat and (b) H3 warp heater checks out as normal according to trouble 9.

11. S1 contacts broken or stuck open—check the S1–A section by turning on the appliance and measuring the voltage reaching the appliance side of the power line (between points **B** and **E**). If full line voltage appears at the line side of the switch (points **A** and **E**), but no voltage appears on the appliance side, the trouble is confirmed.

    Check the S1–B section of the power switch by comparing voltages on both sides of it. The trouble is confirmed if the transformer secondary (points **F** to **J**) has 12 V across it and no voltage appears on the other side of the switch (between points **G** and **C**).

12. Open section of wiring or loose electrical connection—visually inspect the appliance for any loose, broken, burned, or corroded wiring and connections.

Full heat at all temperature settings

1. TH2 contacts shorted—disconnect the 240 V wiring to TH2 (from points **E** to **D**), and check the continuity of the internal contacts with a continuity tester or ohmmeter. TH2 contacts are supposed to be open at room temperature, so that if the test shows good continuity or a very low resistance, the trouble is confirmed. Replace the entire TH2 assembly.

2. Heat sensor shorted—disconnect the wiring to the heat sensor (points **G** and **H**), and measure the resistance of the sensor with an ohmmeter. A reading of zero ohms is a clear indication of a shorted sensing element. Compare other resistance readings with the manufacturer's specifications.

3. Heat selector variable resistor shorted—disconnect the wiring to the variable resistor (points **H** and **I**), and measure the resistance of the component while rotating the shaft between its two extremes. The resistor is indeed shorted if the ohmmeter shows a very low resistance, regardless of the shaft's position. The proper resistance range should appear in the manufacturer's specifications.

4. TH1 contacts stuck closed or H2 shorted—these troubles are best diagnosed by the process of elimination: if the heat sensor and heat selector variable resistor test good as described in troubles 2 and 3, and if TH2 is in good working order, chances are quite good that the trouble is in the contacts or H2 warp heater of TH1. To eliminate the possibility of a short in external wiring, disconnect TH1 from the circuit and apply full power to the appliance. There are no external shorts if the main heating element does not go on.

Appliance draws excessive current or blows fuses

1. Main heating element shorted—disconnect the main heating element from the appliance, measure its resistance with an ohmmeter, and compare the results with the manufacturer's specifications. A resistance of zero ohms is a definite indication of a shorted heating element. See Sec. 5-2.2 for further troubleshooting and servicing hints.

2. Transformer shorted—see the note "To test a transformer" in trouble 2 of "no heat" symptoms in this section.

3. Shorted 240 V section—disconnect the main heating element (points **C** and **D**) and the transformer windings (points **B** and **E**). Apply full power to the appliance. If the appliance still draws excessive current or blows a fuse or circuit breaker, the trouble is definitely in the wiring. Visually inspect the wiring and all electrical connections for shorts. Look especially for bare wires or connectors touching the appliance's metal frame.

Heat too high or too low

Confirm this symptom by monitoring the appliance's operating temperatures as described in the manufacturer's specifications or in the chapters dealing with specific heating appliances.

The most likely causes of this symptom are the thermostats TH1 or TH2. Of these two thermostats, TH1 is the more likely cause of this trouble. If the appliance has been working properly beyond the time limits of the manufacturer's warranty, replace TH1 with a new one.

4-4 QUESTIONS

1. How does a bimetal element respond to changes in temperature?

2. Suppose that a serviceman wants to increase the trip-point temperature of an adjustable bimetal thermostat assembly. Should he increase or decrease the distance of travel between the bimetal's electrical contacts?

3. In what way does a warp heater control circuit mimic the operating temperature of the appliance?

4. What is the primary difference between the ways Robertshaw and King Seeley controls sense changes in temperature?

5. What is a differential thermostat?

5

Electric Motors
and Motor Controls

An electric motor, in a very general sense, is any kind of load device that converts electrical energy into mechanical energy. This definition can be extended to include devices such as relays and solenoids, but common usage of the term *motor* makes it applicable only to devices that convert electrical energy into rotary motion.

This chapter deals with the theory of operation, troubleshooting, and servicing hints for rotary electric motors and their basic control circuits. The discussions are further limited to the types of motors most commonly found in modern major appliances. Relays and solenoids—nonrotary motors—are described in connection with the specific appliances that use them.

A good share of major appliances contain at least one motor. Some motors have heavy-duty applications such as turning the drum in a clothes dryer or the compressor in an air conditioner. In other instances, motors perform light-duty tasks, for example, timing operations in appliances such as clothes washers and dryers and dishwashers.

There are at least four basic types of motors used in the electrical industries today, but only one particular type is found in major appliances. The motor used in major appliances is properly known as an *induction motor*; one of its distinctive features is that it does not have a set of electrical brushes as many small appliance motors do.

5-1 THEORY OF INDUCTION MOTORS

Induction motors belong to a special breed of electric motors that are noted for being especially reliable and simple in construction. The theories behind the operation of induction motors involve the interaction of magnetic fields, transformer action and ac generator action. This section first describes these interactions, then shows how they work together to produce two specific kinds of induction motors.

5-1.1 Magnetic Interactions in Motors

It is a well-known principle of physics that like poles of magnets repel each other while unlike poles attract. Bringing the north pole of a magnet close to the south pole of another, for example, produces a mechanical force that tends to hold the magnets together. This is the case of a pair of unlike poles attracting each other. In the opposite case where two north poles are brought together, they produce a mechanical force that tends to separate them.

Magnets, in other words, are like energy conversion devices that transform magnetic energy into mechanical energy or motion. The amount of motion depends mainly on the strength of the two magnets, whereas the direction of motion depends on the polarities of the magnetic poles.

Permanent magnets, for example, ordinary bar or horseshoe magnets, obey the basic laws of magnetic repulsion and attraction. *Electromagnets*—magnets produced whenever an electric current flows through a coil of wire—follow the same basic laws. In fact there is no real difference between the fields produced by permanent magnets and electromagnets.

It turns out that permanent-magnet motors are very seldom used in modern major appliances. So it is far more important to think in terms of electromagnets and induction motors.

5-1.2 Transformer Action in Induction Motors

A second basic principle behind the operation of induction motors concerns a special kind of transformer action that is called *electromagnetic induction*. Whenever a wire is placed in a fluctuating magnetic field (or the wire is moved within a magnetic field), a current flow is generated, or induced, in the wire. Induction motors, like electric generators and transformers, depend heavily on this principle of magnetic induction.

An induction motor thus uses the principles of induction as well as the laws of magnetic attraction and repulsion. To see how these two effects work together, consider the fact that magnetic energy is converted into motion whenever the poles of two magnets interact with each other. If one of the magnets is fixed so that it cannot move, and the other is arranged so that it can rotate freely within the fixed magnetic field, the movable magnet will always attempt to rotate so that it aligns its north pole as close as possible with the south pole of the fixed magnet.

In an induction motor the fixed magnetic field is created electrically by forcing an alternating current from an outside source through a set of coils. The movable magnetic field is also created electrically, but its current is generated by magnetic induction or transformer action from the fixed electromagnet. In summary, current from an outside power source generates a magnetic field around a fixed coil of wire, and this magnetic field, in turn, sets up a current flow in the movable coil of wire.

The fixed coil of wire in an induction motor is called the *stator* or *field winding*. The movable electromagnet is known as the *rotor* or *armature winding*. The magnetic interaction and transformer action between the field and armature windings is ultimately responsible for making a motor shaft spin.

5-1.3 Generator Action

An induction motor always draws more current from the power source whenever it is first turned on than it does when the shaft is spinning at its normal rate. A generator action between the armature and field windings is responsible for this effect.

Since the alternating current flowing in the field winding of a motor induces a current flow in the armature, is it not possible that the current then flowing in the armature can induce yet another current flow in the field winding? This effect is indeed possible, and it accounts for the higher-than-normal current drain during motor start-up.

Applying ac power to the field winding of an induction motor produces a fluctuating magnetic field that induces an ac current flow in the armature. This armature current, in turn, produces another magnetic field that accomplishes two things: (1) it sets up the magnetic conditions necessary for making the armature assembly spin, and (2) it induces a second ac current flow in the field winding.

The second point is the important one as far as this part of the discussion is concerned. The ac current reinduced into the field winding always opposes the direction of current flow from the main power source. This induced reverse current flow in the field winding results in a partial cancellation of the current drawn from the lines, and the faster the armature spins, the greater this cancelling effect becomes. The overall result is that an induction motor consumes more power from the lines when it is first started than it does after the armature reaches its rated operating speed.

It is possible to demonstrate the effects of this reinduced field current, or *back EMF**, by means of a rather simple experiment. Connect an ac ammeter in series with the field winding of an induction motor, and apply rated line power to it. The instant that power is applied to the circuit, the ammeter shows a large inrush of current that is far above the motor's rated current level. This inrush current begins dropping off as the armature begins to turn, and it eventually drops to the rated level as the motor reaches its specified speed of rotation.

To observe the real significance of back EMF, bind the motor shaft so that it cannot turn. Under this condition, the armature cannot produce the back EMF and the field winding draws its inrush current indefinitely. A good many induction motors "burn out" because the armature does not produce the back EMF required for holding the field current to a safe operating level.

All induction motors draw a relatively large amount of current from the power lines until the armature gets up to its normal operating speed. The current drain usually settles down to its rated level within a second or two, depending on the amount of mechanical load on the armature assembly.

5-2 START-UP FEATURES OF INDUCTION MOTORS

Whenever power is first applied to a simple induction motor, the magnetic field induced in the armature takes on a polarity that tends to lock the motor shaft—unlike magnetic poles are perfectly aligned. A simple induction motor, then, cannot start running without the aid of a special start-up circuit.

The simplest way to start an induction motor is by confusing the direction of the magnetic field set up in the armature. This trick is commonly accomplished by applying the ac power to two separate field windings that are wound so that the magnetic field from one of them is out of phase with the field from the other. A motor using this particular technique for "confusing" the start-up magnetic fields is called a *split-phase* motor.

The second type of induction motor commonly used in major appliances is known as a *shaded-pole* motor. Instead of using two separate field windings to "confuse" the magnetic fields during start-up, a shaded-pole motor uses a single field winding in conjunction with a strip of copper turned around the field assembly.

*EMF is a common abbreviation for electromotive force.

5-2.1   Split-Phase Induction Motors

Figure 5-1 shows schematics for two kinds of self-starting induction motor circuits. Both motor circuits have a pair of field windings labeled *run* and *start*. The two field windings are electrically connected in parallel, but they are wound to produce out-of-phase magnetic fields for the armature.

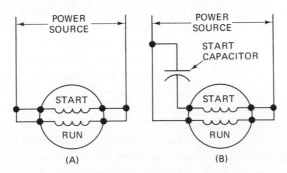

Fig. 5-1   Split-phase induction motors. (A) Simple start winding arrangement, (B) Capacitor-start motor.

The simple split-phase motor in Fig. 5-1(A) relies only on the out-of-phase arrangement of the two field windings to produce the starting torque. The start winding draws less line current than the run winding does, and its magnetic field is relatively weak. But the effect of the start winding is sufficient to make the rotor start turning a little bit in one certain direction; and once the armature turns a little bit, a "chasing" effect in the run winding takes over to keep the armature spinning.

The motor circuit shown in Fig. 5-1(B) is a *capacitor-start* induction motor. It is no accident that the internal wiring of this motor is identical to that of the simple split-phase motor in Fig. 5-1(A). The two motors work on exactly the same principles; in fact, a capacitor-start motor is simply a modified version of the basic split-phase induction motor.

The capacitor connected in series with the start winding tends to create a greater phase offset when power is first applied to the motor. This greater phase offset, combined with a larger amount of inrush field current, gives capacitor-start motors a larger amount of starting torque than a simple split-phase motor of the same general dimensions.

5-2.2   Shaded-Pole Motors

Another type of induction motor, called a shaded-pole motor, works on the same basic principles as the other types of induction motors described thus far in this chapter. The essential difference is the technique used to confuse the interaction of magnetic fields to get the armature spinning.

Instead of using two separate field windings to scramble the magnetic fields during start-up, a shaded-pole motor accomplishes the same effect with one or two copper bands wrapped around the laminated core of the field assembly. These copper bars can behave as the secondary of a transformer whenever line current flows through the field winding. Current flowing through the field winding induces a current in these copper bands; and since the bands form a complete circuit, a considerable amount of current can be induced in them. It is the current flowing through the shading-pole bands that produces the offset magnetic field necessary for starting the motor.

Once the motor shaft approaches its normal operating speed, the resulting loss of field current reduces the shading-pole current to a very small level. Shading-pole current, in other words, is automatically adjusted to the needs of the motor. This current is at its peak during start-up, and it drops off as the motor reaches its operating speed.

Shaded-pole motors are by far the simplest kinds of induction motors, partly because they do not use a separate field winding for start-up and partly because their starting current is self-regulating. The primary disadvantage of a shaded-pole motor is its inherently low starting and running torque.

Small shaded-pole motors do have their place in modern major appliances, however. Such motors are appropriate for conditions calling for a low-cost, simple motor that does not have to handle much of a mechanical load. And because shaded-pole motors tend to run at a very precise speed, they are used most often as the heart of timer assemblies.

5-3 CONTROL CIRCUITS FOR INDUCTION MOTORS

Split-phase and capacitor-start motors are often used in conjunction with three basic types of controls: controls that make the start-up features more efficient, those responsible for reversing the direction of spin, and those designed to alter the running speed. All split-phase motors in major appliances use an external start-up scheme; some motors have either a direction or speed control, and others use all three types of controls.

5-3.1 Start-Up Controls

Once a split-phase or capacitor-start motor begins running close to its normal speed, the run winding takes over all operations and the start winding no longer serves any useful purpose. The start winding, in fact, merely burns up energy that could be better applied to run winding.

Most induction motors having horsepower ratings in excess of 1/8 hp have built-in provisions for removing the start winding from the circuit once the motor builds up some speed. There are two popular techniques for removing the start winding from the circuit: by means of a centrifugal switch or a starting relay. Figure 5-2 shows these two starting circuits as they are used in simple split-phase motors. The ideas work equally well in capacitor-start versions.

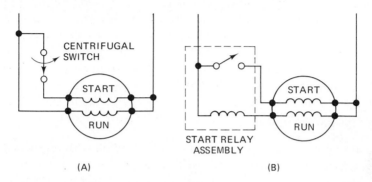

Fig. 5-2 Start-up circuits. (A) Centrifugal switch type, (B) Start relay type.

The centrifugal switch circuit illustrated in Fig. 5-2(A) has a normally closed switch attached to the armature shaft. The contacts of this switch are connected in series with the start winding; when power is first applied to the motor, current flows through both the start and run windings. As the motor speed approaches about 75 percent of the rated running speed, the spinning action of the motor shaft automatically throws the switch contacts open, thus removing the start winding from the circuit. The switch automatically closes again whenever the armature speed drops about 30 percent below the motor's normal running speed.

In short, a centrifugal switch start-up circuit uses the centrifugal force generated by the spinning motor shaft to throw open the switch contacts. Lowering the motor's speed, or stopping it altogether, lowers the centrifugal force and allows the switch contacts to close again.

The theory behind the operation of the relay circuit in Fig. 5-2(B) is a bit more subtle than that of the centrifugal switch arrangement. The relay coil is connected in series with the run winding, and the relay's normally open contacts are connected in series with the start winding. Unless there is a substantial amount of current flowing through the motor's run winding and the relay coil, the start winding receives no current because the relay contacts are open.

When power is first applied to the motor, current cannot flow through the start winding because the relay contacts are open. The relay coil and run winding are connected directly across the power line, however, so that the current through them rises rapidly to a high level.

This surge current through the relay coil and run winding activates the relay, making its contacts close. And as the relay contacts close, the start winding is thrown into the circuit. This action of course forces the motor to start running.

As the armature begins spinning, it generates a back EMF in the two field windings that drastically lowers the amount of line current flowing through the relay coil. This reduction in coil current allows the relay contacts to drop open, once again removing the start winding from the circuit. By this time, however, the run winding has taken over full operation of the motor. The relay is activated again whenever the current through the run winding reaches an above-normal level for any reason.

5-3.2   Direction Controls

A simple induction motor runs equally well in both directions. If the shaft is somehow started in a clockwise direction, for example, it will build up speed and run at full torque in that direction. Starting the motor in a counterclockwise direction makes the motor shaft turn that way at full speed and power.

The point of this preliminary discussion is to emphasize the fact that the direction an induction motor turns depends solely upon the way it is started. An induction motor is very "phase-conscious" at the moment of start-up. The arrangement of the start and run windings assures the necessary phase difference for starting the motor, but the electrical phasing between the two windings determines the direction the motor shaft starts turning. Furthermore, it is possible to reverse the direction of an induction motor by reversing the start winding connections.

The circuit in Fig. 5-3 includes a double-pole switch that actually reverses the electrical connections to the motor's start winding. Whenever this motor

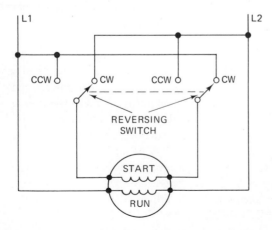

Fig. 5-3 Motor reversing circuit using a double-pole, double-throw switch.

is started with the direction control switch set in its cw (clockwise) position, current flowing through the start winding has a phase that nudges the motor shaft in the clockwise direction; once the motor shaft approaches the rated running speed, a centrifugal switch, or start relay assembly (not shown in the diagram), cuts the direction control and start winding out of the circuit.

Setting the direction control switch to its ccw (counterclockwise) position reverses the phase relationship between the start and run windings, forcing the motor to run in a counterclockwise direction.

A second type of direction control circuit uses a total of three field windings—one run winding and two start windings. As illustrated in Fig. 5-4, one of the start windings is responsible for starting the motor in a clockwise direction, and the other winding starts the motor in the counterclockwise direction. The direction the motor starts and runs depends on which of the two start windings is switched into the circuit as the motor power is applied to the motor.

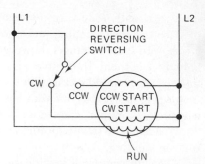

Fig. 5-4 Motor reversing circuit using two start windings.

The two start windings, incidentally, are identical except for one essential feature: they are wound in opposite directions at the time of manufacture. The differences in the direction of winding causes their magnetic fields to take on opposite polarities, and that accounts for the difference in direction of start-up spin.

5-3.3 Induction Motor Speed Controls

The simplest and least expensive way to change the speed of an induction motor is by adding or removing a series-connected coil in the run winding circuit. Adding this speed-control coil reduces the motor's speed; bypassing the coil increases the speed.

Referring to the diagram in Fig. 5-5, the speed-control coil is wound in series with the main run winding inside the motor housing. (Some older motors use an external speed-control coil that looks much like a doorbell transformer.) Setting the switch to its LOW position opens the contacts and allows both windings to share the running current. Changing the switch to its

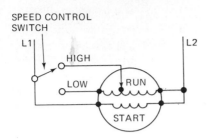

Fig. 5-5 Principle of induction motor speed control.

HIGH position, however, shorts out the speed-control winding, applying full line voltage to the main run winding and letting the motor run at full speed.

5-4 GENERAL SERVICING AND TROUBLESHOOTING HINTS

Usually four wires extend from a split-phase induction motor: one pair for the start winding and another pair for the run winding. (See Fig. 5-6(A).) In some instances, however, the serviceman might find five wires or only three of them. In the five-wire case (Fig. 5-6(B)), chances are that one of the wires is a ground connection to the motor housing. A three-wire induction motor (Fig. 5-6(C)) is one that has an internal start-to-run connection—one wire is the common connection for the two windings, another goes to the "hot" side of the start winding, and the third wire goes to the "hot" side of the run winding.

The manufacturer's specifications and wiring diagram are always the best guides to replacing a split-phase motor or checking its windings. The wires

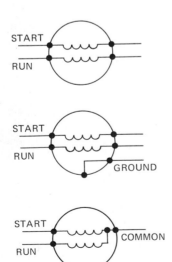

Fig. 5-6 Wiring diagrams for split-phase induction motors. (A) Four-wire version, (B) Five-wire version, (C) Three-wire version.

running out of the motor housing are normally marked or color coded in some manner that is clearly explained in the service bulletin. Because the manufacturer's notes are not always available when they are needed, a serviceman sometimes has to rely on his own understanding of split-phase motors to guide him.

A simple ohmmeter test is frequently adequate to distinguish the start and run windings in a split-phase motor. Assuming that the motor windings are in good order, a serviceman can always distinguish a run winding from the start winding by comparing the electrical resistance of the two. It so happens that a start winding always has a higher resistance than the run winding in the same motor. If one winding measures 50 Ω, for example, and the other reads about 10 Ω, there can be little doubt that the 50 Ω winding is the start winding.

5-4.1 Diagnosing Motor Troubles

The electric motors in many major appliances have to survive under some rather rugged operating conditions, but they normally outlast other mechanical parts such as selector switches, door hinges, and gearing mechanisms. In spite of the "cheap" appearance of many modern electric motors, they are very reliable; and this fact leads to a general rule for troubleshooting and servicing appliance motors: More often than not, a motor that is truly defective becomes that way because of some other trouble.

This general rule contains two essential ideas. The first is that induction motors are usually the victims of a trouble rather than a primary cause. Suppose that a gear train in a clothes washer becomes bound up by a mechanical failure. The resulting overload on the motor overheats the insulation and eventually causes a short circuit in one of the windings. Replacing the motor cures the short-circuit problem; but unless the serviceman cures the primary cause—the bond-up gear train—the new motor will eventually suffer the same fate as the original one. And that is an expensive and frustrating situation that generates poor customer relations.

The second idea contained in the general rule for motor troubleshooting and servicing is that the serviceman is wholly responsible for making certain that a motor is indeed defective before giving the first thought to replacing it. Many troubles in major appliances can mimic the symptoms of a motor trouble and lead an unwary serviceman off the track.

Today's appliance motors are more reliable than ever before, and this important fact is reflected in the construction of large, major appliance motor assemblies. Most modern appliance motors are assembled in such a way that it is virtually impossible to service any troubles inside them. It is still important to troubleshoot appliance motors with skill and competence, but it is no longer practical to attempt motor repairs. Replacing a motor generally costs less than trying to fix it.

The following list summarizes the principal troubles that can be found in split-phase induction motors. Subsequent sections in this chap er describe the troubles in more detail, including some of the appropriate test procedures and observable symptoms. Troubles in direction and speed control circuits are outlined in connection with specific major appliances that use them.

1. Winding troubles—short or open circuits in the run, start, or armature windings.
2. Starting mechanism troubles—(a) centrifugal switch or start relay contacts stuck closed or broken open, (b) start relay coil open or shorted, and (c) start capacitor open or shorted.
3. Miscellaneous mechanical troubles—bad bearings, loose fasteners, and worn or broken parts.

Motor winding troubles normally develop whenever the insulation between adjacent turns of wire is somehow burned or corroded away, allowing a short-circuit condition to develop. The short might not be severe enough to blow a line fuse or trip the motor's circuit breaker. This kind of problem nearly always grows progressively worse, however, creating a more serious short-circuit condition that finally puts the motor completely out of commission.

The insulation on a motor winding is most often burned away by heat generated in the windings themselves. One good way to get the whole problem started is by binding the motor shaft with a heavy mechanical overload. This overload might be caused by user abuse of a mechanical failure of the motor mounting or gear assembly attached to the motor shaft. In any event, the overloading causes the motor to consume above-normal current and thus generate above-normal heat. If the loading condition is not cured in time, the heating eventually burns away a portion of the wire insulation, and the vicious circle is underway.

Another way to get the whole trouble of shorted windings started is by allowing corrosive chemicals to get into the motor. These chemicals might be in water that is saturated with household detergent. Quite often, however, a well-meaning do-it-yourself serviceman lubricates the bearings with an overly generous amount of household oil. The bearings then throw the excess oil all over the motor windings, creating an acid "gunk" that eventually eats away the insulation. *Unless specifically stated otherwise in the appliance manual, never lubricate the motor.* The bearings in most major appliance motors are permanently sealed and contain enough oil to keep the motor properly lubricated far beyond the appliance's normal life expectancy.

Open-circuit troubles in motor windings do not occur very often. When such troubles do appear, they are caused by either a manufacturing defect or a minor winding short that causes the wire to overheat. The "minor" short-circuit condition can lead to an open circuit because the overheated spot that results can eventually melt the wire in two.

Turning attention to the start-up mechanisms, centrifugal switch contacts and start relay contacts can stick closed because of a winding short that forces excessive current to flow through the contacts. This current can actually weld the contacts closed. Open-contact troubles are most often caused by household grime accumulating on them. The grime acts as a good insulator if it builds up thick enough.

Start-up capacitors used in modern appliance motors normally outlast the life of the appliance. After many years of use, however, the electrolytic material in these capacitors can decompose, creating the impression of an open-circuit capacitor.

5-4.2   A List of Motor Troubles and Their Symptoms

**1.   Start winding open—motor does not start,
     but draws excessive current from the line.**

The motor does not start in this instance because induction motors require an initial offset of the magnetic fields that is normally provided by the start winding. The motor draws excessive current because there is no back EMF generated in the field winding. Induction motors rely on this back EMF to limit the operating current.

**2.   Start winding shorted—motor runs slowly
     with low torque, and it draws excessive line
     current.**

A short in the start winding upsets the normal magnetic offset that is needed to get the motor started. The results are that the motor has a lower-than-normal starting torque that might prevent the armature from ever reaching its normal rate of spin. The motor draws excessive current for two reasons: because the short-circuit condition provides a low-resistance path for current flow, and because the armature is not spinning fast enough to generate the necessary amount of back EMF in the field winding assembly.

**3.   Run winding completely open—motor does
     not run but draws excessive current.**

Although the run winding is open and cannot carry current from the power source, the start winding is still connected. And because the motor cannot start with only one winding in the circuit, the shaft does not turn. Furthermore, the motor draws excessive current because there is no back EMF to limit line current.

4. Run winding partially open—motor runs slowly with low torque and draws excessive current.

A run winding can be considered "partially" open because many induction motors have more than one run winding connected in parallel. Opening one of the windings does not stop the motor action altogether, but it certainly reduces the overall efficiency. Again, the motor draws excessive current because the armature is running too slowly to generate the normal amount of back EMF in the field windings.

5. Run winding shorted—motor runs slowly with low torque and draws excessive current.

The motor can run under this fault condition because the start winding is still intact and there is indeed current flowing in the run winding. Because the run winding is shorted, however, it is unable to establish the proper conditions for efficient operation. And because the run winding is shorted, it naturally draws excessive current from the power source.

6. Armature winding partially open—motor runs slowly with low torque, and draws excessive current.

A motor cannot run efficiently unless it is able to pick up the magnetic field from the armature and induce a current flow in the armature. Wire-wound armature assemblies can be considered "partially" open whenever one of several parallel-connected windings is open. One open armature winding reduces the efficiency of the motor and creates the symptoms described here.

This particular trouble, incidentally, applies only to motors having wire-wound armatures. Many motors now appearing in major appliances contain "squirrel-cage" armatures—armatures made up of a laminated core that has between sixteen and twenty-four shorting bars running lengthwise through them. The shorting bars are capable of picking up the current flow induced by the field windings, and they can generate the magnetic fields necessary for making the motor run. The simplicity of squirrel-cage armatures makes them more reliable than their wire-wound counterparts, but they are subject to the same kinds of troubles in the long run.

7. Armature winding shorted—motor runs slowly with low torque and draws excessive current.

As in the case of an open armature winding, this trouble applies mainly to wire-wound armature assemblies. In this case, however, the shorted winding causes excessive current flow in both the armature and field windings, and the subsequent loss of efficiency creates the symptoms.

8. Centrifugal switch or start relay contacts stuck closed—motor draws above-normal current.

Many induction motors run rather well with the start winding connected in the circuit at all times. The efficiency is reduced, however, making the motor draw an above-normal amount of current. This problem can eventually lead to more serious troubles because the excessive current flow overheats the motor assemblies.

9. Centrifugal switch or start relay contacts stuck open, start relay coil open or shorted —motor does not start but draws excessive current.

An induction motor cannot start unless its start winding is connected into the circuit at start-up. An open switch effectively removes the start winding from the circuit. Likewise, a defective relay coil can prevent the start relay contacts from closing as they should during normal start-up. With the start winding disconnected at start-up for any reason, the run winding draws excessive current because the armature has to be spinning in order to generate a back EMF that limits the line current.

10.   Start capacitor open—motor does not start but draws excessive current.

Because the start-up capacitor is connected in series with the start winding, an open capacitor mimics the symptoms of an open start winding, open switch contacts, or a defective start relay coil.

11.   Capacitor shorted—motor starts with low torque and draws excessive current.

The purpose of the start capacitor is to boost the starting torque. If the motor is heavily loaded, it might not start at all under this fault condition. A lightly loaded motor might start, but its start-up time will be abnormally long if the capacitor is shorted out.

12.   Bearings worn—motor is noisy, vibrates, or runs slowly while drawing excessive current.

13.   Loose or broken mechanical parts in the motor assembly—motor noisy.

The troubleshooting notes for specific appliances described elsewhere in this book frequently narrow down troubles to an electric motor or its control circuits. The suggested test procedures in such instances are complete as far as motor control circuits are concerned, and they can leave little doubt that a trouble is in the motor assembly whenever that is the case. Normal testing procedures, however, seldom lead to a knowledge of the exact cause of a trouble within the motor assembly itself.

The question of whether a motor is misbehaving because of a trouble such as an open field winding or shorted armature is actually an academic one. Because it is virtually impossible to repair modern appliance motors economically, the motor has to be replaced, regardless of the nature of the trouble inside it.

5-5   QUESTIONS

In questions 1 and 3 select the words or phrases which make the statements correct.

1.   According to a basic principle of magnetism, two north magnetic poles (attract, repel) each other, while north and south magnetic poles (attract, repel).

2. State the basic principle of electromagnetic induction.

3. In a conventional induction motor, the field windings (remain stationary, spin) while the armature windings (remain stationary, spin).

4. Why is the current drain of an induction motor greater during start-up than it is once the motor is running at normal speed?

5. What is the difference between a split-phase and a shaded-pole induction motor?

6. What is the purpose of the capacitor in a capacitor-start induction motor?

7. What is the purpose of a centrifugal switch in a motor start-up circuit?

8. What is a squirrel-cage induction motor?

6

Principles
of Refrigeration

It is in the nature of things that heat energy flows from a point of relatively high temperature to other points of a relatively low temperature. It makes no difference what the temperature levels are in terms of degrees— the heat naturally flows from the higher to the lower levels.

From the very beginning of civilization, men have been applying this principle of heat transfer to cook food, warm themselves, and produce an endless variety of tools and other useful objects and materials.

Refrigeration, on the other hand, is an "unnatural" process. The basic idea behind refrigeration is to transfer heat energy from an object of a relatively low temperature to one of a relatively high temperature. The principle of refrigeration, in other words, runs counter to the natural process of heat transfer. As it takes a certain amount of technological sophistication to reverse a natural process, it is little wonder that appliances such as refrigerators and air conditioners are newcomers to civilization.

The operation of most consumer refrigeration systems, including air conditioners and dehumidifiers, relies on several general principles of heat physics. Without understanding the essence of these principles, the operation of any kind of home cooling system forever remains a mystery—the kind of mystery that makes good troubleshooting all but impossible.

This chapter deals with the principles of refrigeration in a very general way. Discussions of specific refrigeration systems appear in the chapters on refrigerators, freezers, air conditioners, and dehumidifiers.

6-1 SOME BASIC DEFINITIONS

Much of the confusion that goes along with the study of a new technical subject is caused by an incomplete understanding of the technical terms involved. The main point of this section is to define the most commonly used terms in the refrigeration business and, at the same time, provide some insight into the physics of heat transfer.

6-1.1 The Btu

The *British thermal unit (Btu)* is the most common unit of measure for heat quantity. Just as pints and gallons are units of liquid quantity, the Btu is a measure of heat quantity.

To be precise, a Btu is the quantity of heat required to change the temperature of one pound of water one degree Fahrenheit. One Btu of heat added to a pound of water, for example, should raise the water temperature one degree. By the same token, removing a Btu of heat from a pound of water should lower its temperature one degree.

How much heat is required to warm 10 lb of water 1°F? In this instance, 10 times 1 or 10 Btu's of heat must be added. How much heat must be removed from 1 lb of water to lower its temperature 10°F? Again, 1 × 10 or 10 Btu's must be taken away.

Different substances have different capacities for absorbing and giving up heat energy. A pound of air, for example, requires only about 1/4 Btu of heat to raise its temperature 1°F. And looking at the procedure the other way around, air gives up its heat four times easier than water does. That explains why the water in a lake or swimming pool tends to remain warmer than the surrounding air after the sun sets.

Freon-12, a trade name for the most common kind of refrigerant material, has a heat capacity of about 24 Btu/lb when it is in its liquid state at room temperature. That means this liquid can absorb 24 times as much heat as water can at the same temperature. In its vapor state, a pound of Freon-12 can absorb as much as 85 Btu's of heat.

What is more important, however, is the notion that any material undergoing an increase in temperature by absorbing a certain amount of heat can return to its original temperature only by giving up that same amount of heat. Likewise, a material that gives up a certain quantity of heat and loses some temperature in the process can regain its original temperature only by absorbing the lost heat energy from some other source.

6-1.2   Latent Heat

Basic physics and science books say that matter exists in one of three states: as a liquid, solid, or gas. Ordinary water, for example, is the liquid form of the compound H_2O. The solid form of water is commonly known as ice and the gaseous form is, of course, steam.

People tend to associate a substance with the state it takes on at normal room temperatures and sea-level pressure. The term *water*, for instance, usually calls up an image of H_2O in its room-temperature liquid state. When thinking about carbon dioxide, however, people usually think in terms of a gas; but carbon dioxide can exist as a solid (dry ice) at temperatures below about $-69°F$.

It is important to realize that a substance can exist in any one of its three states, given the right conditions of temperature and pressure. The principles of refrigeration can be quite confusing to anyone who cannot accept the idea that a substance normally considered a gas can also exist as a liquid.

Section 6-1.1 describes how the temperature of a substance changes as heat energy is added or extracted. This principle holds as long as the substance is not making a transition between one of its three states. The temperature of liquid water does indeed increase as heat energy is added—but only up to the point where it begins to boil or change into its gaseous state.

Whenever a liquid is heated to its boiling point, adding more heat energy causes no further increase in temperature. When water is boiling on a stove, for instance, the temperature rises steadily up to the boiling point of $212°F$. Then the temperature stops there. The steam-water mixture remains at $212°F$ until all the water is boiled off. If the steam is confined in a pot at sea-level pressure, adding more heat does indeed make the temperature rise once again.

The very process of changing a liquid into a gas takes up all the heat energy that is added to the liquid-gas mixture. There is no heat energy left to cause any rise in the temperature. Once the liquid is vaporized, however, any additional heat energy is transformed into a temperature rise.

The graph in Fig. 6-1 shows how heat energy added to 1 lb of water influences its temperature. In this case, 100 Btu's of heat are required to raise the water temperature from $112°F$ to $212°F$. Adding another Btu of heat at that point does not cause any change in temperature. Only after adding 970 Btu's more does the temperature begin rising above $212°F$. That 970 Btu's of extra heat energy is used to convert the original 1 lb of liquid water into 1 lb of steam.

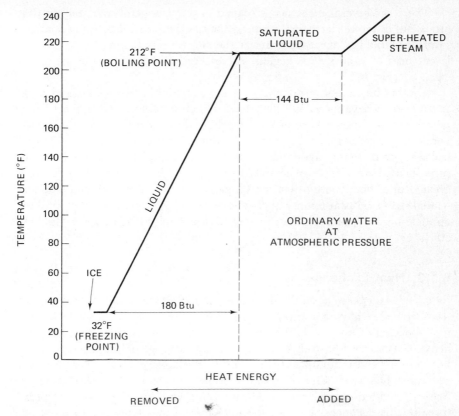

Fig. 6-1 Heat energy-temperature diagram for ordinary water at sea-level pressure.

The entire reaction just described is fully reversible. A pound of steam can give up its heat energy to cooler surroundings, and result in a drop in temperature—up to the point where the vapor begins to condense or change into a liquid. The temperature again remains fixed at the boiling point (212°F in the case of water) until all the steam is condensed. Any further loss of heat energy then results in a corresponding drop in water temperature. The graph in Fig. 6-1, in other words, can be read in either direction: to the right for added heat energy and to the left for lost heat energy.

The amount of heat energy required to transform a boiling liquid into steam is called the *latent heat of vaporization* for that substance. The latent heat of vaporization for water happens to be 970 Btu/lb. A full 970 Btu's must be gained or lost by a pound of water before it can be completely vaporized or liquified. The figure for latent heat of vaporization is different for different substances. Freon-12, for instance, requires only 62 Btu/lb to change from its liquid to gaseous state.

There are several more terms related to the change-of-state process that are useful in the refrigeration business. One of the terms is *saturated liquid*. A saturated liquid is one that exists at the substance's boiling point—in the latent heat of vaporization region where the liquid and gaseous states co-exist. See Fig. 6-1.

Another important term closely related to latent heat is *super-heated vapor*. A super-heated vapor is one that exists at temperatures above the boiling point of the substance. (See Fig. 6-1.) Adding heat energy to a super-heated vapor causes a corresponding rise in the temperature because it is no longer necessary to do work vaporizing a liquid. The most commonly used form of super-heated vapor is super-heated steam. Super-heated steam can store up a great deal of heat energy that can be passed on to a steam turbine. Super-heated steam exists at temperatures above the boiling point of water, and for applications in steam turbines, the temperature might be driven as high as 500°F or more.

6-1.3   Heat Exchange

Heat energy naturally flows from bodies having a higher temperature to other bodies having a lower temperature. A red-hot bar of steel plunged into a bucket of water cools by virtue of the fact that it gives up most of its heat energy to the relatively cool water. This exchange of heat energy—from hot to cold—continues until the bar and water have precisely the same temperature. The same kind of heat exchange operation takes place when a freezing cold bar of steel is dropped into a bucket of water at room temperature. In this instance, however, the heat flows from the water to the steel. The steel absorbs heat energy from the water until the bodies have the same temperature.

A somewhat more elaborate example of heat exchange system is the cooling system found in a typical water cooled automobile engine. The engine block normally operates at temperatures well above that of the water circulated through it. As a result the water absorbs some of the heat energy. The heated water has a higher temperature than the air forced through the radiator, so that the water gives up much of its heat content to the open atmosphere. Two heat exchange operations take place continuously in a water cooled auto engine: the hot engine gives up its heat to the moderately cool water, and the moderately cool water gives up its heat to the cooler air.

The notion that heat travels from hot to cold bodies is the most important facet of the principles of natural heat exchange. The process has another feature, however, which contributes to the success of modern cooling systems: the bigger the temperature difference, the faster the rate of heat exchange.

When two bodies having widely different temperatures come into contact with one another, the hotter body begins giving up its heat at a fairly rapid rate. As the heat exchange process continues and the temperature difference grows smaller, the rate of heat exchange begins to slow down. And when the two bodies have temperatures that are within several degrees of one another, the rate of heat exchange slows to an almost imperceptible pace.

6-1.4 The Pressure-Temperature Relationship

Virtually all consumer refrigeration appliances have sealed refrigerant systems that operate under pressure. The pressure in some instances is as low as 5 psig*, but it can rise as high as 160 psig in other parts of the same system.

Changes in refrigerant pressure play a vital role in the operation of refrigeration appliances. Generally speaking, every change in refrigerant pressure is accompanied by a heat exchange process. In one instance the pressure change makes the refrigerant absorb heat from the cooling space, and in another instance a pressure change makes the refrigerant give up its absorbed heat to some other medium.

It so happens that the boiling point of a substance is directly related to its pressure as well as its temperature. The fact that water boils at 212°F only holds true at atmospheric pressure. Actually water can boil at 60°F if the surrounding air pressure is low enough, and it can handle temperatures as high as 500°F before boiling if the surrounding pressure is high enough.

The law of physics that says the boiling point of a substance is proportional to the gas pressure upon it is one of the key features of the refrigeration process. Without it, it would be impossible to draw heat from a relatively cool space and deliver it to a warmer one—a process that runs directly against the natural laws of heat exchange described in Sec. 6-1.3.

To get a better feeling for the effects of pressure change on the boiling point of a substance, consider the fact that a tank of pressurized gas grows cold if the gas is bled off at a fairly high rate. A bottle of propane gas, for example, gets quite cold—even to the point of gathering frost—when the valve is turned full open. A refrigerant material such as Freon-12 produces an even more pronounced chilling effect.

Suppose that a container of Freon-12 is charged to 135 psig. According to the vapor pressure chart in Table 6-1, the boiling point at that pressure is 110°F. At normal room temperature, about 75°F, the refrigerant in the container is below its boiling temperature and thus exists as a liquid.

When the valve on the container is opened, the escaping gas undergoes a pressure drop from 136 psig to 0 psig. Table 6-1 shows that the boiling point of Freon-12 at 0 psig is about −20°F—well below room temperature. Lower-

---

*Psig is "gauge pressure," or a standard pressure scale that takes sea-level atmospheric pressure of 14.7 psi as the zero point.

TABLE 6-1   Temperature-pressure chart for Freon-12 refrigerant.

Temperature (°F)	Vapor Pressure (psig)
−40	−5.4
−30	−2.7
−20	0.6
−10	4.5
0	9.2
10	14.6
20	21
30	28.5
40	37
50	46.7
60	57.7
70	70.1
80	84
90	100
100	117
110	136
120	157

ing the pressure thus allows the gas to boil, and as described in Sec. 6-1.2, a boiling substance is tightly held at its boiling point temperature. In this instance, the boiling point temperature is −20°F. So it is little wonder that the tank feels cold. The tank and escaping gas are so cold, in fact, that they can "burn" human skin by freezing it.

A gas subjected to high pressures can thus exist in its liquid state at room temperatures, and a sudden drop in pressure lets the fluid boil at subzero temperatures. That explains at least one half of the normal two-phase refrigeration process.

The other half of the refrigeration process takes advantage of the fact that a gas can be liquified once again by applying high pressure by means of an external source of energy. Adding some sort of outside energy usually means warming the substance well above normal room temperature; but as long as the pressure is sufficiently high, the substance will liquify or condense. Applying a pressure of about 167 psig to Freon-12, for example, allows it to remain in its liquid state up to 120°F.

In a typical refrigeration cycle, a mechanical pump raises the gas pressure of Freon-12 to about 160 psig. The pump action raises the fluid temperature somewhat above 100°F, but the refrigerant still remains in its liquid state. The liquid is forced through a small orifice into a cooling section that has a low pressure on the order of 5 psig. This sudden drop in pressure makes the

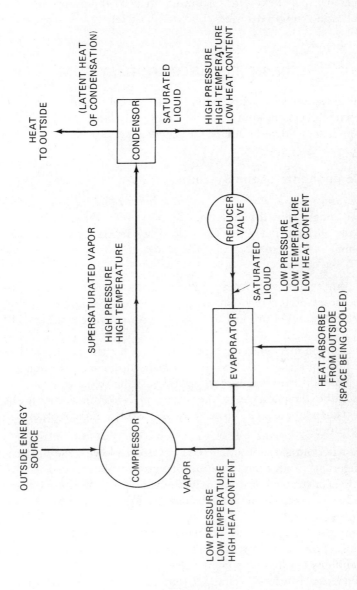

Fig. 6-2 Basic elements and stages of a closed refrigeration system.

Freon-12 boil at about $-10°F$. If the appliance happens to be a refrigerator, the low temperature fluid absorbs heat energy from the cooling cabinet. The fluid carries away the heat and is again liquified by the pump.

The following section describes this two-phase refrigeration cycle in more detail.

6-2 THE BASIC REFRIGERATION SYSTEM

This section deals with the basic refrigeration system in a very general way. The discussions apply equally well to any kind of consumer refrigeration appliances—dehumidifiers, air conditioners, refrigerators, freezers, and so on.

6-2.1 Components of the System

Figure 6-2 is a block diagram of a basic refrigeration system. It is a simplified diagram in the sense that it shows only the components most crucial to the refrigeration cycle. The following paragraphs describe the purpose and some of the general specifications for each of the four basic components.

1. THE COMPRESSOR STAGE.   The compressor raises both the pressure and temperature of the incoming vapor, producing a hot supersaturated vapor. Typical values of pressure and temperature for Freon-12 are 140–160 psig at 115°–125°F.

In the case of a mechanical compressor, or pump, the mechanical energy applied to the vapor raises its pressure which, in turn, causes the temperature to rise. A flame-operated compressor works just the other way around: the flame raises the temperature of the vapor in a confined space, thereby increasing its pressure as well. Either way, the result is higher vapor pressure and temperature.

2. THE CONDENSER STAGE.   The condenser lowers the heat content of the refrigerant, producing a mixture of saturated liquid and vapor. The condenser is constructed so that only the liquid refrigerant can leave it. Typical values of pressure and temperature for Freon-12 are 140–150 psig at $+115°F$.

In theory, lowering the temperature of the vapor should cause a corresponding loss in pressure. In a closed refrigeration system, however, the compressor maintains the high vapor pressure.

The condenser is a heat exchanger that uses some mechanism for transferring some of the refrigerant's heat to another medium having a lower temperature. Most home refrigeration and air-conditioning appliances use a blower to force cooler room air across the condenser. Larger commercial air conditioning systems accomplish the same task more efficiently by passing chilled water around the condenser coils.

3. THE REDUCER VALVE.   The reducer valve flushes high-pressure saturated refrigerant into the low-pressure part of the system. This sudden drop in pressure lowers the liquid's boiling point, letting a portion of it vaporize from its own stored-up heat. The temperature of the refrigerant thus plunges down to its low-pressure boiling point, and a mixture of cold liquid and vapor emerges from the reducing stage. Typical pressures and temperatures for Freon-12 are on the order of 5 psig at $-10°F$.

The reducing stage represents a high resistance between the high- and low-pressure sections of the refrigeration system. In principle, the reducing valve has to be nothing more than a very small hole between the two sections of the system. In practice, however, the reducer is often a capillary tube having a length and inside diameter adjusted to maintain a reasonably even flow of refrigerant. The reducer in more elaborate refrigeration systems is a control valve that adjusts the flow of refrigerant to maintain an even temperature in spite of changes in the cooling demand.

4. THE EVAPORATOR STAGE.   The evaporator boils off low-pressure liquid refrigerant remaining in the system, absorbing the necessary heat from some outside medium. Freon-12 vapors leave the evaporator and enter the compressor with pressures and temperatures on the order of 5 psig at $-10°F$.

The evaporator stage is the section responsible for actually doing the cooling work in a refrigeration or air-conditioning system. In a refrigerator, for instance, the evaporator boils the refrigerant by draining heat from the air in the cooling compartment. The evaporator in an air conditioner works by absorbing heat from room air passed through the evaporator coils and fins.

It is important to realize that the refrigerant undergoes a measurable temperature change at only two points in the refrigeration cycle: at the compressor and at the reducer. The compressor elevates the temperature, while the reducer lowers it.

The condenser and evaporator do not cause temperature changes. Rather, they change the amount of latent heat carried by the refrigerant. The condenser lowers the latent heat content to prepare it for the evaporator stage. The evaporator stage then adds latent heat by extracting it from a surrounding medium.

6-2.2   The Refrigerant Cycle

The refrigerant leaves the compressor under high pressure. This high pressure condition elevates the boiling point of the substance to a temperature well above normal room temperature—something on the order of about $115°F$. The compression process, whether taking place by mechanical pumping or heating action, warms the refrigerant to its boiling point and adds enough heat energy to make it a supersaturated vapor. See Fig. 6-3(A).

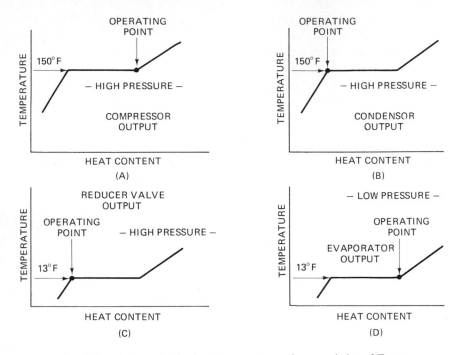

Fig. 6-3 Changes in the heat-temperature characteristics of Freon-12 (R-12) in a closed refrigeration system.

Most of the latent heat absorbed by the refrigerant in the compression process is removed at the condenser. Removing the latent heat causes the refrigerant to liquify without reducing its temperature. See Fig. 6-3(B). The fluid leaving the condenser stage is thus a saturated liquid.

The refrigerant undergoes a sudden drop in pressure as it passes through the reducer valve. This drop in pressure drastically lowers the fluid's boiling point, and its own heat content supplies the energy to make it boil. The fluid temperature is normally below the freezing point of water during this part of the cycle; and as shown in Fig. 6-3(C), it enters the next stage as a saturated liquid—one containing very little latent heat.

While circulating through the evaporator, the chilled refrigerant absorbs heat energy from the surrounding air or water, and carries it away as latent heat. The absorbed latent heat vaporizes most of the fluid by the time it reaches the input side of the compressor. See Fig. 6-3(D).

6-2.3 A Simplified Refrigerator System

The refrigerator diagrammed in Fig. 6-4 contains only the most essential parts of any refrigeration system. Secondary features, such as temperature controls and defrosting devices, are not described in this section.

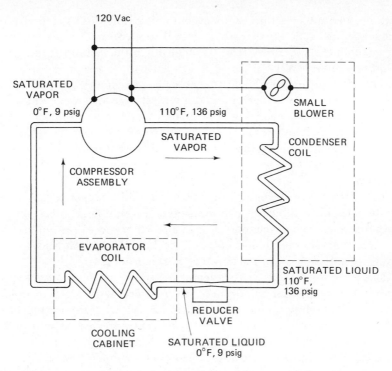

Fig. 6-4 Electrical-mechanical schematic of an all-electric refrigeration system (controls not included).

The refrigerant in this example is assumed to be Freon-12—the most common refrigerant material in use today. Referring to the table of Freon-12 boiling points (Table 6-1) can aid in the understanding of the pressures and temperatures specified for this refrigerator.

The compressor assembly contains a 120 Vac motor that turns the shaft of a vane-type gas pump. The compressor appears to be a single unit; and for all practical servicing purposes, it is indeed a single unit.

What is important to this explanation is the fact that the compressor motor provides the mechanical force necessary to pump the refrigerant vapor to a high pressure. Figure 6-4 shows that the vapor pressure created by the compressor is on the order of 136 psig.

According to Table 6-1, the boiling point of Freon-12 at 136 psig is 110°F. The mechanical compressing action raises the temperature of the refrigerant vapor to that point, and adds even more heat energy to create a saturated vapor.

The vapor passes through a section of tubing to the condenser portion of the system. In a typical home refrigerator, the condenser consists of about

30 ft of coiled tubing set into a honeycomb of cooling fins. A second 120 Vac motor operates a blower that picks up cool room air and drives it across the hot evaporator "radiator." The warmed air is then dumped into the surrounding atmosphere.

The air forced through the condenser coils removes most of the latent heat energy from the refrigerant, causing most of it to condense into a saturated liquid without changing its temperature by any significant amount. A combination of gas pressure and gravity forces the condensed liquid into the bottom portion of the evaporator. The refrigerant is still hot at this point, but it cannot boil because of the high vapor pressure exerted from the upper section of the condenser.

The gas pressure behind the condenser liquid forces it through a short section of capillary tubing. When the fluid emerges, it encounters a relatively low pressure created at the input side of the compressor. This sudden change in pressure causes the boiling point of the fluid to drop drastically, and it begins to boil off at a low temperature in the evaporator.

The evaporator, like the condenser, contains a long, coiled section of tubing. The evaporator tubing in a refrigerator covers much of the inside surface of the cooling cabinet. The pressure in the evaporator is on the order of 9 psig, and according to Table 6-1, this vapor pressure should make the refrigerant boil at about 0°F. Most of the heat energy for boiling fluid is extracted from the cooling compartment. The temperature in the cooling compartment thus drops to a low level that approaches the boiling temperature of the refrigerant—about 0°F in this example.

The vaporized refrigerant leaves the evaporator and returns to the intake side of the compressor pump where the entire cycle begins all over again.

6-3   QUESTIONS

1.   What is a Btu (British thermal unit)?

2.   Why does the temperature of a heated pan of water stop rising at the boiling point, 212°F?

3.   What happens to the boiling temperature of a liquid when the surrounding vapor pressure is increased?

4.   What is the natural direction of heat exchange between two bodies having different temperatures—from the hotter to the colder or from the colder to the hotter?

5.   What are the four basic stages or components of a mechanical refrigeration system?

6.   What is meant by a *saturated vapor*?

7

Garbage Disposers

Garbage disposers are among the simplest major appliances in the home today, but it happens that they are also the target for more user-created troubles than any other appliance. This means a serviceman's job does not end as soon as he gets a disposer running again—he is obliged to educate the user in the proper use and care of this accident-prone appliance.

As illustrated in Fig. 7-1, modern garbage disposers are made up of three major mechanical parts: a drive motor, a set of fixed shredding elements, and a set of impellor blades. The motor spins the impellor blades in such a way that they force the waste material against the sharp blades of the shredding element. Fresh water flowing into the shredding chamber washes the ground-up material through the disposer and into the home's sewage system.

Most troubles in garbage disposers occur whenever some sort of nondis-posable object or material gets jammed between the shredding element and impellor blades. Hard objects such as pieces of silverware, bones, stones, and finger rings are some of the more common causes of motor jamming. A long piece of string, however, can be even more troublesome than the more solid kinds of foreign objects. At any rate, the disposer is normally put back into

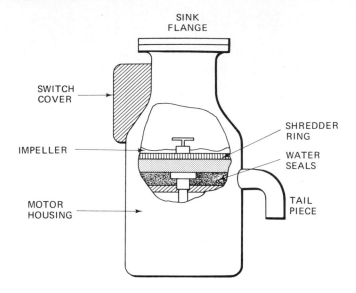

Fig. 7-1 Simplified cut-away view of a typical garbage disposer.

operation after reversing the impellor blades to dislodge the object and removing it by hand.

A second kind of trouble arises whenever the user fails to flush the disposer with fresh, *cold* water while the motor is running. The water performs two important tasks: it washes ground material out of the system and cools the motor. The second function is often overlooked; users who have a habit of flushing the disposer with hot water while it is in operation eventually find they must replace the entire unit because of a burned-out motor.

Garbage disposers vary somewhat with respect to mechanical features, and a serviceman should always consult the manufacturer's specifications and servicing notes before beginning an in-depth troubleshooting procedure on an unfamiliar model. The electrical features do not vary quite as much from one make of model to another; therefore, the circuits described in the following two sections are representative of most disposers in use today.

7-1 SIMPLE GARBAGE DISPOSERS

The garbage disposer circuit illustrated in Fig. 7-2 consists of an ordinary wall-mounted on/off switch, a split-phase motor, and a small control unit containing an overload circuit breaker and a start relay. This particular model is considered a rather simple garbage disposer because it contains nothing other than the most basic parts.

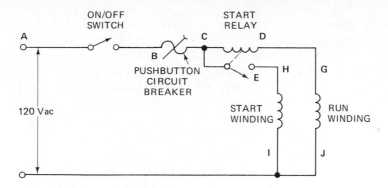

Fig. 7-2 Schematic diagram of a simple garbage disposer unit.

7-1.1 Theory of Operation

Whenever the user places the on/off switch into its ON position, full line power is applied to the appliance. Current flows through the overload circuit breaker, the coil of the start relay, and the run winding of the motor. Since the start winding in the motor is not initially in the circuit (the normally open contacts in the start relay cut off current to the start winding), the motor draws an abnormally large amount of current at first. This current is sufficient to activate the start relay, pulling the contacts closed and applying full line power to the start winding.

With the start winding thus connected into the circuit, the motor begins to run. And as soon as the motor reaches about 75 percent of its normal operating speed, the back EMF from the stator windings reduces the input current to a level that allows the start relay to drop open again. The motor then runs at its rated speed and at its normal efficiency until the user turns off the on/off switch. See Chapter 5 for a more complete discussion of relay-start motors.

The overload circuit breaker trips open whenever an abnormally large amount of current flows through the motor windings for a dangerously long period of time. The purpose of the breaker is to shut down the appliance before the fault current can start a fire or seriously damage the motor windings. The breaker normally remains latched open after it is activated, making it necessary for the user to manually reset it before power can be applied to the motor again. It is hoped that the user will attempt to remedy the cause of the fault current before resetting the breaker and trying the motor again.

As mentioned earlier in this chapter, most disposer troubles are caused by foreign objects jammed in the shredding chamber. Curing this kind of trouble usually involves rotating the impellor in the reverse direction far enough to dislodge the object. The disposer circuit illustrated in Fig. 7-2 has no provisions for electrically reversing the direction of the motor. Such disposers are generally equipped with an emergency hand crank that fits into a slot in the bottom or side of the disposer unit. This crank makes it possible to manually reverse the rotation of the impellor and dislodge the trapped object. Obviously the disposer must be turned off when cranking the unit by hand.

The garbage disposer circuit in Fig. 7-3 represents something of an improvement over the simpler model described in connection with Fig. 7-2. The essential feature of the better model is that it does away with the "crank-and-sweat" technique for momentarily reversing the direction of the impellor blades whenever they are jammed with a foreign object.

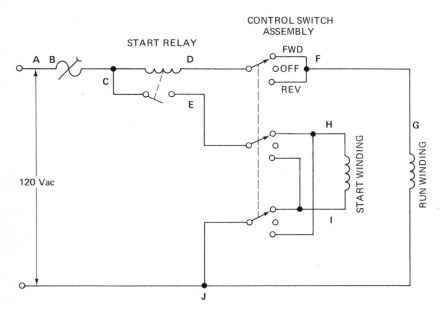

Fig. 7-3   Schematic diagram of a garbage disposer with a manual reversing switch.

The main control switch in this instance is a three-position wall switch. The switch positions might vary from one manufacturer to another, but the basic idea is that one position is the normal OFF position, one is for the normal ON position, and the third is for momentarily *reversing* the direction the motor turns. This REV position on the switch is usually spring-loaded so that the user must hold it in that position to keep the motor running.

Whenever the control switch is placed into its FWD (forward) position (as shown in Fig. 7-3), line current flows to the run winding in the motor via the overload circuit breaker and the start relay coil. An initial surge of line current through the run winding also flows through the relay coil, closing the relay connection to the start winding. Current for the start winding thus flows through the reversing switch path between points **F** and **K**. The motor responds by turning in its normal forward direction, and as the motor comes up to speed, the corresponding drop in stator current lets the relay contacts drop open. Removing the start winding from the circuit allows the motor to continue running as its rated power and efficiency until the user turns it off.

Reversing the direction of the motor is a matter of flipping the control switch to its REV position. The start-up and stop sequences are exactly the same as they are in the FWD case—the operation of the start winding being completely controlled by the start relay. The main difference is that the polarity of the start winding is reversed. Instead of flowing between points **F** and **G** in the control switch (as is done for FWD operations), start current for REV flows between points **G** and **L** in the control switch. Providing a current path between points **G** and **L** effectively reverses the polarity of the power applied to the start winding, making the motor turn in the opposite direction.

7-1.2 Troubleshooting Guide

This troubleshooting guide applies to garbage disposers of the type illustrated in Figs. 7-2 and 7-3.

Motor does not run—seems dead

1. No power reaching the appliance—check the supply voltage at the circuit connection points (between points **A** and **J**). The trouble is confirmed if no voltage appears at those points.

2. Overload circuit breaker open—connect a voltmeter across the breaker's terminals (between points **B** and **C**). Depressing the reset pushbutton on the breaker normally makes any voltage across these terminals disappear. If the voltage is present and if it remains after attempting to reset the breaker, it is indeed suffering from an open circuit trouble.

3. On/off switch open (Fig. 7-2 only)—connect a jumper wire across the switch contacts (between points **A** and **B**). If the motor runs, the trouble is confirmed. Doublecheck this conclusion by removing the switch from the circuit and testing its continuity. A switch having broken contacts will show no continuity or infinite resistance, regardless of the switch setting.

4. Open contact in the control switch (Fig. 7-3 only)—connect a voltmeter across the run portion of the control switch (between

points **D** and **F**), and note the readings while flipping the switch through all its positions. If the switch shows 120 V in all switch positions, chances are quite good that part of the switch is defective.

Remove the switch from the circuit and doublecheck the contacts with an ohmmeter or continuity tester. If any set of poles—especially the run winding poles—show infinite resistance, the trouble is confirmed.

5. Start relay coil open—connect a voltmeter across the start relay coil (between points **C** and **D**), and turn on the disposer. The trouble is confirmed if full line voltage appears across the coil.

    Note: there will be a small voltage across the relay coil under normal operating conditions. Consult the manufacturer's service notes if there is any reason to question the amount of voltage found there.

    Doublecheck the conclusion by removing the relay assembly from the circuit and checking the coil with a continuity tester or ohmmeter. Again, the manufacturer's service notes show the proper resistance level. The coil is indeed open, however, if this test shows infinite resistance.

6. Open section of wiring or bad connection—systematically check the voltage between pairs of points throughout the circuit. Voltage should appear only across open switches and load devices—never across sections of wiring.

Motor does not run, but draws heavy current

1. Impellor blades jammed—visually inspect the grinding chamber and clean out any foreign material.

2. Defective start relay—connect a jumper wire across the relay contacts (between points **C** and **E**), and apply full power to the disposer. The trouble is confirmed if the motor starts normally.

3. Motor run or start winding open—see Chapter 5.

4. Motor run winding shorted—see Chapter 5.

Motor seems sluggish

1. Undisposable material in the chamber—visually inspect the grinding chamber and clean out any foreign material.

2. Motor run winding open—see Chapter 5.

Motor does not run in reverse (Fig. 7-3 only)

The trouble is definitely associated with the control switch. Visually inspect the switch for external troubles such as broken or shorted wires. If nothing is apparent, replace the entire switch assembly.

7-2 DELUXE DISPOSERS

The garbage disposer described in this section and illustrated in Fig. 7-4 has some "extras" that set it apart from its simpler counterparts in the previous section. The main feature of this disposer is that the motor automatically reverses in the event of a jamming condition. Another feature is that the motor cannot start unless cold water is running into the grinding chamber or a chamber lid is latched into place.

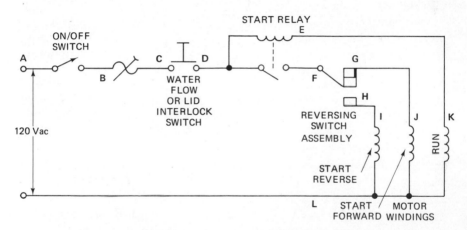

Fig. 7-4   Schematic diagram of a garbage disposer that features a lid or water interlock switch and an automatic reversing assembly.

7-2.1 Theory of Operation

The circuit in Fig. 7-4 contains the same sort of start relay mechanism and on/off switch found in simpler units. The essential differences are: a double-section start winding in the motor, a thermostatically operated reversing switch, and a safety interlock switch.

Like the disposer in Fig. 7-3, the motor in this unit is reversible. Rather than switching around the phase of the applied power, however, this unit is reversed by applying the same phase to an entirely different start winding—one that is wound in the opposite direction. The result is that the motor starts in the normal forward direction when start power is applied to the FWD winding, and the motor starts in the reverse direction when power is applied to the REV winding.

An interlock switch, shown connected in series with the main power source, prevents the disposer from starting until the user carries out some operation that is necessary for closing the switch contacts. In some models, this interlock is activated by a stream of cold water running into the grinding chamber. The interlock switch on some other models can be closed only by fitting a special drain cover into place. In any event, the on/off switch and the interlock must be closed to start the motor and keep it running.

The purpose of the reversing switch is to restart the motor in the reverse direction whenever the motor stalls while running in the normal direction. The switch works much like an ordinary circuit breaker; in other words, the switch changes from one state to another in response to an excessive current flow through it. Under normal current conditions, the automatic switch is in the position shown in Fig. 7-4.

Normally, closing both the on/off and interlock switches feeds full line power to the run winding on the motor. Since there is not yet any power applied to the start winding via the relay assembly, the run winding draws a large amount of current from the lines. This overcurrent condition energizes the start relay, the contacts in the relay close, and the FWD start winding finally receives power via the normally closed contacts of the automatic switch.

The motor thus begins running in its normal forward direction. As the motor comes up to speed, current through the run winding drops off to a normal level, de-energizing the start relay and removing power from the start winding. And everything remains in this condition until (1) the user turns off the power or (2) a serious jamming condition arises.

Whenever a jamming condition arises, the motor stalls and causes the run winding to draw excessive current. This overcurrent condition activates the start relay, which, in turn, applies power to the FWD start winding. The motor thus tries to start in the normal forward direction. If the motor does not restart, the continuing heavy current drain soon activates the automatic switch mechanism.

The automatic switch transfers starting power from the FWD start winding to the REV winding. This operation reverses the direction of the motor starting torque, freeing it from its jamming condition in most instances. As the motor comes up to speed in the reverse direction, the start relay drops open once again, and all power is removed from the REV start winding. With no power applied to the REV winding, the automatic switch soon springs back to its normal position, setting the stage for the next starting cycle. The motor continues to run in the reverse direction until the user turns off the power.

7-2.2 Troubleshooting Guide

The following troubleshooting and servicing notes apply to "deluxe" garbage disposers similar to the one illustrated in Fig. 7-4.

Motor does not run—seems dead

1. No power applied—check the voltage at the "hot" lead to the on/off switch and the "neutral" lead on the disposer (between points **A** and **L**). The trouble is confirmed if no voltage is present.

2. Circuit breaker open—connect a voltmeter across the terminals on the circuit breaker (between points **B** and **C**). Depress the reset pushbutton and note the response on the voltmeter. Depressing the reset button normally makes any voltage across these terminals disappear. If the voltage is present and if it remains after attempting to reset the breaker, the unit is suffering from an open circuit condition. Doublecheck the diagnosis by pulling the breaker out of the circuit and running an ohmmeter or continuity test.

3. On/off switch open—connect a jumper wire across the switch contacts (between points **A** and **B**), and close the interlock switch. If the motor runs, the trouble is confirmed. Doublecheck the diagnosis by removing the switch from the circuit and testing its continuity. A switch having broken contacts will show no continuity or infinite resistance.

4. Interlock switch contacts broken open—connect a jumper wire across the interlock switch contacts (between points **C** and **D**), and turn on the power to the disposer. If the motor starts normally, the trouble is confirmed.

5. Start relay defective—connect a jumper wire across the start relay coil (between points **D** and **E**), close the interlock switch, and apply power to the appliance. The trouble is confirmed if the motor starts normally.

6. Open run winding in the motor—disconnect the wiring to one side of the run winding (at point **L**), and check the resistance of the winding. If this test shows infinite resistance, the diagnosis is correct.

7. Faulty wiring or loose connection—visually inspect the wiring for signs of broken cables and bad connections. Systematically check the voltage between pairs of points throughout the circuit.

Voltage should appear only across open switches and load devices
—never between two connections separated by only a length of
wire.

Motor does not run, but draws excessive current

1. Defective start relay—connect a jumper wire across the relay
   contacts (between points **D** and **F**), and turn on the disposer.
   The motor will run normally if this diagnosis is correct.

2. Open reversing switch—connect a jumper wire across the
   normally closed contacts in the automatic switch (between points
   F and **G**). Apply power to the disposer, and note the response.
   If the motor runs normally, the trouble is confirmed.

3. Open FWD start winding—disconnect the wiring to one of the
   start winding terminals (at point **J**), and check the resistance of
   the winding. If the test shows infinite resistance, the trouble is
   indeed caused by an open motor winding.

4. Shorted reversing switch—disconnect all wiring to the reversing
   switch, and connect a jumper wire between the FWD start winding and the run winding (between points **J** and **L**). If the motor
   starts and runs in the forward direction, the trouble is confirmed.

Motor runs in reverse at all times

The most likely cause of this trouble is a defective reversing switch.
Disconnect all wiring to the reversing switch, connect a jumper wire
between the FWD start winding and the run winding (between points
J and **L**), and apply power to the disposer. If the motor runs in the
normal forward direction, the trouble is confirmed.

7-3 QUESTIONS

1. Name the three basic mechanical parts of a typical garbage disposer.

2. Why is it important to run *cold* water through a garbage disposer while
   it is in use?

3. What is the most common cause of troubles in garbage disposers?

4. What causes a disposer motor to apply extra torque whenever a jamming
   condition occurs?

8

Trash Compactors

A trash compactor uses about one ton of squeezing force to transform all kinds of household trash—bottles, cans, boxes, and wastepaper—into a single block of concentrated junk. A typical kitchen compactor can reduce the equivalent of two or three twenty-gallon cans of trash into a bag about the size of an ordinary wastebasket.

One of the main selling features of trash compactors is that they eliminate the daily trip to outside trash cans. In fact, these relatively new appliances practically do away with trash cans altogether. Many people still consider trash compactors luxury appliances, but today's luxuries tend to become tomorrow's necessities, and we can expect to see trash compactors in most kitchens of the future.

The general procedures for using trash compactors are much the same for all the popular makes and models. The idea is to slide open a drawer in the front of the unit and drop the trash into it. If the trash is properly loaded, the user starts the compacting operation after the drawer is closed and a START pushbutton is depressed.

During the compacting operation, a heavy-duty ram descends slowly into the trash drawer, applying an increasing pressure that reaches about 2000 lb before the ram is lifted away. The compacting cycle is complete when the ram has returned to the top of the unit. The entire cycle normally takes about one minute.

To keep the operation as tidy as possible, the compacting area is lined with a plastic-lined paper bag. Trash coming out of the compactor is thus neatly done up in a sturdy, relatively watertight container that is easy to handle. Another important feature is an automatic deodorizer made up of a can of aerosol deodorant that is triggered every time the ram is operated. The idea is to reduce unpleasant odors that might otherwise fill the kitchen whenever the compactor drawer is opened.

8-1 THEORY OF OPERATION

Mechanically speaking, trash compactors work on the same general principles as a vise or wine press. A trash compactor has two vertical power screws that are threaded through a set of power nuts on the ram assembly. As the power screws turn, the ram assembly moves up or down along the screws.

The two power screws are driven by a chain-and-sprocket assembly consisting of a main drive chain, a drive sprocket, and a smaller sprocket on each power screw. As the drive sprocket turns, it forces the two drive screws to turn in the same direction and at exactly the same rates.

The drive sprocket is, itself, driven by a reducing gear or belt-and pulley arrangement connected to the main drive motor. The main drive motor turns at about 1700 rpm, but the connections to the drive sprocket and power screws reduce the turning speed to something on the order of 250 rpm. Gearing down the speed, by the way, vastly increases the torque available at the power screws. Most compactors are capable of applying up to one ton of ram pressure.

The circuit diagram in Fig. 8-1 clearly shows how much the electrical operation of a trash compactor depends on switches. In fact, taking away the switches leaves nothing but a simple motor and an overload circuit breaker to worry about. Switches thus play a vital role in the electrical operation of a trash compactor; and understanding the function of each of the switches automatically leads to a good understanding of how a trash compactor works from an electrical point of view.

8-1.1 Description of Switches

The following description of switches uses part numbers specified in Fig. 8-1.

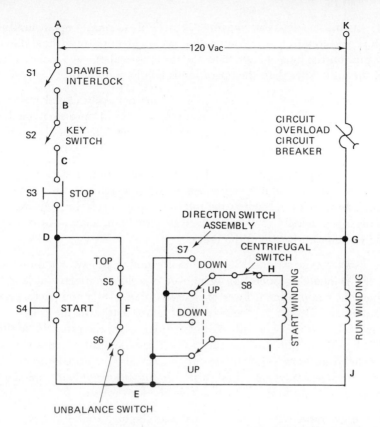

Fig. 8-1 Schematic diagram of a trash compactor.

DRAWER INTERLOCK SWITCH (S1). This normally open switch is capable of totally shutting down the compactor whenever its contacts are opened. The contacts are operated by the drawer on the compactor, and the only way to close the contacts is by completely closing the drawer. In other words, the user cannot start the unit with the drawer open, and the unit automatically shuts off if the drawer is ever opened during an operating cycle.

KEY SWITCH (S2). This normally open switch is manually operated by means of a special lock-and-key arrangement on the control panel. The user closes this switch by inserting a special key and turning it about one-half turn in the clockwise direction. The switch then remains closed until the user rotates the key to its original position. The key cannot be removed without opening the key switch contacts. This particular switch acts as a safety feature aimed at preventing unauthorized users (especially small children) from activating the compactor cycle.

START PUSHBUTTON SWITCH (S4).   This normally open pushbutton switch is used to initiate the compacting cycle. The user must hold down the START pushbutton long enough to let the ram move about two inches from the top of the unit. After that, the operation is wholly automatic.

STOP PUSHBUTTON SWITCH (S3).   This normally closed pushbutton switch is one of the user's manual control switches. Depressing this button stops the ram at any point in the compacting cycle. The ram always rises as soon as the STOP button is released.

TOP LIMIT SWITCH (S5).   This particular control switch is responsible for keeping the unit running when the user releases the START pushbutton. The switch is located at the top of the power screws; and since it is a normally open switch, it closes only when the ram moves away from its resting position at the top of the unit.

UNBALANCE SWITCH (S6).   This normally open switch immediately stops the compacting operation whenever a serious unbalancing condition occurs in the compacting drawer. The user's manuals for compactors recommend placing large objects such as thick glass bottles in the center of the drawer. If they are very far off-center for any reason, the ram can be thrown out of alignment. The unbalancing switch rests against the drawer and is forced closed under normal circumstances. If a serious unbalance condition makes the drawer move out of position, the unbalance switch stops the ram. Depressing the START button then causes the ram to rise.

DIRECTION SWITCH (S7).   This double-pole, double-throw switch is responsible for changing the direction of the motor. See Chapter 5 for further details about the theory of motor direction controls. The essential idea here is that the direction switch is located at the top of the unit along with the top limit switch. The direction switch is placed in its DOWN position as long as the ram is within an inch or two of the top of the unit. The direction switch is thus in its UP position except at the very beginning and the very end of a normal compacting cycle.

CENTRIFUGAL SWITCH (S8).   The centrifugal switch takes the motor's start winding out of the circuit whenever the motor reaches about 70 percent of its normal operating speed. The centrifugal switch in a trash compactor, however, plays an especially important role in reversing the direction of the ram at the lower end of its cycle. As the ram reaches the bottom of the guides or its force applied to the trash reaches about 2000 lb, the motor stalls out, letting the centrifugal switch close. The motor then starts in the opposite direction and continues to run until the ram reaches the top of the power screws.

8-1.2 Compactor Operating Cycles

The trash compactor illustrated in Fig. 8-1 uses the same operating sequence for every normal compacting operation. There are, however, other operating cycles that go into effect whenever the load becomes badly unbalanced or the user depresses the STOP pushbutton during a compacting cycle. Table 8-1 lists the operations included in a normal compacting cycle. The fault-condition cycles outlined in Tables 8-2 and 8-3 are described in the last part of this section.

A normal cycle begins as the user closes the drawer, turns on the key switch, and depresses the START pushbutton. According to Table 8-1 these three actions close S1, S2, and S3. As the third switch closes, line power reaches the motor, and it begins to run.

As the motor comes up to speed (Step 4), the centrifugal switch opens, taking the start winding out of the circuit. By this time the motor is driving the ram downward (Step 5); and as the ram drops about 1 in. below the top of the guides, it allows the top limit switch S5 to close. Closing S5 completes a circuit around the START pushbutton, thus making it possible to release the START button without having the appliance shut down (Step 6).

As the ram is driven about $1^1/_2$ in. below the top of the compactor, it releases the direction control switch S7. This operation changes the electrical connections on the motor's start winding from DOWN to UP, but there is no outward sign of any change because the centrifugal switch, S8, is open at the time.

The ram continues its slow downward travel without making further changes in the status of switches until it makes contact with the trash and eventually stalls the motor. Of course the motor stops turning as soon as the system is stalled, and the centrifugal switch responds by falling closed (Step 9). Recall that the direction switch had been set to UP earlier in this cycle, so that the motor's start winding receives power that makes the motor start in the UP direction. The ram then begins rising toward the top of the power screws (Step 10).

As the ram approaches the top of its travel, it first makes contact with the direction switch, changing its setting to DOWN; because the motor's start winding is disconnected from the circuit, however, there is no outward response. The ram does respond when it finally makes contact with the top limit switch (Step 12). The top limit switch cuts off all power to the motor, ending the compacting cycle and leaving all the switches ready for another cycle. The user must depress the START pushbutton to get the next cycle underway.

Table 8-2 lists the operations involved in a compacting cycle that is aborted by an unbalance condition during the downward stroke of the ram.

TABLE 8-1 A normal operating cycle

	User Action	Automatic Action	Electrical Response	Outward Response
1.	Close drawer	—	S1 closes	—
2.	Turn key switch	—	S2 closes	—
3.	Depress START button	—	S4 closes	Motor starts
4.	—	Motor up to speed	S8 opens	Ram moving downward
5.	—	Ram releases top limit switch	S5 closes	—
6.	Release START pushbutton	—	S4 opens	—
7.	—	Ram releases direction switch	S7 to UP	—
8.	—	Ram stalls at the bottom	Motor current rises	Motor stops
9.	—	Centrifugal switch closes	S8 closes	Motor starts in reverse direction
10.	—	Motor up to speed	S8 opens	Ram moves upward
11.	—	Ram activates direction switch	S7 to DOWN	—
12.	—	Ram opens top limit switch	S5 opens	Motor stops
13.	—	Centrifugal switch closes	S8 closes	—
14.	Turn off key switch	—	S2 opens	—

TABLE 8-2   A cycle interrupted by an unbalanced load condition

	User Action	Automatic Action	Electrical Response	Outward Response
1.	Close drawer	—	S1 closes	—
2.	Turn key switch	—	S2 closes	—
3.	Depress START pushbutton	—	S4 closes	Motor starts
4.	—	Motor up to speed	S8 opens	Ram moving downward
5.	—	Ram releases top limit switch	S5 closes	—
6.	Release START pushbutton	—	S4 opens	—
7.	—	Ram releases direction switch	S7 to UP	—
8.	—	UNBALANCED LOAD	S6 opens	Motor stops
9.	—	Centrifugal switch closes	S8 closes	—
10.	Depress START pushbutton	—	S4 closes	Motor starts
11.	Hold down START pushbutton	Motor up to speed	S8 opens	Ram moving upward
12.	Hold down START pushbutton	UNBALANCE CLEARED	S6 closes	—
13.	Release START pushbutton	—	S4 opens	—
14.	—	Ram activates direction switch	S7 to DOWN	—
15.	—	Ram opens top limit switch	S5 opens	Motor stops
16.	—	Centrifugal switch closes	S8 closes	—
17.	Turn off key switch	—	S2 opens	—

This condition often arises whenever the user fails to place sturdy objects such as large glass bottles and aerosol cans in the center part of the drawer. As the ram descends, these off-center objects tend to place unbalanced stresses on the power screws and drive nuts. The unbalance switch, S6, is responsible for stopping all operations whenever these stresses occur. The only way the situation can be remedied is by pressing and holding down the START pushbutton until the unbalance condition is cleared. The ram then continues moving upward to end the cycle. The door can be opened and the trash balanced a bit better.

Referring to Table 8-2, the first seven operations are identical to those of a normal compacting cycle. When the unbalance condition occurs in Step 8, however, the unbalance switch, S6, opens to interrupt the power supplied to the motor circuit. Of course the motor stops running immediately and, as a result, the centrifugal switch, S8, drops closed. For all practical purposes, the whole unit is shut down. The door cannot be opened in this condition, either, because of a mechanical interlock that always latches the door closed when the ram is situated away from its resting position.

Starting the operation of the system again is a matter of raising the ram to its resting position. This operation would serve two purposes: (1) it relieves the pressures that caused the unbalance condition in the first place and (2) it unlatches the drawer so that the user can open it to redistribute the load properly. Once the motor stops because of an unbalance (Step 8), depressing the START pushbutton reapplies power to the drive motor. From a previous operation (Step 7), the direction switch is in its UP position; therefore, the power applied to the drive motor makes it turn in a direction that causes the ram to move upward.

The unbalance condition is normally cleared the instant the ram moves away from the trash. This means that the unbalance switch drops closed again (Step 12), completing the circuit around the START switch and making it possible for the cycle to end automatically if the user releases the START pushbutton (Steps 13, 14, and 15).

On rare occasions, especially when a serious trouble occurs, the unbalance switch might not fall closed as the ram pulls away from the trash. In such cases the user has to hold down the START button until the ram reaches the top of its travel and the drawer can be opened.

Table 8-3 illustrates the processes involved in manually interrupting a compacting cycle. The operating cycle starts out normally, but the user decides to interrupt the cycle at Step 8. At that point, S3 opens to interrupt power to the motor. The motor stops and the centrifugal switch falls closed (Step 9). The direction switch has been set to UP in Step 7, however, and as soon as the user releases the STOP pushbutton, power is immediately reapplied to the motor, making it turn in a direction that moves the ram upward (Steps 10 and 11).

TABLE 8-3   A cycle manually interrupted by the user

	User Action	Automatic Action	Electrical Response	Outward Response
1.	Close drawer	—	S1 closes	—
2.	Turn key switch	—	S2 closes	—
3.	Depress START pushbutton	—	S4 closes	Motor starts
4.	—	Motor up to speed	S8 opens	Ram moving downward
5.	—	Ram releases top limit switch	S5 closes	—
6.	Release START pushbutton	—	S4 opens	—
7.	—	Ram releases direction switch	S7 to UP	—
8.	Depress STOP pushbutton	—	S3 opens	Motor stops
9.	—	Centrifugal switch closes	S8 closes	—
10.	Release STOP pushbutton	—	S3 closes	Motor starts
11.	—	Motor up to speed	S8 opens	Ram moving upward
12.	—	Ram activates direction switch	S7 to DOWN	—
13.	—	Ram opens top limit switch	S5 closes	Motor stops
14.	—	Centrifugal switch closes	S8 closes	—
15.	Turn off key switch	—	S2 opens	—

This compactor cannot be completely shut down by pressing the STOP pushbutton—the system always restarts on the upward stroke as soon as the STOP button is released. The only ways to completely shut down the system during a compacting cycle is either by turning off the key switch to, or unplugging, the appliance.

8-2 TROUBLESHOOTING GUIDE

The troubleshooting notes in this section refer to the schematic diagram in Fig. 8-1. The boldface letters indicate convenient test points found in similar models.

Motor does not start—unit seems dead

1. No power applied—make certain that portable units are plugged into live outlets of the proper voltage rating. Check the condition of service line fuses or circuit breakers.

2. Drawer interlock switch open—make certain that the key switch is turned off, and connect a jumper wire across the interlock's terminals (between points **A** and **B**). Close the drawer and activate the compactor. If the motor starts, the trouble is confirmed.

3. Key switch open—make certain that the drawer is open, and connect a jumper wire across the key switch terminals (between points **B** and **C**). Close the drawer and activate the compactor. The trouble is confirmed if the motor starts while the jumper is in place.

4. STOP switch open—make certain that the key switch is turned off, and connect a jumper wire across the contacts on the STOP switch (between points **C** and **D**). Attempt to start a compacting cycle in the normal manner. If the compactor cycles one time, the trouble is indeed caused by a faulty STOP switch.

5. START switch open—make certain the key switch is turned off, and connect a jumper wire across the contacts of the START switch (between points **D** and **E**). CAUTION: The compacting cycle may start as soon as the key switch and drawer interlock are closed. The diagnosis is correct if the motor runs when the jumper is in place and does not start whenever the jumper is removed.

6. Overload circuit breaker open—check the overload breaker to

make certain it is latched down. If the breaker seems to be properly set, connect a voltmeter across the terminals (between points **G** and **K**), and perform the normal start-up routine. The circuit breaker is open if the voltmeter shows full line voltage whenever the START button is depressed while the drawer and key switches are closed.

Overload circuit breakers do not "go bad" on their own accord. A bad breaker is thus a good indicator of a more serious trouble elsewhere in the appliance. A prudent serviceman seeks out the more serious trouble—paying special attention to the motor—before replacing a breaker that has gone bad.

Unit draws excessive current—does not compact trash

1. Top limit switch set too low—visually inspect the action of the switches while the compactor is cycling. As the ram approaches the top of its travel, it should contact the direction switch before it touches the top limit switch. If it appears that the top limit switch is being activated first, consult the manufacturer's specifications and servicing notes for the correct switch adjustments. A trial-and-error adjustment is recommended only in emergencies.

2. Direction switch set too high—visually inspect the operation of the compactor as described in the previous diagnosis.

3. Centrifugal switch open—disconnect the wiring to either end of the motor's start winding (at either point **H** or **I**), and check the continuity of the centrifugal switch (between points **H** and **L**). If the test shows a lack of continuity or infinite resistance, the trouble is confirmed and the switch must be replaced.

4. Motor winding open—disconnect the wiring to the motor's start winding (at either point **H** or **I**), and check the resistance of the winding with an ohmmeter. The start winding is open if this test shows infinite resistance. If the winding appears to be in good order, reconnect the wires and perform the same test on the run winding (points **G** and **J**). Replace the motor if either winding is open.

5. Mechanical binding—remove all cover panels from the compactor and carefully inspect the mechanical sections. Look especially for loose sprockets, a broken drive chain, or defective power screws. Consult the manufacturer's service notes for recommended lubrication procedures.

6. Direction switch defective—if the five previous tests do not uncover the trouble, there is a very good chance the direction
switch is defective. Normally it is a poor practice to "troubleshoot" a component by replacing it with a new one, but this
happens to be one of those rare instances when it is cheaper and
easier to do so.

7. Motor windings shorted—See Chapter 5.

**Motor does not stop automatically at the end of a
cycle**

1. START switch shorted—if this is the case, the compactor tends to
start running the instant that the drawer is closed and the key
switch is turned on. The unit, in other words, begins running
before the START button is depressed.

   This diagnosis can be doubly confirmed by disconnecting the
START switch from the circuit and checking its continuity with
an ohmmeter. The switch should show zero resistance when the
pushbutton is depressed and infinite resistance when it is not.
A shorted switch, however, shows zero resistance at all times.
The best repair procedure is to replace the entire switch assembly with a new one.

2. Top limit switch set too high—visually inspect the action of the
switches while the compactor is cycling. The ram should touch
the top limit switch and stop as it approaches the top of its
travel. But if the top limit switch has been somehow moved or
bent upward, the ram cannot make contact with it, and the
system continues cycling up and down until the key switch is
turned off.

   If it appears that the ram is not making contact with the top
limit switch, lower the switch a little bit and try cycling the
system again. If there is any doubt about the exact adjustment
or adjustment procedure, consult the manufacturer's specifications.

3. Top limit switch shorted—turn off the appliance and disconnect
all the wiring to one terminal on the top limit switch (at either
point **D** or **F**). Reapply power and attempt a normal starting
operation. If the top limit switch is shorted, the motor runs only
as long as the START pushbutton is depressed.

   Doublecheck this diagnosis by removing the top limit switch
from the unit and testing the continuity of the contacts. As this
is a normally closed switch, the test would normally show infinite

resistance when the button is depressed and zero resistance when it is not. A shorted pushbutton switch, however, shows zero resistance whether it is depressed or not.

Motor runs only while start button is depressed

1. Top limit switch open—remove the wiring to one of the terminals on the top limit switch (at either point **D** or **F**), and check the continuity of the switch contacts. Since this is a normally closed pushbutton switch, the test would normally show infinite resistance when the button is depressed and zero resistance when it is not. An open switch of this type, however, shows infinite resistance whether the button is depressed or not.

2. Unbalance switch open—disconnect the wiring to one of the terminals on the unbalance switch (at either point **E** or **F**), and check the continuity of the switch contacts. The unbalance switch on the model shown in Fig. 8-1 is a normally open switch that is usually kept closed by the drawer assembly. If an unbalance condition arises, however, the switch is allowed to open. Other compactors may use normally closed switches for the same application. In either case, the switch is at fault if it shows infinite resistance whether it is depressed or not.

3. Top limit switch set too low—hold down the START pushbutton and visually observe the operation of the top limit and direction switches. As the ram approaches the top of its travel, it should make contact with the direction switch before it touches the top limit switch. This trouble is confirmed if the ram touches the top limit switch first. Consult the manufacturer's specifications for the proper adjustment procedures. A trial-and-error approach should be reserved for emergency cases.

4. Mechanical binding—remove all cover panels and carefully inspect the mechanical sections. Look especially for damaged power screws. Lubricate the assembly according to the manufacturer's servicing notes.

Drawer cannot be opened

The chief cause of this particular problem is the mechanical interlock system that latches the drawer closed as long as the ram is anywhere but in its topmost resting position. Any trouble that causes the ram to stop midcycle is thus going to cause the drawer to stick closed as well.

1. Direction switch set too high—this trouble becomes a likely candidate whenever the ram can be moved up and down by means of the usual panel controls. Visually inspect the action of the top limit and direction switches while the compactor is cycling. As the ram approaches the end of a cycle, it should contact the direction switch before it touches the top limit switch. If this is not the case, consult the manufacturer's specifications for the appropriate adjustments. Use a trial-and-error adjustment only if absolutely necessary.

2. Direction switch defective—if the previous test shows the direction switch is fixed in its proper position, there is a very good chance this switch is defective—especially if the ram tends to bind at the bottom of its travel.

   It is normally a poor practice to "troubleshoot" a component by replacing it with a new one. This happens to be one of those instances, however, when it is cheaper and easier to replace the switch than it is to troubleshoot it.

3. Mechanical binding or broken linkages—remove all cover panels and carefully inspect the unit for broken, loose, or missing mechanical parts. Consult the manufacturer's specifications for the recommended tension on belts and chains and proper lubrication procedures.

8-3 QUESTIONS

1. What three switch conditions must be met before a normal compacting cycle can begin (refer to Fig. 8-1)?

2. The direction switch changes to the UP position shortly after the downward stroke begins. What prevents the motor from reversing direction at that time?

3. What causes the motor and ram to reverse their direction of travel the moment the trash is compacted?

4. Why is it necessary to hold down the START pushbutton until an unbalance condition is cleared?

9

Automatic Dishwashers

When automatic dishwashers first appeared on the consumer scene some years ago, cartoonists had a heyday depicting an incredible imaginary diswashing machine that picks up a dirty dish, scrubs it with a sponge and soap, rinses it in a tub of hot water, and dries it with a towel. Of course our mental picture of automatic diswashers is much more sophisticated today, but the result of the process is the same: a clean, dry dish.

Modern automatic dishwashers are compact machines that have very few moving parts. The scrubbing action is carried out by jets of hot water, and the drying is done by electrically generated heat. A basic dishwasher is actually a rather simple appliance. The addition of selectable or programmable washing cycles in the past few years, however, has done much to increase the impression of electrical complexity.

9-1 GENERAL OPERATING PRINCIPLES

A dishwashing cycle can be broken down into about five basic operations. Some of the operations are repeated two or more times, giving the

127

novice serviceman the idea that the dishwashing cycles might be rather involved processes. This section describes these basic dishwashing operations in general terms. Section 9-2 outlines the main electrical and mechanical components in greater detail, while Secs. 9-3 and 9-4 combine the basic principles to produce complete pictures of several operational dishwasher systems.

9-1.1 Dishwashing Operations

The simplest dishwashers use a combination of five separate operations: fill, drain, wash, rinse, and dry. The fill and drain operations are responsible for getting fresh water into the washer and then removing it after it has served its purpose. The wash and rinse steps are both cleaning operations, and the drying step uses electrically generated heat to evaporate any rinse water remaining on the dishes.

More elaborate dishwashers can have up to three additional automatic features: a detergent dispenser, a drying agent dispenser that injects a special drying agent into the final rinse water, and an air valve that mixes air with the water jets.

All automatic dishwashers use some sort of detergent dispensing mechanism, but the simpler models use a purely mechanical version and better models have an electrically operated dispenser.

A drying agent is sometimes injected into the final rinse water. This chemical breaks up beads of rinse water remaining on the dishes after the final rinse, making the drying job take place faster and more effectively.

The jets of water that are sprayed onto the dishes during normal wash and rinse operations often jostle the dishes together. Of course this is a risky situation in the case of delicate china and glassware, and so some dishwashers have an optional setting that automatically mixes air with the water jets. This air tends to break up the streams of water into a finer spray that strikes the dishes with less impact than plain water does.

Automatic dishwashers use combinations of wash, rinse, drain, and dry operations to clean and dry the dishes. The timing and sequencing of these operations can vary from one make and model to another, and the sequences can be varied by means of pushbutton selector switches on the deluxe models. A complete sequence of dishwashing operations—from the beginning of the first fill operation to the end of the drying operation—is properly known as a *dishwashing cycle*.

9-1.2 Dishwashing Cycles

Figure 9-1 illustrates a complete dishwashing cycle in a popular diagram form. This particular cycle is typical of the least expensive dishwashers and includes single wash, rinse, and drying operations. The cycle diagram is

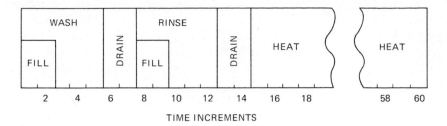

Fig. 9-1 A diagram showing the operations included in a single dishwashing cycle.

broken up into one-minute intervals running from left to right. The operations taking place during these times are blocked out above the interval marks and numerals.

This particular dishwashing cycle begins with two operations taking place at the same time: fill and wash. The fill operation occupies two minutes; during that time, a water valve is opened to let fresh water run into the dishwasher from the home's hot water system. At the end of the first two minutes of operation, the fill valve closes, but the washing operation continues.

During any washing operation, water is pumped from the bottom of the dishwasher and through a set of spinning nozzles that direct the water against the dishes. Since this is an example of a rather simple dishwasher cycle, the soap is probably injected into the water by mechanical means—by means of a little door that opens to release detergent the moment a jet of water strikes against it.

The drain operation begins at the sixth one-minute interval, and for two minutes, the dishwasher does nothing more than pump the used-up wash water out of the machine and into the home's sewage system.

The fill and rinse operations begin at the eighth time increment. In the case of a simple dishwasher, the only difference between the rinse and wash operations is the fact that detergent is not injected into the rinse water. The fill operation thus occupies two minutes, whereas the rinsing takes until the end of the twelfth minute.

The dishwasher is drained during increments 13 and 14, and the drying operation takes over at the fifteenth minute. The machine then completes its cycle with a drying operation that lasts through the sixtieth increment.

Figure 9-2 illustrates a more complicated dishwashing cycle. In this instance, there are two washing operations followed by a double rinse and the drying operations. Detergent is automatically injected into the water during the second wash operation by means of an electrically operated dispenser. The drying agent is mixed with the water in a similar fashion during the last rinse operation.

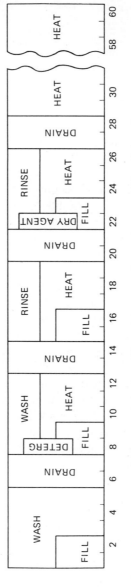

Fig. 9-2 A typical dishwashing cycle for moderate-quality dishwashing machines.

The cycle begins with fill and wash operations that cover the first two and five minutes, respectively. The water is then drained for two minutes before the second washing cycle begins at increment 8.

Three operations take place during the fifth increment: the filling operation begins, the spray nozzles initiate the washing step, and the detergent dispenser feeds soap into the water. The detergent valve closes at the end of increment 8, and the fill valve closes one minute later. The second washing operation continues through increment 12, however.

It is important to note that a heating operation begins at increment 7 during this second washing operation. The heating coil, normally used for drying operations, is thus turned on to keep the water hot throughout the entire washing step. The simpler dishwashing cycle illustrated in Fig. 9-1 does not have this water heating feature, and the water temperature in such machines tends to drop off drastically as the washing operation progresses. Of course the dishwashing operation is far more effective when the water is kept hot by the heater.

When the second washing step ends at the end of the twelve-minute mark, the dishwasher is drained for two minutes before the first rinse-with-heat step begins. The second rinse operation beginning at increment 22 is much the same as the first rinse operation. A drying agent is mixed with the water in this instance, however.

The final drain operation takes place during increments 27 and 28, and the drying step completes the hour-long dishwashing cycle that characterizes this machine.

All dishwashers are set up to operate according to a basic cycle similar to the ones illustrated in Figs. 9-1 and 9-2. Many dishwashers are programmable, however. This means that the user can set up variations of the basic cycle by means of some pushbuttons on the control console. The basic cycle is the same in any event, but the programming allows the machine to do things such as hurry some operations and skip over others.

Automatic dishwashers can be described in terms of the number of different cycles they offer. Machines that have only one operating cycle, for example, are considered single-cycle machines. This does not mean that the dishwasher has only a single wash and rinse operation programmed into its normal sequence. Rather, it means that it is built to perform one and only one particular sequence of operations.

By the same token, a two-cycle dishwasher is one that lets the user select one out of two possible cycles of operation—normal and gentle wash, for instance. Top-of-the-line washers can have as many as six or seven choices of operating sequences. These six- or seven-cycle machines give the user choices of normal cleaning, rinse-and-hold, rinse-and-dry, special gentle wash, and so on. Specific operating cycles are described more fully in Secs. 9-3 and 9-4.

9-2 GENERAL THEORY OF OPERATION

This section describes the principal electrical components of modern dishwashers and shows how they are applied to the basic dishwashing operations.

9-2.1 Electrical Components

TIMING SWITCHES.   A timing switch assembly is the "brain" of an automatic appliance, and the timers found in automatic dishwashers are not much different from those found in some other major appliances, including automatic clothes washers and dryers. Such switches are responsible for starting and stopping nearly all routine operations, leaving the user little to do but start the cycle and remove the dry dishes about one hour later.

The basic elements of a timing switch assembly are a split-phase motor, a set of cams, and some contact switches. The motor, usually geared down to a speed of about one-half revolution per hour, turns a set of cams that open and close banks of switch contacts. The switch contacts control the flow of line power to the various electrical devices in the dishwasher.

Figure 9-3 shows a pictorial diagram and schematic of a simple timer demonstration circuit. The cam rotates one-half turn every hour. In Fig. 9-3(A), the operating cycle starts with both switch contacts open and neither light goes on. After about fifteen minutes, however, the cam closes switch 1 (Fig. 9-3(B)) and turns on lamp 1. Lamp 1 remains on for about fifteen minutes, then goes out as the cam allows contact 1 to open again. But as the cam lets switch 1 open, it closes switch 2, thus turning on lamp 2. (See Fig. 9-3(C).) Lamp 2 remains on to the end of the cycle where the cam lets switch contact 2 open once again (Fig. 9-3(D)).

THE MOTOR/PUMP ASSEMBLY.   Just as the timing switch assembly can be considered the "brain" of an automatic dishwasher, the motor/pump assembly is its "heart." Only the drying operation takes place without some kind of active role by the motor and pump.

The motor/pump assembly performs two opposing kinds of operations, depending on which way the motor shaft is turning. When the motor turns in one direction, it makes the centrifugal water pump draw water from the bottom of the dishwasher and force it through the spinning spray nozzles. When the motor is reversed, however, the same pump draws water out of the dishwasher and forces it out into the home's sewerage system.

The motor in an automatic dishwasher is usually a single-speed, two-direction split phase motor having electrical ratings between 1/4 and 1/3 hp at 120 Vac. The motor normally has a basic operating speed of approximately 1700 rpm, and it uses a relay-type starting mechanism. See Chapter 5

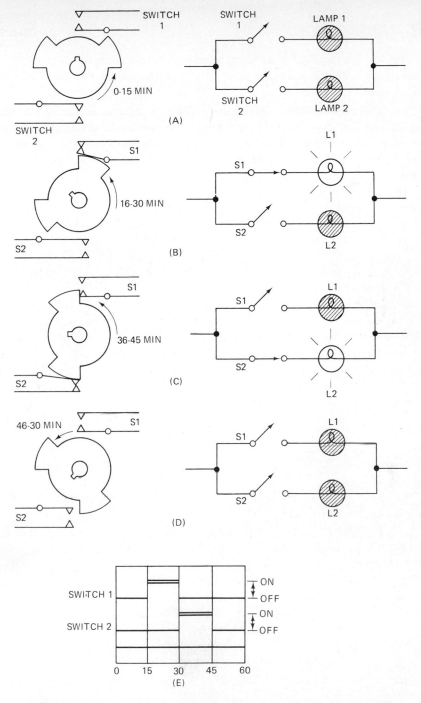

Fig. 9-3 Timing cam operations: (A) First fifteen minutes, (B) Second fifteen minutes, (C) Third fifteen minutes, (D) Final fifteen minutes, and (E) Corresponding switch contact timing diagram.

133

for further details about these starting and direction control features. As in most major appliances, the motor is equipped with a current overload circuit breaker.

SOLENOID VALVES. Automatic dishwashers contain at least one solenoid valve and as many as four. Such valves are made up of a coil of wire that generates a magentic field whenever current flows through it. This magnetic field attracts a bar of soft iron, which, in turn, opens a mechanical valve.

The solenoid valve that is common to all automatic dishwashers is the one that is connected to the home's hot water supply. Whenever electrical power is applied to this valve, called the FILL valve in most dishwasher systems, it allows hot water to flow into the dishwasher under the normal water system pressure. Removing the electrical power to the solenoid allows the valve spring to close, thus turning off the water. Such a valve is actually an electrically operated hot water spigot.

Two other solenoid valves open a small door that lets powdered dishwashing detergent and a drying agent fall into the washing space. These valves, like the FILL valve, open whenever electrical power is applied to them. For the purposes of this discussion, the detergent valve is labeled DETERG and the valve that dispenses the drying agent is called DRY AGENT. The user normally must fill these valve chambers with the appropriate chemicals before beginning a dishwashing cycle.

A fourth solenoid valve that is found in some of the better dishwasher models merely opens a small orifice that draws outside air into the spray nozzle assembly. The idea in this case is to provide a gentler spray pressure for washing delicate china and glassware. This valve will be labeled AIR in this chapter.

All these solenoid valves operate on 120 Vac and are controlled by switches in the timer switch assembly.

HEATING ELEMENT. All modern automatic dishwashers contain a tubular heating element that is rated at about 800 W at 120 Vac. See Sec. 3-2.1 for further details about such elements.

One of the main functions of the heating element is to provide heat for drying the cleaned and rinsed dishes. And in most dishwashers, the heating element is also used to maintain the wash and rinse water at a temperature in the neighborhood of 120°–140°F.

The heating element generates full heat whenever line voltage is applied to it. Better dishwasher models have a thermostat control connected to the heating circuit. Chapter 4 deals with the general principles of such heat control circuits.

THE FLOW WASHER AND OVERFILL SWITCH. Every wash and rinse operation requires about $2^1/_2$ gallons of fresh water from the home's hot water system. Too little or too much water leads to inadequate washing, rinsing, or drying.

The fill operation is normally controlled by the timer assembly. Water is allowed to flow into the machine for a certain period of time. If the water pressure is too low, the machine doesn't fill as much as it should; and if the pressure is too high, the machine can overfill.

The flow washer, a special plastic washer usually located in the fresh water connection to the dishwasher, helps maintain an even flow of water into the machine, regardless of the home's water pressure. The opening in this special kind of washer increases under low supply pressure and it decreases in response to higher-than-normal water pressure. The overall effect is a fairly constant rate of water flow into the machine during every fill operation. And this constant rate of flow means that the machine fills about the same amount every time.

The dishwasher must also have provisions for automatically ending a fill operation in the event of a trouble that otherwise makes the FILL valve stay open. If would be rather unsettling to open the dishwasher door, only to have about thirty gallons of hot water gush out onto the floor.

The overfill switch is a pressure-operated switch located beneath a plastic diaphragm in the bottom of the washing chamber. If the water level ever rises above a certain critical level, the resulting increase in water pressure on the diaphragm makes the switch activate a circuit that turns off the FILL valve.

DOOR INTERLOCK SWITCH.   The door interlock switch automatically interrupts the power supplied to all of the electrical sections whenever the door is opened. Looking at this feature from the user's point of view, it means that the door must be closed and latched before a dishwashing cycle can be started. It also means that all operations come to an immediate halt if the door is opened at any time during a dishwashing cycle.

RUN-AHEAD TIMER.   A second timer motor, called the run-ahead timer, is used in some of the more elaborate dishwasher models. Whenever the main timer activates this motor, the ongoing operation is rapidly advanced to the next operation.

9-2.2 The Basic Electrical Operations

As described in Sec. 9-1, a dishwashing cycle is made up of a relatively few basic operations. Every dishwashing cycle, no matter how simple or complex it might seem, is nothing more than a set of basic operations strung together and controlled by the timer switch assembly.

Most dishwashing operations include a particular timing step that has not been discussed thus far in this chapter. This special step occurs during the first ten or fifteen seconds of most wash, rinse, and drain operations, and its purpose is to completely turn off the main drive motor long enough to let the timer switches change the start windings.

Note that a drain operation has to be fit between consecutive rinse and wash operations. Also consider the fact that the motor/pump assembly turns in one direction for wash and rinse operations and in the opposite direction for a drain operation. This means that the system must reverse the motor's direction of spin at the end of every operation except the last drain step. (The final drain step is followed by a drying operation that does not require a motor function.)

Figure 9-4 shows the portion of an automatic dishwasher that is directly involved in this special short-interval step. Suppose for the purpose of this illustration that the system is just completing a wash operation and that contacts 1, 2, and 3 are closed. The motor is thus operating at its normal speed and in a direction that forces water through the spray nozzles. Because the motor is running at its normal operating speed, the RUN winding current is too low to hold in the start relay contact, and there is no power to the WASH START winding.

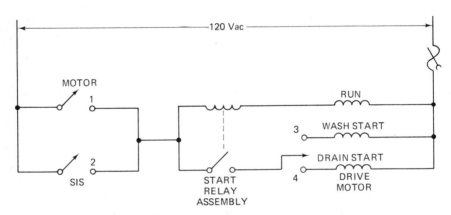

Fig. 9-4 Dishwasher elements included in the short-interval step (SIS).

The timer assembly now ends the wash operation and initiates a drain operation. It is at this point that the special short-interval step goes into effect; this whole step centers around timer contact 2 which is noted as the SIS (*short-interval switch*) on the schematics. The timing cam for the SIS is cut with finer timing intervals than the others. Whereas the other cams operate for even one-minute intervals or on multiples of one minute, the SIS cam is machined down to operate at intervals as short as five seconds.

As the drain operation begins in this example, the timer allows contacts 1 and 3 to open and contact 4 to close. The motor continues running as it was throughout the wash operation because it is still receiving full line power through the SIS contact, contact 2.

Approximately 5 seconds into the drain operation, the SIS cam opens switch contact 2. Since contact 1 has been opened previously, line power is finally removed from the motor circuit. The motor then stops running.

The SIS cam holds contact 2 open for about ten seconds—just long enough to make certain the motor has stopped turning. At the end of that ten-second interval, the SIS cam closed contact 2 once again, reapplying full line power to the motor circuit.

The current through the RUN winding during restart is considerably higher than it is during normal operations, and the start relay assembly responds by closing the relay contact to the START windings. The timer in this case closed contact 4 about fifteen seconds before, so that the DRAIN START winding is the one connected into the motor circuit, and the motor/pump assembly responds by forcing water out of the machine. The timer then closes contact 3 so that line power is applied continuously to the motor circuit, in spite of the on-off effect of the SIS that takes place throughout most of the dishwashing cycle.

A TYPICAL WASH OPERATION.   Figure 9-5 illustrates the main components commonly involved in a dishwasher's wash operation. The operation begins with wash and fill steps. The fill step occupies the first two minutes of the operation, while the wash step runs the full five minutes.

The heat step begins one minute into the operation and runs to the end. The DETERG solenoid is activated at the end of the fill step to inject detergent into the water. This particular step lasts only one minute.

Turning attention to the timing diagram and schematic in Fig. 9-5, note that this wash operation begins with an SIS step. The main motor contact, contact 4, is initially open; but since the SIS cam is activated, the motor circuit undergoes the on-off-on cycle that is necessary for reversing its direction. Since contact 5 to the START WASH winding is closed and contact 6 is open, the motor starts in a direction appropriate for a washing operation.

Contact 2 to the FILL solenoid valve closes at the very beginning of the operation and remains closed throughout the two-minute fill step. The contact for the DETERG solenoid is closed for one minute at the end of the fill operation; and the contact to the heater, contact 1, closes at the end of the first minute.

The positions of the contacts for the fill, detergent, and heat steps fall directly in line with the timing blocks at the top of the timing diagram. Only the wash step is directly influenced by the SIS step at the beginning of the operation. Note that the SIS operations are not actually shown as short-interval on-off steps on the switching diagram. The switch line for the SIS simply appears to be activated at all times, although it is cycling on and off at its short-interval rate.

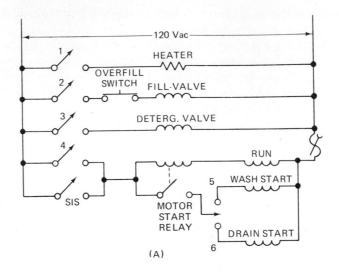

(A)

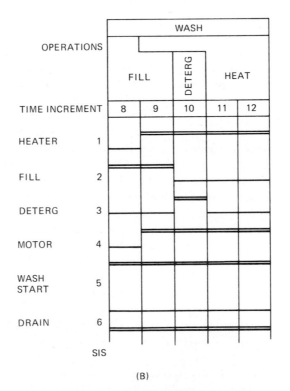

(B)

Fig. 9-5 Elements of a wash operation: (A) Simplified dishwasher schematic, (B) Wash operation timing diagram.

All wash operations have this same general format. Only one of the wash operations, however, will include the detergent step, and the first wash operation in the cycle has no need for an SIS step (because the motor is already stopped at the beginning of the first wash).

A TYPICAL RINSE OPERATION. It is no accident that the rinse operation diagrammed in Fig. 9-6 is almost identical to the wash diagram in Fig. 9-5. The fact is that a rinse operation involves the same timing sequence and many of the same electrical components as a wash operation. The only real difference is that one of the rinse operations might include a drying agent step rather than a detergent step.

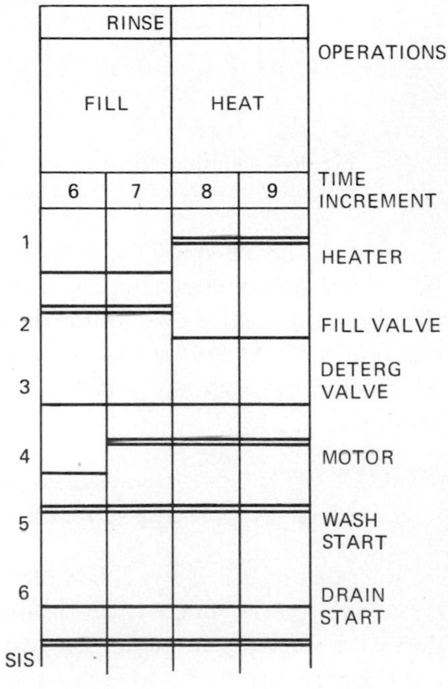

Fig. 9-6 Timing diagram for a rinse operation.

A TYPICAL DRAIN OPERATION. The drain operation diagrammed in Fig. 9-7 runs for two minutes. The most complicated part of any drain operation is the SIS step already desribed in detail at the beginning of this section. The whole idea of the drain operation is to (1) change the motor's START windings from WASH to DRAIN, (2) stop the motor by removing line power for a few seconds, and (3) restart the motor by applying line power again. The switch diagram shows how the SIS is turned off for a short time during the drain operation.

THE DRYING OPERATION. A dishwashing cycle normally concludes with a drying operation that runs through the sixtieth minute. The only

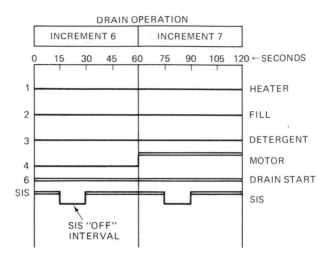

Fig. 9-7 Timing diagram for a drain operation. Time scale is expanded to show details of the SIS.

components involved are the timer switch assembly and the heating element. The timer simply closes the electrical contact to the heating element until the drying interval is over. Some dishwashers end the drying operation with a run-ahead step that resets the timer for the next dishwashing operation. This particular step is described in connection with the deluxe washer in Sec. 9-4.

9-3 A SINGLE-CYCLE, SINGLE-WASH DISHWASHER

Figure 9-8 shows a complete schematic diagram and timing chart for a single-cycle, single-wash dishwashing machine. The machine is considered a single-cycle model because it is capable of performing only one particular sequence of dishwashing operations. This is in contrast to the four-cycle machine described in Sec. 9-4. The machine described here is also considered a single-wash model because its sequence of operations includes only one washing operation.

The dishwasher featured in this section is thus the simplest possible machine on the market today. Leaving out any one of the steps would make the dishwashing operation incomplete.

9-3.1 Theory of Operation

The user initiates a complete dishwashing cycle by closing the door on the unit and manually rotating the timer mechanism to the starting point.

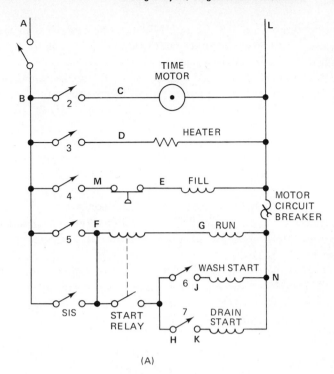

(A)

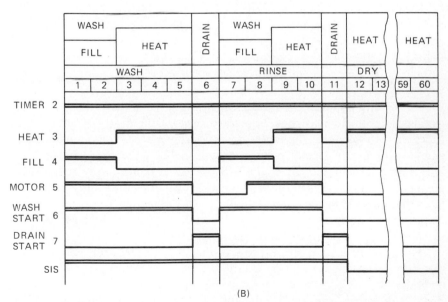

(B)

Fig. 9-8 A single-cycled dishwasher: (A) Schematic diagram, (B) Timing diagram.

More elaborate models, for example, the one described in Sec. 9-4, requires the user to depress the timer control knob once it is set to the appropriate starting point. In any case, closing the door on the dishwasher unit completes the power circuit as far as the timer assembly; setting the timer closes contact switch 2 to complete the circuit to the timer motor itself. Opening the door at any time during the operating cycle interrupts all ongoing activity, including the timing operation. When the user closes the door again, the interlock switch is closed and the cycle picks up exactly where it left off.

The timing diagram in Fig. 9-8 shows that switches 2, 4, 5, and 6 are closed at the very beginning of the cycle. Contact 2 merely keeps line power applied to the timer motor, while contact 4 activates the FILL solenoid, letting fresh hot water flow into the dishwasher. Contact 5 completes the circuit to the motor's run winding and the start relay. Contact 6 places the WASH START winding into the circuit, starting the motor in a direction that forces water into the spray nozzles.

This rather simple dishwasher model does not contain a DETERG solenoid, thus it is safe to assume that the washer uses a purely mechanical detergent dispenser. If the user has filled the dispenser with detergent prior to starting the cycle, the water forced through the spray nozzles washes the detergent into the washing space.

The timing diagram shows that fresh water continues flowing into the dishwasher throughout the first two minutes of the wash operation. At the end of that time, switch contact 4 opens and 3 closes. This particular step allows the FILL valve to close off the supply of fresh hot water and applies full line power to the heating element. During the third and fourth time increments, then, the motor is pumping water through the spray nozzles and the heater is maintaining the water temperature at a satisfactory washing level—approximately 140°F.

The drain step takes over during the fifth minute of the cycle. And as the timing diagram shows, switch 3 opens to turn off the heat, contact 5 opens to let the SIS take over the motor operations, contact 6 opens, and 7 closes to place the motor's DRAIN START winding into the circuit.

As described in Sec. 9-2.2, the SIS operation momentarily removes all power to the motor. When the switch contact closes again about ten seconds later, the DRAIN START winding actually starts the motor. The SIS continues its on-off cycling throughout most of the washing cycle; as long as the main motor switch (contact 5) is closed, the motor is not affected by the SIS action.

The drain operation is timed to finish at the end of the fifth minute, and the rinse operation takes over. Contact 4 closes to activate the FILL valve again, contact 6 closes and 5 opens to set up the motor for starting in the "wash" direction, and the SIS begins its short on-off-on sequence. When the motor is restarted about fifteen seconds into the rinse operation, it turns in the direction that makes the pump force fresh, clean water through the spray nozzles.

After two minutes of filling, contact 4 opens to shut off the fresh water supply and contact 3 closes to apply power to the heating element. This rinse operation continues until the end of the ninth time interval.

The drain operation taking place during the tenth minute of the cycle is identical to the one scheduled for the fifth increment.

The dry operation then takes over at the beginning of the eleventh increment. Only contacts 2 and 3 remain closed to keep the timer running and the heater turned on. At the end of the sixtieth increment, both these switches open, stopping the timer motor and turning off the heater.

The system is thus reset for the start of another cycle.

9-3.2 Troubleshooting Guide

This troubleshooting guide applies to single-cycle, single-wash dishwashers of the type illustrated in Fig. 9-8. The basic ideas, however, can be extended to just about all the moderate- and middle-cost automatic dishwashers on the market today.

Machine does not start—seems dead

1. No power applied to the appliance—measure the voltage applied to the unit (between points **A** and **L**). If this test shows no voltage, the trouble is confirmed. Check the service line fuses or circuit breaker. Open wiring outside the appliance is possible, but not likely, under normal circumstances.

2. Door interlock switch broken open—set the timer control knob to OFF, and connect a jumper wire across the door switch contacts (between points **A** and **B**). Close the door, and rotate the timer knob to start a wash operation. The trouble is confirmed if the machine starts. Immediately turn off the machine by rotating the timer knob to OFF. Replace the defective interlock switch.

3. Timer contact 2 broken open—connect a voltmeter across the timer motor contacts (between points **C** and **L**), close the door, and rotate the timer knob to initiate a wash operation. The trouble is confirmed if no voltage appears on the voltmeter.

   Inspect the timer assembly for a possible "easy fix." If it appears impractical to repair contact 2, replace the entire timer assembly.

Water does not drain from machine

1. Motor not being switched to DRAIN START winding—set the timer control knob to OFF, and connect a voltmeter across the DRAIN

START winding on the motor (between points **K** and **N**). With the door closed and full power applied to the dishwasher, set the timer knob to a DRAIN position and note the response on the meter. The trouble is confirmed if the voltmeter shows zero volts.

It is possible to doublecheck this conclusion by connecting the voltmeter across the timer contacts for switch 7 (between points **H** and **K**). Start the machine in a DRAIN position and note the response on the meter. The trouble is doubly confirmed if the reading remains at full line voltage throughout the drain cycle.

Inspect the timer assembly for a possible repair in the area of contact 7. If a repair job appears impractical, replace the timer assembly.

2. DRAIN START winding open—disconnect the DRAIN START wire to the motor (at point **K**), and check the continuity of the DRAIN START winding (between points **K** and **N**). If this test shows infinite resistance, the diagnosis is correct. Replace the motor's field assembly or the entire motor.

3. Pump assembly jammed with a foreign object—visually inspect the pump for foreign objects, for example, pieces of silverware, long pieces of string, or particles of food such as bones or orange peels. Suggest that the user make the same check periodically.

4. Obstructed drain line—visually inspect the drain line for kinks. Disconnect the drain line and run a plumber's snake through it to clear any foreign materials that might have passed through the filter screen.

5. Motor contacts in the timer assembly stuck closed—if power is always applied to the motor, it cannot be reversed to begin a drain operation. This trouble becomes apparent at the end of a wash operation where the motor is supposed to stop for about five or ten seconds. The trouble is confirmed if the motor does not stop when transferring from a wash or rinse operation to a drain step. Replace the timer assembly if necessary.

Water does not enter dishwasher

1. Water supply valves turned off—inspect the home's hot water supply to make certain that all valves from the water heater to the dishwasher are open.

2. Power failing to reach the FILL valve coil—connect a voltmeter across the FILL valve's contacts (between points **E** and **L**), close the door on the unit, and set the timer knob to a WASH operation. The trouble is confirmed if the motor runs but no voltage appears across the FILL valve.

    The trouble in this instance is most likely in the timer assembly. Inspect the timer for a possible "easy fix" such as loose wires or broken connections. Replace the entire timer assembly if necessary.

3. FILL valve coil open—set up the test described in the previous trouble. The FILL valve coil is probably open if line voltage appears across it, but it still does not open. Doublecheck this diagnosis by removing the FILL valve from the unit and checking the continuity of the winding with an ohmmeter. The trouble is doubly confirmed if the test shows infinite resistance. Replace the entire valve assembly.

4. FILL valve defective—set up the test conditions described in the previous two troubles. This trouble is confirmed if full line voltage appears across the valve coil and the coil shows good continuity, but water still fails to enter the system. Replace the valve assembly if a close inspection does not reveal an easily repaired trouble.

5. Overfill switch contacts stuck open—connect a voltmeter across the overfill switch contacts (between points **M** and **E**), and initiate a WASH operation. The trouble is confirmed if full line voltage appears across the overfill switch when there is no water in the system. Replace the entire overfill switch assembly.

Dishes not properly cleaned

1. Water level too low—start a wash operation, keeping track of how long the fill step runs. Open the door at the end of the fill step, and check the water level. The water level is indeed too low if it does not cover the heating element in the bottom of the dishwasher. Consult the manufacturer's specifications for other possible criteria for a low water condition.

    Low water levels can be caused by either an electrical or a purely mechanical problem. The electrical troubles can occur in either the overfill switch or the timer assembly. Mechanical problems include abnormally low water pressure in the home, a defective flow valve, or a pinched supply line.

The trouble is in either the overfill switch or timer if the fill time is more than five or ten seconds short of the time specified for a fill operation on the manufacturer's timing chart. The trouble is a mechanical one if the timing is right, but the water level is low.

Suppose that the fill interval is too short. To determine which component is causing the trouble, connect a voltmeter across the contacts on the overfill switch (between points **M** and **E**). Close the door on the dishwasher, and rotate the timer knob to a DRAIN step. After the water is drained, reset the timer to the beginning of a WASH operation. Watch the reading on the voltmeter while the machine performs the fill step. If the voltmeter shows a sudden change in voltage from zero volts to full line voltage during the fill step, the trouble is in the overfill switch. If, on the other hand, the voltmeter shows zero volts throughout the fill step and at least one minute into the wash step that follows, the short-fill trouble is in the timer assembly.

Visually inspect the suspected component for a possible "easy fix" such as a broken or loose connection. Replace the troubled part if a repair job appears to be too costly.

If the fill time is correct, but the water level is low, look for kinks in the water supply line, and make certain that all hot water valves in the home are fully open. Check the flow valve for signs of wear or damage. Replace the flow valve with one having a higher flow rating if everything else appears to be in good order.

2. Low water temperature—consult the manufacturer's specifications for the appropriate techniques for checking the water temperature in the dishwasher. If this information is not readily available, start a wash operation and open the door about halfway through the wash step. Place a thermometer into the water in the bottom of the dishwasher. Note: Do not start the unit while the thermometer is inside the unit. Read the temperature after three or four minutes. If the temperature is below 130°F, a low-temperature trouble is apparent.

Low water temperature can be caused by either a defective heating element (in units that electrically heat the water during wash and rinse operation) or timer. To check the heating element, connect a voltmeter across the heating element connections (between points **E** and **L**). Drain all water out of the dishwasher and set the control knob to a dry operation. If the voltmeter shows full line voltage, but the element remains cool, the trouble is indeed in the heating element. Visually inspect the heater and its connections for loose or broken wiring. If there are no obvious signs of trouble, disconnect the heating element and test its resistance with an ohmmeter. The element is indeed defective if this test shows infinite resistance.

If, on the other hand, the heating element becomes hot during the dry operation, set the timer knob to a wash operation, and note the voltmeter reading again. The trouble is in the timer if this test shows zero volts.

3. Detergent dispenser not working—if the dishwasher has a purely mechanical dispenser, place the recommended amount of detergent into it and start a normal washing cycle. Open the door during the first wash operation, and note whether or not the unit has deposited the detergent into the water. The mechanical dispenser can be repaired or replaced as necessary.

   If the unit happens to employ an electrical detergent dispenser (not shown on the schematic in Fig. 9-6), connect a voltmeter across the dispenser coil, drain the water from the unit, and restart the washing cycle. If the voltage does not jump to full line voltage at some time during the wash operation, the trouble is in the timer. But if the voltage jumps to full line voltage for about one minute during the wash operation, the trouble is in the detergent valve assembly.

   Replace the defective component if a visual inspection does not uncover a simple repair job.

4. Rinsing with dirty water—fill the detergent dispenser with the recommended amount of detergent, and start a normal washing cycle. When the cycle is about halfway through the rinse operation, open the door and inspect the water. The water should be clean and clear of any traces of detergent. If the water is not clear, the trouble is confirmed.

   Dirty water can be caused by a clogged drain filter, incomplete draining, or backfilling of water that was previously pumped out of the unit. Visually inspect the drain filter, and replace it if it shows signs of wear or damage. Check the draining by opening the door just as the rinse operation begins. More than a slight trace of water in the unit indicates inadequate draining. Observe the water level for several minutes. If the level rises, the trouble is caused by backfilling from the sewerage system. In the case of backfilling, consult the manufacturer's installation instructions for the proper drainage setup.

Dishes not drying properly

1. Low water temperature—see the same trouble under "Dishes not properly cleaned," p. 145.

2. Heating element open—connect a voltmeter across the heater terminals (between points **D** and **L**), close the door on the dishwasher, set the timer knob to DRY, and note the response on the voltmeter. The heating element is most likely open if the meter shows full line voltage, but the heater remains cool. Disconnect the heating element from the unit and measure its resistance with an ohmmeter. The diagnosis is doubly confirmed if the ohmmeter test shows infinite resistance.

3. Defective timer assembly—repeat the previous test conditions. If the test shows zero voltage across the heater during the DRY operation, the trouble is in the timer or in its wiring and connections. Visually inspect the timer assembly for possible loose wires or broken connections. Replace the timer if there are no obvious causes for the difficulty.

4. Incomplete water drainage—start a normal washing cycle, and open the door about halfway through the dry operation. The trouble is confirmed if water remains in the bottom of the unit. See further test procedures under "Water does not drain from machine," p. 143.

Water enters machine, but motor does not run

1. Motor circuit breaker open—depress the motor circuit breaker, and attempt to restart the wash operation. If the circuit breaker opens again, the trouble is in the motor assembly. See troubles 2 and 3 below.

    It is unlikely that the circuit breaker itself is the cause of this trouble. To check the operation of the breaker, connect a voltmeter across its terminals (between points **N** and **L**), apply power to the dishwasher, and observe the voltage across the breaker terminals. The breaker is defective if it shows full line voltage when the reset button is depressed.

    To doublecheck the operation of the breaker, remove it from the motor assembly and check the contacts with an ohmmeter. The breaker is indeed defective if it shows infinite resistance when the button is depressed. Replace the circuit breaker assembly.

2. RUN winding shorted—check for a shorted winding as described in Chapter 5.

3. WASH START or DRAIN START winding shorted—check for shorted windings as described in Chapter 5.

4. Open motor winding—disconnect all power from the dishwasher and set the timer control knob to OFF. Check the continuity of the RUN winding by connecting an ohmmeter between points **G** and **H**. An infinite reading indicates an open winding. Check the WASH START and DRAIN START windings in a similar fashion between points **J** and **H**, and **K** and **H**, respectively.

   Replace the entire motor assembly if any of these tests indicate an open winding.

5. Motor mechanically bound or frozen—disconnect the motor shaft from the gear assembly, and attempt to turn the motor shaft by hand. If the shaft does not turn freely, the mechanical binding is in the motor assembly, and it must be replaced.

   If, on the other hand, the motor seems to be in good working order, check the operation of the gear assembly by turning the spray nozzles by hand and noting the action of the gears. The trouble is in the gear/nozzle assembly if they cannot be turned easily. Repair or replace this unit as necessary.

6. Motor start relay assembly defective—turn off the dishwasher, connect a jumper wire across the start relay contacts (between points **H** and **F**) and a voltmeter across the RUN winding (between points **G** and **H**). Apply power to the dishwasher, and set the timer control to the middle of the wash or rinse operation.

   The trouble is confirmed if the motor runs or if the motor does not run, but full line voltage appears across the RUN winding.

   Replace the start relay assembly.

9-4 A MULTICYCLE DISHWASHER

Multicycle dishwashers differ from the single-cycle model featured in Sec. 9-3 in that the multicycle units allow the user to select a program of operations suited to a particular dishwashing task. Food-encrusted pots and pans, for instance, require a more vigorous washing cycle than stemware does. The program is usually selected by depressing one of several buttons labeled with descriptive names such as NORMAL WASH, RINSE AND DRY, SHORT CYCLE, and so on. (See Fig. 9-9 for a typical multicycle dishwasher.)

Fig. 9-9   A typical multicycle dishwasher with pushbutton selectors for NORMAL or SHORT WASH and RINSE AND HOLD. (Courtesy of General Electric Major Appliance Group)

The six-cycle dishwasher described in this section is typical of most multicycle machines on the market today. Many models have fewer programming options, and many use different descriptive names for the various cycles. The principles of operation are essentially the same, however; and a good understanding of this particular machine makes it possible to work on a wide variety of slightly different models.

9-4.1   Theory of Operation

Figure 9-10 shows a complete electrical schematic for a six-cycle dishwasher. The switch contacts numbered from 1 through 14 are contacts controlled by cams in the timer assembly. The switches labeled P1 through P10 are the programming switches.

Whenever the user depresses one of the programming buttons on the control console, several programming switch contacts are closed. Depressing a program button labeled NORMAL WASH, for example, closes programming contacts P3, P4, P7, P9, and P10. Depressing a different program button closes an entirely different combination of program contacts.

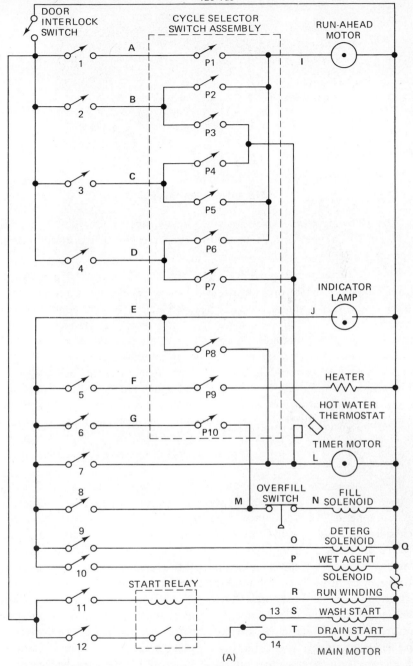

Fig. 9-10 A six-cycle dishwasher: (A) Complete schematic diagram, (B) Program switch contact diagram.

PROGRAM CONTACTS

CYCLE NAME	P1	P2	P3	P4	P5	P6	P7	P8	P9	P10
NORMAL WASH	0	0	X	X	0	0	X	0	X	X
SHORT WASH	0	0	X	0	X	0	X	0	X	X
RINSE AND DRY	0	0	X	X	0	X	0	0	X	X
RINSE AND HOLD	0	X	0	X	0	X	0	0	0	X
GENTLE WASH	0	0	X	X	0	0	X	X	X	X
CHINA CRYSTAL	0	0	X	0	X	0	X	X	0	0
CANCEL	0	X	0	0	X	X	0	0	0	0

X = Closed
0 = Open

(B)

Fig. 9-10 (Continued)

The following paragraphs describe the various cycles that the machine in Fig. 9-10 can perform. The timing diagram for this particular model appears in Fig. 9-11.

THE NORMAL WASH CYCLE. The NORMAL WASH cycle is programmed into the machine when programming contacts P3, P4, P7, P9, and P10 are closed. Figure 9-12 shows the switches and electrical components directly involved in the NORMAL WASH cycle. All other switch contacts and components have been eliminated from the diagram for the sake of greater clarity.

The NORMAL WASH cycle uses all the operations diagrammed along the top of the timing chart in Fig. 9-11. This cycle begins with four five-minute rinse and wash operations. Detergent is finally added to the water in the fourth operation; after completing yet another rinse operation, the machine rinses the dishes with hot water which has a wetting agent added to it. All the rinse and washing operations occupy the first thirty-two minutes of the complete cycle. The cycle ends with a drying cycle that lasts through the sixtieth minute.

Referring to the simplified NORMAL WASH schematic in Fig. 9-12 and the main timing diagram, the cycle begins with contact 3 applying line power to the components and their controls—assuming, of course, that the door interlock switch is also closed. Contact 7 to the timer motor closes immediately and remains closed throughout the entire cycle, except for the twenty-ninth time increment. The reason for turning off the timer motor during the twenty-ninth increment will be explained later in this discussion.

Switch contacts 8, 11, and 13 also close as soon as the cycle is initiated. Contact 8 begins the fill step and 12 applies continuous power to the motor circuit. Contact 13 closes to start the motor turning in the wash direction. The SIS, contact 11, begins its short-cycling operation, but its influence on the motor circuit is cancelled out by contact 12 for the time being.

Contact 8 to the FILL solenoid opens at the end of the first minute, but contact 6 closes at the same instant to maintain power to the FILL valve for a

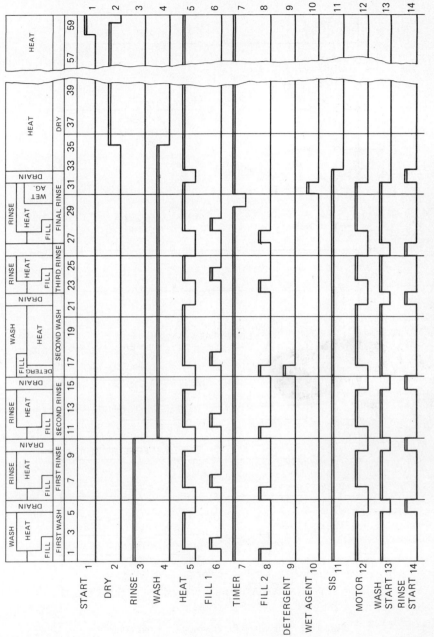

Fig. 9-11 A complete timing diagram for a six-cycle dishwasher.

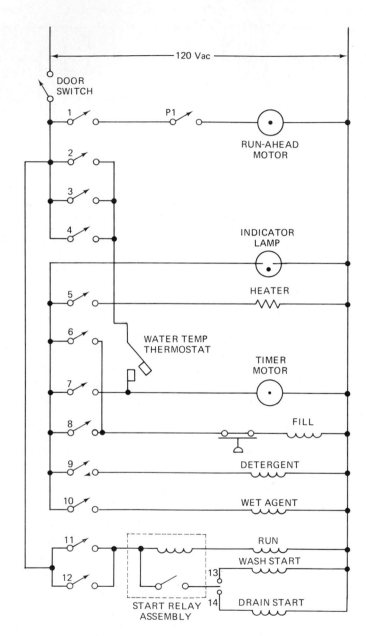

Fig. 9-12 Circuitry for a NORMAL WASH cycle.

total of two minutes. The reason for this switch-over of FILL valve contacts will become apparent during the discussion of several other dishwashing cycles.

Contact 5 to the heating element closes at the beginning of the second minute and remains closed throughout the washing step.

The first drain step begins at the fifth time increment. At that time, contacts 5, 12, and 13 open and contact 14 closes. Opening contact 5 removes power from the heating element, and opening 12 removes continuous power to the motor circuit, letting the SIS take over those operations. When contact 14 closes, it connects the DRAIN START winding to the motor.

About ten seconds into the drain step, the SIS cycles open for about five seconds, giving the motor a chance to stop turning in the wash direction. When the SIS closes again, the motor restarts in the drain direction, and it continues running in that direction until the end of the drain step.

The two rinse operations that follow the first wash operation repeat these same basic steps with one exception: Contact 3 opens at the end of the first rinse step. This step would tend to remove line power from most of the switch contacts and electrical components in the dishwasher; however, the fact that contact 4—which is connected in parallel with 3—closes at the same instant keeps full line power applied to the system. Again, the reason for this seemingly pointless switch-over of power contacts will become apparent during the study of other operating cycles.

The second wash operation differs from the first only by the activation of the DETERG solenoid through the sixteenth time increment. The third rinse operation works the same way as the first two, except that it is one minute shorter.

The final rinse operation occupies six time increments on the timing diagram. As shown on the diagram in Fig. 9-11, contact 10 closes during the thirty-first increment to apply power to the WET AGENT solenoid, and thereby inject a wetting agent into the final rinse water.

The really unique part of the final rinse operation takes place during the thirtieth time increment, however. At the beginning of the thirtieth increment, contact 7 to the timer motor opens, removing all power to that motor. The timer motor stops turning, freezing all washing operations in the state they hold at the beginning of the thirtieth increment—the motor is running in the wash direction, and the heater is turned on.

The timer motor begins running and resumes the dishwashing cycle only when the thermostat contacts close to reapply power to the timer. This thermostat is located in the bottom of the dishwasher, and it responds to the water temperature. The overall effect is that the cycle sticks in the final rinse operation until the heater has a chance to boost the water temperature to about 160°F. When the water reaches this higher-than-normal temperature, the timer begins running again. The thermostat provides the only path for power to the timer motor until the end of the thirtieth increment when contact 7 closes again. The thermostat can open at any time after that without making the cycle come to a halt.

The whole point of this delay during the last rinse cycle is to make certain the rinse water is hot enough to make the drying job more efficient and effective. Few homes can provide tap water at 160°F, and the heater is not large enough to make the water that hot within three or four minutes. Of course the length of the delay during increment 30 depends on how far the heater has to raise the water temperature.

The drying operation begins at the thirty-third time increment. Contact 5 to the heating element is closed, and so is contact 7 to the timer. Contact 4 provides a path for line power to the control switches and components through the first two minutes of the drying operation. That contact opens at increment 35, but contact 2 closes at the same instant to maintain a source of power. The state of the switches then remains unchanged until the fifty-ninth increment when contact 1 finally closes.

Closing contact 1 applies full line power to the run-ahead motor, but unless the programming contact P1 is closed during that time, the run-ahead motor cannot start.

Contact 2 drops open at the beginning of the sixtieth increment, removing all line power from the control contacts, heater, and timer. For all practical purposes, the cycle is finished. The system remains turned off in the sixtieth increment until the user depresses one of the programming buttons to start another dishwashing cycle. At that time, P1 is closed and power is applied to the run-ahead motor. This motor rapidly turns the timer assembly to the beginning of the first minute where contact 3 closes to apply continuous power to the main control section and components.

THE SHORT WASH CYCLE.   The SHORT WASH cycle is the same as a NORMAL WASH except that the shorter version skips over the first wash and rinse operations. SHORT WASH begins at the eleventh time increment and cycles normally until the end. The reason for including a SHORT WASH cycle is to save time, electricity, and hot water when cleaning dishes that are not soiled with stubborn stains or burned-on food.

The schematic in Fig. 9-13 shows the switches and components that play a special role in the SHORT WASH cycle. The solenoids and motor/pump circuits are not shown because they respond in the same way as they do during NORMAL WASH.

The programming switches closed for this cycle are P2, P4, P7, P8, and P9. Referring to the timing diagram in Fig. 9-11, every cycle begins with contact 3 closed (at the beginning of increment 1). Closing contact 3 in the SHORT WASH mode applies line power directly to the run-ahead motor which, in turn, rapidly advances the timer assembly through increment 10.

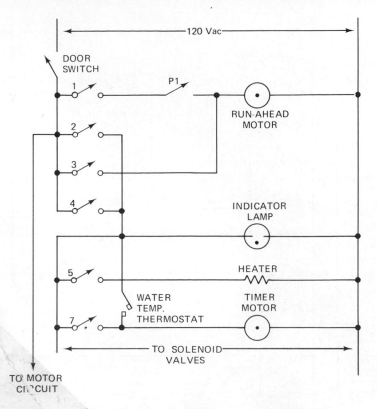

Fig. 9-13 Circuitry for a SHORT WASH cycle.

Contact 3 opens at the end of increment 10 to remove power for the run-ahead motor. At that same instant, however, contact 4 closes, applying line voltage to the timer motor and the other switches and components in the circuit. The operations from increment 11 through the end of the cycle follow the NORMAL WASH pattern.

THE RINSE AND DRY CYCLE. This dishwashing cycle performs the first wash and rinse operations, then skips to the dry operation. The wash-with-soap operation is thus completely eliminated. Such a cycle can be used to rinse dishes that might only be water spotted.

The schematic in Fig. 9-14 shows the switches and components that play a special role in the RINSE AND DRY cycle. The solenoids and motor circuit have been eliminated because they perform the same way as described for NORMAL WASH. Depressing the RINSE AND DRY programming button automatically closes programming contacts P3, P4, P6, P9, and P10; and these switches set up the programming circuitry in Fig. 9-14.

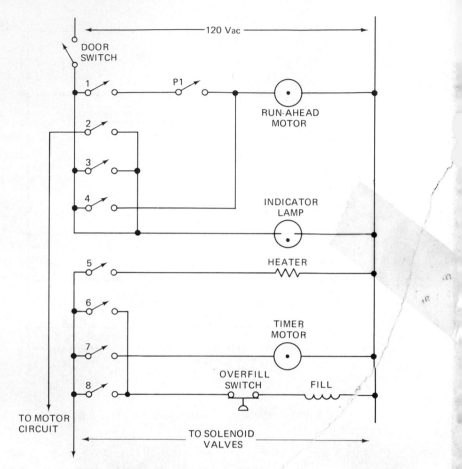

Fig. 9-14   Circuitry for a RINSE AND DRY cycle.

Referring to the timing diagram in Fig. 9-11, contact 3 closes at the beginning of the cycle, applying full line power to the timing switches connected to active components. Contact 7 is also closed at this time, so the timer motor begins running at its normal rate.

The cycle proceeds through the first wash and rinse operations in the same manner as in the NORMAL WASH mode. At the end of increment 10, however, contact 3 opens and 4 closes. This particular switch-over of power removes line voltage from the timer circuit to the run-ahead motor.

The run-ahead motor rapidly advances the timer assembly through increment 34 where contact 3 opens and 2 closes. Opening contact 3 effectively turns off the run-ahead motor, and closing contact 2 reapplies power to the regular timer and its switches. The system then completes the drying operation in the normal fashion.

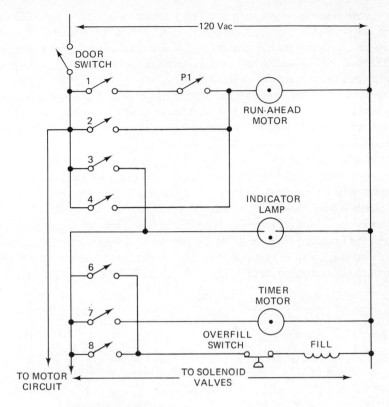

Fig. 9-15 Circuitry for a RINSE AND HOLD cycle.

THE RINSE AND HOLD CYCLE.   This particular cycle carries out the first wash and rinse operations, then skips to the end of the timing sequence. The dishes are thus rinsed in clear, hot water two times and then left wet.

Depressing the RINSE AND HOLD program control button closes programming contacts P2, P4, P6, and P10. The simplified diagram appears in Fig. 9-15.

As shown in the timing diagram in Fig. 9-11, contact 3 closes at the beginning of increment 1 to apply full line power to the timer. The washing cycle proceeds in the normal way to the end of increment 10 where contact 3 opens and 4 closes. Closing 4 applies power to the run-ahead motor, and opening 3 removes power to the normal timing circuit. As a result, the sequence of operations rapidly advances until contact 4 opens at the end of increment 34 in the drying operation. Contact 2 closes as 4 opens, however, and line power is maintained to the run-ahead timer.

The run-ahead timer continues advancing the program until contact 2 opens at the end of increment 59. The system turns itself off at that time and stands ready for the next washing cycle.

THE GENTLE WASH CYCLE.   The GENTLE WASH cycle uses the same timing sequence as NORMAL WASH. The only real differences in overall operations are that only half the normal amount of water is introduced into the machine during all fill operations and that the thermostat operation in the last rinse (increment 30) is eliminated.

Whenever the user depresses the GENTLE WASH program button, programming contacts P3, P4, P6, and P10 are closed. The timer contacts and components uniquely involved in the GENTLE WASH cycle are shown in the simplified schematic in Fig. 9-16.

Referring again to the timing diagram in Fig. 9-11, the cycle begins at increment 1 with the closure of contacts 3, 7, and 8. Other contacts are closed at the same time, but because they affect normal motor operations, they are not described here. See "The NORMAL WASH cycle" for motor details.

The cycle actually proceeds according to the NORMAL WASH cycle plan through the first time increment. At that moment, contact 8 to the FILL valve opens, shutting off the source of hot water to the machine. Contact 6 closes at the end of increment 1 in all of the cycles described at this point, extending

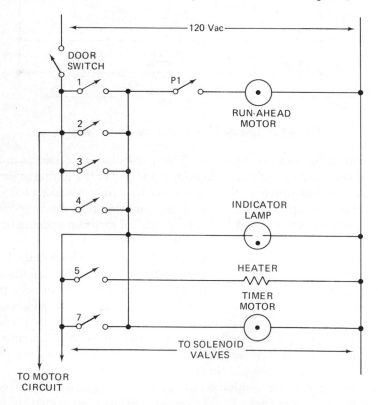

Fig. 9-16   Circuitry for a GENTLE WASH cycle.

the FILL time to two minutes. The effect of turning off the water after the first minute of the fill step is that the machine has only half its normal load of water. The low water condition lowers the spray pressure on the dishes to produce the desired gentle wash effect.

The cycle continues according to the basic timing diagram, leaving out the second minute of FILL solenoid power during each fill step. At increment 30 where the system normally pauses until the heater brings the water temperature up to about 160°F, contact 4 closes to short out the thermostat contacts. The system cannot pause at increment 30 under this condition, and the final rinse operation takes place at whatever water temperature is available.

THE CHINA CRYSTAL CYCLE.   The CHINA CRYSTAL cycle is the same as GENTLE WASH, except that the CHINA CRYSTAL cycle bypasses the first wash and rinse operations. CHINA CRYSTAL is something like a short GENTLE WASH.

Depressing the CHINA CRYSTAL program button on the control console closes programming contacts P3, P5, P7, and P8. The simplified diagram that results appears in Fig. 9-17.

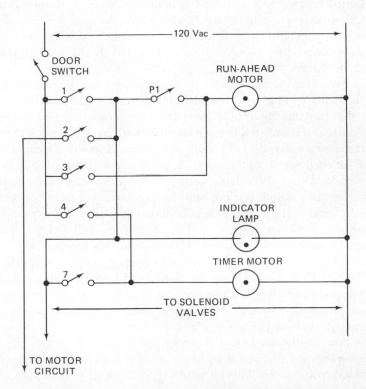

Fig. 9-17 Circuitry for a CHINA CRYSTAL cycle.

Contact 3 is closed at the beginning of increment 1, forcing the run-ahead motor to drive the timer to the beginning of the second rinse operation (at increment 11). The cycle then progresses just like a GENTLE WASH cycle.

THE CANCEL CYCLE. The CANCEL cycle is a special cycle that is used to abort any other washing cycle while it is in progress. What the CANCEL cycle does is automatically run any ongoing cycle to the end of the program. This is a handy feature in the event the user wants to change the cycle that has just been selected.

Depressing the CANCEL program button during a cycle closes programming contacts P2, P5, and P6. This switch configuration effectively turns off the timer motor and switches power to the run-ahead motor. Power then remains applied to the run-ahead motor until it quickly runs the cycle to the sixtieth time increment where everything is shut down and reset for the start of the next cycle.

9-4.2 Troubleshooting Guide

The six-cycle dishwasher (Fig. 9-10) featured in this section is so complicated that a component-by-component analysis of troubles is impractical. Of course it is possible to troubleshoot even the most complex electrical devices in a systematic manner, and the discussions in this section show how to go about organizing a troubleshooting task that would seem impossible to an untrained serviceman.

In a device having the complexity of the dishwasher diagrammed in Fig. 9-10, the first step in a good troubleshooting procedure is to determine the section that contains the trouble. After that, the general cause of the problem can be narrowed down to a few possibilities; and finally, a quick check with a voltmeter or similar kind of testing device can pinpoint the exact trouble.

For the purposes of troubleshooting, the six-cycle dishwasher in Fig. 9-10 can be divided into three basic sections: the active-electrical-components section, the timer switch section, and the programming switch section. The active-electrical-components section includes the drive motor/pump, timer and run-ahead motors, solenoid valves, heater, overfill switch, hot water thermostat, motor starting relay, and the door interlock switch.

The timer switch section includes all switch contacts controlled by the timer motor. These switches are numbered 1–14 on the schematic in Fig. 9-10. The programming switch section, the section responsible for setting up the cycle programs, contains ten manually operated switch contacts that are numbered P1–P10 on the schematic.

The first step in the troubleshooting procedure, identifying the section containing the trouble, begins by observing the behavior of the machine in the NORMAL WASH cycle. This particular cycle uses all of the timer contacts at one time or another; therefore, if that cycle proceeds according to specifications, the trouble cannot be in the timer switch assembly—it has to be in either the programming switch assembly or in one of the active electrical components.

Suppose for the time being that the NORMAL WASH cycle proceeds normally. Any legitimate customer complaint must involve one of the other cycles, but it is a good idea to confirm the complaint by running the faulty cycle again. If the NORMAL WASH cycle runs according to plan, but any other cycle does not, the trouble has to be in the programming switch section.

Visually inspect the programming switch assembly for obvious troubles such as loose wires and broken contacts. If the area around the switch assembly shows signs of accumulated kitchen grime, spray some aerosol contact cleaner into the switch assembly, and operate all the switch contacts manually to clean off the grease and dirt.

The troubleshooting procedure is somewhat more involved if the NORMAL WASH cycle does not run according to plan. In such a case, the trouble is most likely in either the timer switch assembly or in one of the active components. To make matters a bit worse, there is still an outside chance that the trouble is in the program switch assembly, but in a place that has no effect upon the other cycles.

To eliminate the possibility of a trouble in the programming switch assembly, turn the timer knob to OFF and open the door on the dishwasher. This step completely removes all power to the appliance. Depress the NORMAL WASH button on the control console and check the continuity of the programming switch contacts as follows:

P1   (between points **A** and **H**)—infinite resistance.
P2   (between points **B** and **H**)—infinite resistance.
P3   (between points **B** and **J**)—zero resistance.
P4   (between points **C** and **J**)—zero resistance.
P5   (between points **C** and **H**)—infinite resistance.
P6   (between points **D** and **H**)—infinite resistance.
P7   (between points **D** and **J**)—zero resistance.
P8   (between points **E** and **L**)—infinite resistance.
P9   (between points **F** and **L**)—zero resistance.
P10 (between points **G** and **H**)—zero resistance.

Any departure from this set of test results indicates a trouble in the programming switch assembly. Of course this list applies only to dishwashers having the programming assembly shown in Fig. 9-10. The basic idea is to determine whether or not the contacts are open or closed as prescribed by the NORMAL WASH cycle program. Closed switches show zero resistance and open switches show infinite resistance; and by knowing whether a given switch is supposed to be open or closed (either by consulting the manufacturer's specifications or by visually inspecting the mechanical workings of the switch assembly), the serviceman can generate his own test sequence.

Repair or replace the programming switch assembly if it does not check out according to the resistance tests on the contacts.

After eliminating the possibility of a trouble in the programming switch assembly, the next troubleshooting step is to eliminate the chance of troubles in the timer switch assembly. The following list of timer troubles are unique to the timer—only a timer trouble can cause them. Recall that these tests are to apply only to the NORMAL WASH cycle.

1. Timer rapidly advances through the entire NORMAL WASH cycle, then stops at the end—contact 1 shorted or stuck closed.

2. The NORMAL WASH cycle stops completely in the dry operation (at the end of increment 34)—contact 2 stuck open or broken.

3. Unit does not stop cycling—contact 2, 3, or 4 shorted or stuck closed.

4. NORMAL WASH cycle stops at the end of the first rinse operation (at the end of increment 10), but the drive motor/pump may continue running—contact 4 stuck or broken open.

5. Heat turned on at all times during NORMAL WASH cycle—contact 5 shorted or stuck closed.

6. FILL valve open only one minute, instead of two, in NORMAL WASH— contact 6 or 8 stuck or broken open.

7. Detergent injected into first wash—contact 9 shorted or stuck closed.

8. Wetting agent injected into first wash—contact 10 shorted or stuck closed.

9. Pump does not run during any drain operation (water does not drain out at all)—contact 11 or 14 stuck or broken open.

10. Drive motor runs continuously in the "wash" direction until the dry operation (motor does not change direction for drain, and water does not drain out)—contact 11 or 12 shorted or stuck closed.

11. Drive motor cycles on and off at one-minute intervals throughout all the rinse and wash operations—contact 12 stuck or broken open.

A dishwasher displaying any one of these eleven symptoms is suffering from a trouble in the timer assembly. Visually inspect the timer for obvious troubles such as loose wires and broken contacts. Clean the assembly with an aerosol contact cleaner and tighten any loose connections. Replace the entire timer assembly in instances where a repair job is not feasible.

There are also some symptoms that indicate a defective active component—they have no direct relationship to troubles in either the timer or programming switch assembly. Assuming that the trouble is electrical, the following list of symptoms points directly to the components indicated.

Unit does not cycle out of final rinse

The hot water thermostat is broken or stuck open. To doubly confirm the trouble, connect a jumper wire across the thermostat contacts (between points **J** and **L**), and initiate the final rinse operation. If the machine moves through the entire operation without pausing, the thermostat is indeed the cause of the trouble.

No water

Always check first for obvious mechanical troubles, for example, clogged feed lines, valves that are turned off, and dirty water filters.

1. FILL valve solenoid defective—connect a voltmeter across the FILL valve coil (between points **N** and **Q**), start a NORMAL WASH cycle, and note the response on the meter during the fill operations. If the meter shows full line voltage, but water does not run into the machine during scheduled fill operations, the valve is defective.

2. Overfill switch stuck or broken open—connect a voltmeter across the overfill switch contacts (between points **M** and **N**), and start a NORMAL WASH cycle. The trouble is confirmed if the meter shows line voltage at any time when water is not in the machine.

Timer runs, but drive motor/pump does not

1. RUN winding in the motor is open—disconnect the RUN winding from the motor circuit and check its continuity with an ohmmeter. A reading of infinity confirms the diagnosis.

2. Motor start solenoid coil open—disconnect the start relay assembly and check the resistance between the terminals. A reading of infinity across the coil confirms the trouble.

Motor runs, but draws excessive current

1. Start relay contact shorted—disconnect the start relay and check the continuity of the contacts with an ohmmeter. Good continuity under these conditions confirms the diagnosis.

2. Partially shorted motor winding—see Chapter 5.

Motor does not run, but draws heavy current

1. Start relay contact stuck or broken open—replace any wiring disconnected during previous troubleshooting steps, make certain that the dishwasher is completely turned off, and connect a jumper wire across the contacts in the start relay. Apply power to the machine and start a NORMAL WASH cycle. The diagnosis is correct if the motor/pump assembly runs.

2. Shorted motor winding—see Chapter 5.

Finally, there is a small set of symptoms that can indicate a trouble in either the timer assembly or an active component.

No heat at any time

1. Heating element open—connect a voltmeter across the heating element (between points K and Q), close the door on the dishwasher, and set the timer knob to DRY. If full line voltage appears on the voltmeter, but the heater does not get warm, chances are quite good that the heating element is open. Turn off all power to the appliance, remove the heating element from the circuit, and check its continuity with an ohmmeter. The diagnosis is doubly confirmed if the test shows infinite resistance.

2. Contact 5 in the timer assembly stuck or broken open—set up the test conditions described in the previous paragraph. The timer contact is at fault if *no* voltage appears across the heating element.

Cycle does not delay for water heating during final rinse

1. Hot water thermostat shorted or stuck closed—remove all power to the appliance and disconnect the wiring to one terminal of the thermostat assembly (at point L). Set the timer control knob to FINAL RINSE in the NORMAL WASH cycle, and apply power to the dishwasher. The trouble is confirmed if the unit times up to increment 30, then pauses indefinitely.

2. Contact 7 in the timer is shorted or stuck closed—set up the test conditions described in the previous paragraph. The timer is at fault if the unit still times through the FINAL RINSE without pausing for a time in increment 30.

Drive motor/pump runs, but unit does not cycle

1. Timer motor winding open—connect a voltmeter across the timer motor (between points **L** and **Q**), and start a NORMAL WASH cycle. The trouble is confirmed if the meter shows full line voltage, but the timer motor still does not run.

2. Contact 7 in the timer switch assembly broken or stuck open— set up the test conditions just described. The timer switch is at fault if the voltmeter shows zero volts instead of full line voltage.

No detergent

1. DETERG solenoid coil open—connect a voltmeter across the DETERG solenoid coil (between points **O** and **Q**). Set the timer control knob to the SECOND WASH operation (or any operation using the DETERG coil), and apply power to the appliance. The trouble is confirmed if the meter shows full line voltage during a scheduled detergent-dispensing interval, but the valve does not respond.

2. Contact 9 in the timer switch assembly broken or stuck open— set up the test conditions described in the previous paragraph. The timer switch is at fault if the voltmeter shows zero volts throughout the detergent-dispensing operation.

No wetting agent

1. WET AGENT solenoid coil open—perform the tests for an open DETERG coil specified under the "no detergent" symptom. Be sure to connect the voltmeter across the WET AGENT coil (between points **P** and **Q**), however.

2. Contact 10 in the timer switch assembly broken or stuck open— confirm this trouble in a fashion similar to the DETERG problem.

Motor/pump does not run during any wash or rinse step, but runs during a drain step

1. Motor's WASH START winding open—connect a voltmeter across the WASH START winding (between points **R** and **Q**), and initiate a NORMAL WASH cycle. There is a good chance that the WASH START winding is open if full line voltage appears on the meter, but the motor does not run. Doublecheck the diagnosis by dis-

connecting the WASH START winding from the circuit and checking its resistance with an ohmmeter. A reading of infinity confirms the trouble.

2. Contact 13 in the timer switch assembly stuck or broken open— set up the power-on test described in the previous paragraph. If the voltmeter shows zero voltage at all times, this trouble is confirmed.

Motor/pump does not run during any drain step, but runs normally during rinse and wash operations

1. Motor's DRAIN START winding open—connect a voltmeter across the DRAIN START winding (between points **T** and **Q**), and start a NORMAL WASH cycle. There is a good chance that the winding is open if full line voltage appears on the meter, but the motor does not run during a drain step. Doublecheck the diagnosis with a continuity test on the DRAIN START winding.

2. Contacts 11 or 14 in the timer switch assembly stuck or broken open—set up the test condition just described. This trouble is confirmed if the meter shows no voltage during any scheduled drain step.

9-5 QUESTIONS

1. From the user's point of view, what is the difference between a single-cycle dishwasher and a multicycle version?

2. How is fresh water forced into a dishwasher?

3. How is wash water circulated through a dishwasher?

4. What mechanism is responsible for pumping the used-up wash water out of a dishwasher?

5. What is the purpose of a run-ahead motor in an automatic dishwasher?

6. Name two reasons why a heating element is included in an automatic dishwasher.

7. What is the purpose of including a wetting agent in the final rinse water?

10

Automatic
Clothes Washers

Automatic clothes washers run a close third in popularity behind ranges and refrigerators. History books depict the earliest clothes washers as women kneeling beside a stream beating wet clothing between two rocks. This primitive form of clothes washing was eventually replaced by the washboard and tub. Washboards are still available in some hardware stores, but there is good reason to believe that more of them are used as musical instruments than as washing tools.

Wringer-type washing machines with a motor-driven agitator were the mainstay of the home laundry for several generations. Some inventive engineers in the 1940s attempted to automate the wringer process, but they had no real success. The agitation feature is still used in modern automatic washers, but the wringer assembly has been replaced by a high-speed spin cycle that lets centrifugal force drive most of the water out of the laundry.

The automatic washers described in this chapter are typical of the machines on the market today. There is no attempt to follow one particular make or model in these discussions; instead, the circuits and timing diagrams are composites of the more common features found in several different models.

The troubleshooting procedures in this chapter are likewise very general, and do not necessarily apply word for word to any particular automatic clothes washer on the market. The intent in this case is to present and demonstrate a logical approach to troubleshooting that can apply in all cases.

10-1 GENERAL OPERATING PRINCIPLES

Many automatic clothes washing cycles can be broken down into four basic operations: fill, agitate, drain, and spin. Almost all these operations are repeated two or three times throughout a complete washing cycle; and for the most part, they are controlled by a timing assembly.

The fill operation is responsible for getting water into the laundry tub. The water normally enters the machine from the home's fresh water system and under the pressure that system provides. Some models use timed fill operations that start and end under the control of the machine's timer. Other models start fill operations from the timer, but depend on a water level sensing switch to end the fill operation when the water level is right.

The agitate operation is the one that is responsible for washing and rinsing the laundry once the tub is filled with water. Most automatic washers intended for use in the home are of the agitator, top-loading variety. Commercial front-loading washers, in contrast, often use a continuous tumbling action in place of the agitation.

The purpose of the drain operation is to pump used wash and rinse water out of the machine and into the home's sewage system.

The spin operation is responsible for removing excess water from the laundry fabrics. During this operation, the main drive motor spins the laundry tub at a relatively high rate of speed, forcing water out of the tub and fabrics by means of centrifugal force. The spin operation actually replaces the wringer action that was a standard part of laundry machines of an earlier generation. The drain pump removes this spun-out water from the machine.

Some automatic washers have an additional soak or pause operation in which the laundry is allowed to stand for a moment or two in the wash or rinse water without any sort of agitation or spin action.

Figure 10-1 shows a timing diagram and the user's timer dial for a simple automatic washer. The operations on the timing diagram are blocked out with the time increments shown directly below. The increments in many instances are equal to one minute, but some models have time increments as long as two minutes and others as short as forty-five seconds.

The user initiates the cycle by rotating the timer dial just beyond the OFF position and turning on the machine by either pulling or depressing a knob in the center of the timer dial.

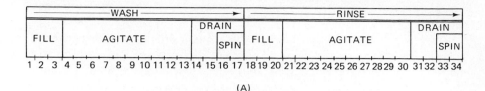

Fig. 10-1 A simple washing cycle. (A) Timing diagram, (B) Timer control knob.

The washing phase in this machine begins with a timed fill operation that runs through the first three time increments. The agitation then begins and continues through the thirteenth increment when the first drain operation takes over.

The system runs on the drain operation alone during increments 14 and 15, then it is joined by a two-increment spin operation. The first two increments of the drain operation are necessary in this machine for getting the bulk of the wash water out of the tub before the spin operation begins. The drain pump continues running through the spin operation, however, to remove the water spun out of the laundry.

The rinse phase of the cycle begins with another fill operation at increment 18. The entire washing sequence just described is simply repeated in this machine through increment 34 where the timer ends the cycle. The only real difference between the wash and rinse phases of the cycle is that the user adds a detergent to the water during the washing phase and adds a fabric softener, if desired, during the rinse phase.

Figure 10-2 shows a timing diagram and a timer dial for an automatic washer that features four different washing and rinsing cycles: EXTRA WASH, NORMAL WASH, RINSE ONLY, and DELICATE WASH. The EXTRA, NORMAL, and RINSE ONLY cycles are actually defined as different starting points on a forty-two-increment timing cycle. The EXTRA WASH starts at increment 1, the NOR-

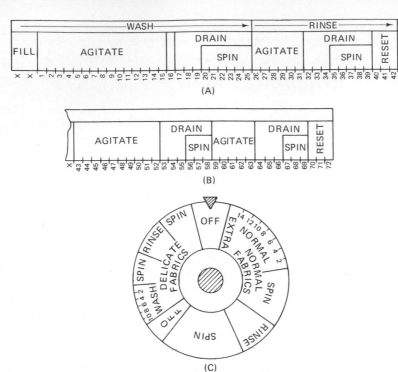

Fig. 10-2 A four-cycle automatic washer. (A) Timing diagram, (B) Timer control knob.

MAL WASH begins at increment 8, and the RINSE ONLY starts at increment 26 of the same long timing cycle. Only the DELICATE WASH cycle occupies its own portion of the timing diagram—an interval running from increments 43–72.

Also note that there are no timed fill operations. This machine uses a nontimed fill feature that is initiated by the timer, but terminated whenever a water level sensing switch closes. Aside from assuring a proper water level in spite of variations in the amount of laundry in the machine, this nontimed fill feature lets the user initiate the washing cycles at any point.

Suppose, as an example, that the user only wants a 10-minute wash step. The timer dial can be manually rotated to the 10 digit on the timer, and then started. Setting the timer dial to "10" in this instance actually advances the washing operation to the sixth time increment, thus leaving only ten full minutes of washing time.

The fill operation begins immediately upon starting the machine, but the timer does not start until the water level is right. And when the water level sensing switch is finally activated, the timer starts running and the agitation operation commences from time increment 6.

The washing phase then runs normally through increment 15, followed by a one-increment pause interval during which the laundry is simply soaked in the wash water. The drain and spin operations then occupy the machine through increment 25.

At increment 26, the timer is again stopped for a fill operation. Once the laundry tub is filled to the proper level, the timer starts running and the agitation operation for the rinse phase begins. All operations after that are under the control of the timer.

With this type of machine, the user can select any washing time between zero and a full fifteen minutes. A second advantage is that the cycle can be started at any point during the rinse operation. This is not normally done, but this RINSE ONLY cycle can be used in cases where the user wants to skip over all the washing phase and merely rinse and spin the laundry.

The reset interval between increments 40 and 42 is used to reset all of the machine's electrical contacts for another complete washing cycle. The timer automatically shuts off the on/off switch at the end of the seventy-second increment, making it impossible for the machine to advance to the DELICATE WASH cycle on its own accord. The reset interval is labeled OFF on the timer control knob.

The portion of the timing diagram allocated for the DELICATE WASH cycle begins at increment 43. This cycle is actually a shortened-up version of the normal cycles just described. The idea is to reduce the wear and tear on the laundry by shortening the agitate and spin operations. In this machine, there are only ten time increments available for the washing phase and five increments for the following rinse. The spin operations for the DELICATE WASH cycle take up only three time increments apiece.

Modern automatic clothes washers can include a number of optional features that do not appear as necessary parts of a timing diagram. The more common options are listed here. (See basic clothes washer in Fig. 10-3.)

WATER TEMPERATURE SELECTOR SWITCHES.   The user normally has access to a set of switches, pushbuttons, or a dial, which allows a choice of water temperatures. In the simplest machines, the switch might only permit a selection of either hot or cold water for both the washing and rinsing phases of the wash cycle. Better machines have separate selectors for the wash and rinse phases: hot, warm, or cold for the washing phase and warm or cold for the rinsing phase.

AGITATION SPEED SELECTOR.   This control lets the user select a NORMAL or GENTLE speed for the agitation action. The GENTLE speed is used only in instances in which there is a chance that the NORMAL speed might harm certain kinds of fabrics.

It is important to note that this speed selector switch does not influence the timing in any way. If the user sets up a five-minute wash operation, for

Fig. 10-3 This top-of-the-line clothes washer features three basic cycles (NORMAL, SOAK, and PERMANENT PRESS) and a number of water temperatures, speed, and water level options. (Courtesy of General Electric Major Appliance Group)

example, the operation will occupy a full five minutes, whether the agitator speed is set to NORMAL or GENTLE.

WATER LEVEL SELECTOR SWITCH.   The purpose of such a switch is to conserve water whenever the laundry tub is only partially filled with laundry.

Some machines do not have a water level selector switch, and all wash and rinse phases run with the tub filled to capacity. Other machines have a HIGH/LOW selector, some give the user a choice of HIGH, MEDIUM, and LOW water levels, and a few machines have an "infinite" water level adjustment that lets the user set the water to any desired level.

AUTOMATIC DETERGENT, BLEACH, AND SOFTENER DISPENSERS. Better machines have provisions for automatically dispensing measured amounts of liquid laundry detergent and bleach into the wash water. The main advantage of this system is that the user does not have to load the machine with detergent and bleach prior to starting every wash load. The dispenser reservoirs need to be filled only when they run dry.

The dispensers are operated by solenoids that are energized by timer switches at the appropriate times during the washing step.

Many modern-day users like to add a bit of fabric softener to the final rinse water. The objective is to give the fabrics a certain softness that cannot be achieved without the help of this special chemical process.

During the first days that such softeners were available, users had the problem of remembering to add the material at the right time in the cycle. There are now several ingeneous softener dispensers on the market that spill out the softener at the right time in the cycle; but built-in automatic softener dispensers provide the best solution.

The automatic softener dispenser works exactly like the detergent and bleach dispensers. The operation of the softener dispenser, however, is keyed to the rinse phase of the cycle.

WASH WATER SAVE-AND-RETURN CONTROLS. Washing machines equipped with this special feature allow the user to store the wash water from one washing cycle so that it can be used again for the next cycle. Suppose, for example, that the user wants to wash two full loads of laundry; in this case, the machine can pump the wash water from the first load into a temporary storage space such as an ordinary laundry basin. The remainder of the first washing cycle then takes place normally, dumping the rinse water into the sewage system. When the second load of laundry is started, however, the machine draws its wash water from the storage basin instead of the home's fresh water supply.

This "suds-saver" feature does indeed save the cost of a fresh supply of water and detergent. The only difficulty is that the water stored in the basin during the first laundry cycle is likely to cool slightly before it is pumped back into the machine. Of course this is not a real problem in instances where the first load is to be washed in hot water and the second calls for a warm or cold water temperature.

Most machines equipped with the suds save-and-return system have two additional switches on the user's control panel. One of these switches determines whether or not the wash water will be stored. Setting this particular switch to its NORMAL position lets the machine pump the used wash water into the sewage system; but setting it to SAVE energizes a valve that bypasses the used wash water to the storage basin. The second switch energizes a separate pump that draws the stored wash water back into the machine during the wash fill operation. The user must set this switch to its SUDS RETURN position whenever the stored water is to be used in a laundry cycle.

10-2 GENERAL THEORY OF OPERATION

An automatic clothes washer can be an elaborate piece of electro-mechanical equipment. Most modern washers have a number of basic electrical and mechanical parts that work very much the same way in every make and model. Such parts include a timer assembly, solenoids for controlling the inflow of hot and cold water, a main drive motor and transmission for providing the powerful agitation and spin actions, a water pump assembly for recirculating and removing water from the machine, and a host of other controls and switches.

This section describes these basic components in terms of what they do and how they do it.

TIMER ASSEMBLY.   A timer assembly is the "brain" of an automatic clothes washer, and it is actually no different from the type of timer described in connection with automatic dishwashers (Sec. 9-2.1). The cam-operated switch contacts are responsible for starting and stopping most of the basic machine operations, leaving the user little to do but start a washing cycle and remove the laundry at the end of the cycle.

The cam assembly is driven by a small shaded-pole induction motor that runs at a very precise speed under normal loading conditions. Section 5-2.2 deals with the operation of these little motors in some detail.

MAIN DRIVE MOTOR.   The main drive motor is responsible for converting electrical energy into the kind of mechanical power that is necessary for carrying out the machine's agitation, spin and pumping actions. The motor is normally a split-phase induction motor that is rated at about 1/2 hp. Washer motors, almost without exception, operate from 120 V line power.

A capacitor-start feature is not necessary for washing machines using fractional horsepower drive motors, but a centrifugal switch or relay-start mechanism is always an integral part of the main drive motor's control system. The washer motors are also reversible in come cases, and they sometimes have built-in speed control windings. See Sec. 10-3 for basic motor control details.

TRANSMISSION ASSEMBLY.   The transmission in an automatic clothes washer is the most complex piece of mechanical machinery in the home appliance industry. The transmission is wholly responsible for converting the rotary motion of the main drive motor into either an agitation motion or spinning action. Although there is often a direct linkage between the drive motor shaft and the cam assembly that produces the agitation motion, the motor is connected to the spin section of the transmission by means of a friction clutch that lets the laundry tub reach its normal spinning speed gradually, without overloading the motor.

In a few current models, the transmission is shifted from one type of action to the other by means of a solenoid-operated gear shift. Most models, however, shift between agitate and spin according to the direction the drive motor spins. Whenever the drive motor turns in one particular direction, the transmission is shifted to the spin gear. Reversing the motor then automatically shifts the transmission to its agitate gear.

Many washing machine transmissions also have a neutral gear that allows the drive motor to turn without causing either the spin or agitate action to occur. This feature is used during drain operations that call for running the water pump by itself.

WATER PUMP ASSEMBLY.   The main purpose of the water pump is to draw used water out of the machine at the end of the washing and rinsing steps and during the spin operations. The same pump, however, can also be used to recirculate the wash and rinse water—usually through a lint filter.

The water pump in an automatic washer is mechanically driven by the transmission and main drive motor. Generally speaking, the pump is operating whenever the main drive motor is running.

Consider now the fact that the main drive motor is reversible in many models—it runs in one direction for agitate operations and in the opposite direction for spin operations. This means that the water pump runs in both directions as well; and the logical conclusion is that the pump moves water in two different directions, depending on which way the main drive motor is turning.

It is possible to take advantage of this two-direction characteristic of the water pump by using it in conjunction with a two-way flapper valve assembly. The idea is to recirculate the wash or rinse water during agitate operations and pump the water out of the system during spin operations. As shown in Fig. 10-4(A), turning the drive motor and pump in the agitate direction opens valve A and forces valve B closed. The water is thus routed through the water recirculation system inside the machine. Turning the drive motor and pump in the spin direction as shown in Fig. 10-4(B) closes valve A and opens B. Since valve B leads to the home's sewage system, moving the water in that direction effectively drains it all out of the machine.

It is thus possible to use a flapper valve assembly for routing the water without using extra electrical controls and timer switches. Some machines control the routing of the pump water by means of solenoid valves, however;

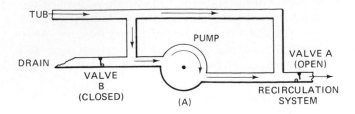

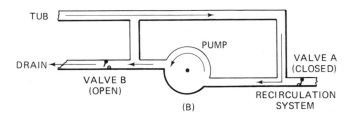

Fig. 10-4   Operation of a flapper-valve water control system. (A) Pump turning in the agitate direction to recirculate the water. (B) Pump turning in the spin direction to pump water out of the machine.

and machines having a suds save-and-return feature must have an additional solenoid valve that opens whenever water is to be pumped to or from an outside storage tub.

FRESH WATER VALVES.   The fresh water valves control the inflow of fresh hot and cold water during the fill operations. As shown in Fig. 10-5,

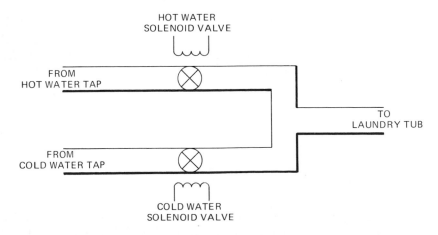

Fig. 10-5   Hot and cold water solenoid valve control system.

the valves are electrically operated. The solenoids are turned off most of the time, keeping their respective valve ports closed. The ports open only when electrical power is applied to the solenoid windings.

The two fresh water valve solenoids can be operated individually or at the same time. Activating the "hot" valve, for instance, fills the machine with hot water. Energizing the "cold" valve fills the machine with cold water, and energizing both valves at the same time fills the laundry tub with warm water—a mixture of hot and cold.

The water temperature selector switch determines which water valves are operated during any given fill operation; timer contacts are responsible for energizing the selected solenoids at the appropriate times.

Figure 10-6 shows a typical water fill circuit for modern automatic

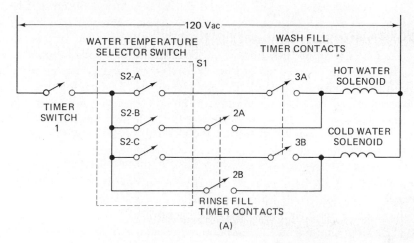

SELECTED WATER TEMPERATURE		S1 CONTACT CONFIGURATION		
WASH	RINSE	S1-A	S1-B	S1-C
HOT	WARM	X	X	0
HOT	COLD	X	0	0
WARM	WARM	X	X	X
WARM	COLD	X	0	X
COLD	WARM	0	X	X
COLD	COLD	0	0	X

X = CLOSED
0 = OPEN

(B)

Fig. 10-6 Water temperature selector circuit. (A) Circuit diagram. (B) Switch closures for different combinations of wash and rinse water temperatures.

washers. The hot and cold water solenoid valves are energized through several sets of timer contacts and a water temperature selector switch assembly.

Timer contact 1 is closed whenever the washing cycle calls for a fill operation. Note that it is connected in series with the entire water control circuit; and whenever contact 1 is open, it is impossible to energize either of the water solenoid valves. Timer contact 1, in other words, is the contact that determines *when* a fill operation is to take effect.

Timer contacts 3A and 3B close during a wash fill operation, while contacts 2A and 2B close during each rinse fill step. These contacts are used to establish a difference between the wash and rinse water temperatures.

It is the temperature selector switch assembly, however, that actually determines *which* valves will be operated during any fill operation. If S1A is closed during a wash fill step, for example, the hot water solenoid valve is energized through timer contact 1, S1A and timer contact 3A. In this example, the machine would fill with hot water during every wash fill operation.

The wash temperature can be lowered to a warm level by closing contacts S1A and S1C. During each wash fill step, hot water will flow into the machine as just described. Cold water also flows into the machine in this instance, however, because the cold water valve is energized through timer contact 1, S1C, and timer contact 3B. With both water valves closed in this manner, the machine would fill with warm water—a mixture of hot and cold.

The rinse fill operations take place in a similar fashion through timer contacts 2A and 2B. The table accompanying the circuit in Fig. 12-6 shows the selector switch configurations necessary for programming six different combinations of wash and rinse water temperatures.

The switch contacts in the temperature selector switch assembly are not operated directly from the control panel. Instead, the user operates a set of switches or a dial that automatically closes the appropriate combination of selector switch contacts. If, for example, the user rotates a selector dial for WARM WASH-COLD RINSE, a mechanical linkage between the panel control and the S1 assembly automatically closes contacts S1A and S1C.

WATER LEVEL SENSING SWITCH.   Machines that do not use a timed fill interval must have provisions for sensing the water level and turning off the water supply whenever a given water level is reached. This sensor normally takes the form of a pressure switch that is activated either directly by the water pressure on the bottom of the laundry tub, or indirectly activated by air pressure in a tube located at the rear of the machine.

The diagram in Fig. 10-7 illustrates the operation of the indirect, or air pressure, sensing mechanism. The water level in the tube is always the same as the water level in the machine. And as the water levels rise, the air pressure at the top of the tube increases. A pressure switch at the top of the tube can

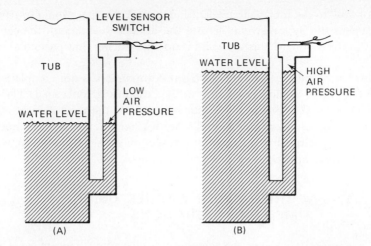

Fig. 10-7 A water level sensor scheme. (A) Water level below set point on the sensor. (B) Water level at the set point.

be adjusted to close at various pressure levels representing different water levels in the machine.

DOOR INTERLOCK SWITCH. The door interlock switch is a safety feature that completely shuts down the washer whenever the loading door or lid is opened during a spin operation. Opening the door during any other part of the cycle does not affect the ongoing operation.

The diagram in Fig. 10-8 shows how the door interlock switch is bypassed by a timer contact. The timer contact is closed throughout most of the machine's cycle, allowing the lid switch to be opened without interrupting

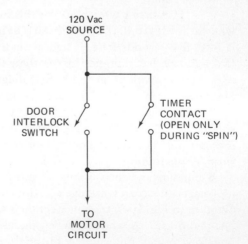

Fig. 10-8 Door switch and override circuit.

current flow to the motor circuit. During every spin operation, however, the timer opens the bypass switch, letting the lid switch interrupt the complete circuit to the motor whenever the lid is opened during that particular operation.

This list of mechanical and electrical components is not complete as far as the full range of modern clothes washer models is concerned. The list is complete, however, in the sense that it describes the most critical components and those that are unique to clothes washers. Some of the components that are not specifically mentioned in this section are described in connection with appliances appearing elsewhere in this book.

10-3   A THREE-CYCLE WASHER USING TIMED FILL OPERATIONS

Figure 10-9 shows the schematic and timing diagram for a three-cycle washer that uses timed fill operations and a transmission that shifts between agitate and spin according to the direction the main drive motor spins. There is no drain operation specified on the timing diagram because this machine uses the spin operation itself to throw all the water out of an inner laundry tub and into a surrounding drum that is emptied by a water pump.

The user's controls include only a water temperature selector switch and a timer control knob that has an on/off switch built into it. Better versions of this same machine would include a water level selector, an agitation speed selector, and a shorter wash/rinse cycle for delicate fabrics.

10-3.1   Theory of Operation

The EXTRA WASH cycle for this machine begins at time increment 1, whereas the NORMAL WASH cycle starts at increment 9. If each time increment is forty-five seconds long, it figures that the EXTRA WASH cycle runs about five and one-half minutes longer than the NORMAL WASH cycle does. The remaining operations on the timing diagram—pause, spin, rinse, and reset operations—are identical for both the normal and extra wash cycles.

There is really nothing special about the RINSE ONLY cycle because it is simply the tail end of the wash cycles. When setting up the RINSE ONLY cycle, the user merely starts the operations at increment 25—the beginning of the rinse fill operation.

To understand the workings of this particular machine, suppose that the user starts an EXTRA WASH cycle at time increment 1. As shown in the timing diagram in Fig. 10-9, the timer contacts that close during increment 1 are 1, 5A, and 5B, 7, 8A, and 8B. When the user turns on the on/off switch, then, line power is fed immediately to the timer motor via contact 1; and power reaches the water solenoids through the closed centrifugal switch contact CS1A, the water temperature selector switch assembly S3, and timer contacts 5A and 5B.

The timer motor thus begins running and wash water starts flowing into the machine the moment increment 1 is initiated. Whether the water is hot,

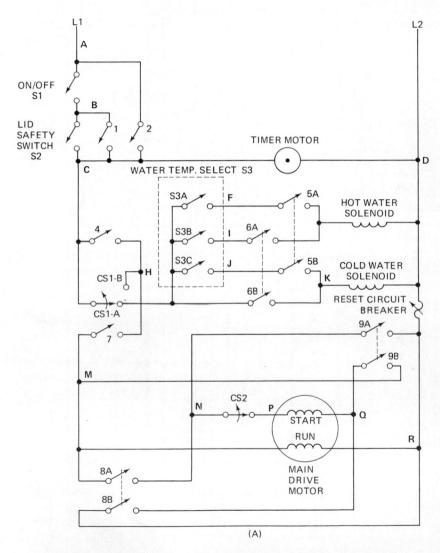

(A)

Fig. 10-9 A typical washing machine featuring timed fill operations: (A) Schematic diagram, (B) Timing diagram, (C) Water temperature selector switch configurations.

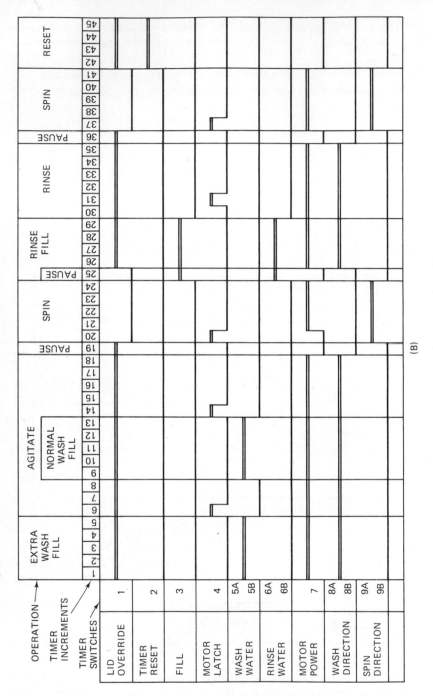

Fig. 10-9 (Continued)

(B)

SELECTED TEMPERATURE		SWITCH CONDITIONS		
WASH	RINSE	S3A	S3B	S3C
HOT	WARM	X	X	0
HOT	COLD	X	0	0
WARM	WARM	X	X	X
WARM	COLD	X	0	X

WATER TEMPERATURE SELECTOR
SWITCH PROGRAMMING
X = CLOSED
0 = OPEN

(C)

Fig. 10-9 (Continued)

warm, or cold depends on the setting of the water temperature selector switch. See the water temperature switch table in Fig. 10-9(C). If the wash temperature is set for HOT, for example, S3A is the only water selector contact that is closed, and the hot water solenoid is the only one that is energized.

The machine maintains this switch status through the first five time increments. This adds up to a time interval of three and three-quarters minutes.

At the beginning of time increment 6, the timer opens contacts 5A and 5B to turn off the flow of fresh water into the machine. At the same time, the timer closes contact 4 which completes a circuit to the motor via contacts 7 and 8. The motor thus begins running in a direction that shifts the transmission to the agitate mode.

As the motor approaches its normal running speed, centrifugal switch CS2 opens to cut out the start winding. A second centrifugal switch assembly, made up of contacts CS1A and CS1B, changes state so that CS1B is closed and its counterpart is open. Activating CS1 in this manner effectively transfers the main power from the water solenoid lines to the motor circuitry.

Timer contact 4 drops open again at the end of increment 6, but there is no outward change in operations because CS1B is now closed to maintain line power to the drive motor circuit. The agitation operation is thus in full swing, and there are no further changes in the timer circuitry until the beginning of increment 9.

At increment 9, timer contacts 5A and 5B to the water solenoids close again. The solenoids are not energized in this instance, however, because CS1A is open. What then is the reason for closing timer contacts 5A and 5B? The reason is that increment 9 is the starting point for the NORMAL WASH cycle, and if the drive motor is not running to keep centrifugal switch CS1A open at increment 9, a fill operation begins. The fill operation for the EXTRA WASH cycle in progress has already been completed, however, so that there is no need for additional water in the machine. The closing of contacts 5A and 5B between time increments 9 and 13 thus pass without affecting the cycle at all.

Timer contact 4 closes during increment 14; but again there is no effect as far as the ongoing EXTRA WASH cycle is concerned. Closing contact 4 at increment 14 starts the agitation operation for a NORMAL WASH cycle.

The washing portion of the EXTRA WASH cycle thus proceeds uninterrupted through increment 18—about ten and one-half minutes.

All motor operations come to a halt at increment 19. This pause interval lasts only one timer increment, but that is plenty of time to allow the motor to stop spinning and to set up the timer contacts for the next operation. When the motor stops spinning, CS2 closes to reconnect the start winding into the circuit, CS1B opens and CS1A closes to reset the motor for another start-up operation. The only timer contact that is closed during this interval is contact 1 connected across the lid safety switch. The timer motor still runs through the pause interval, however, receiving its power through the closed on/off switch and timer contact 1 or the lid switch.

The first spin operation begins at increment 20. At that moment, the timer closes contacts 4, 7, 9A, and 9B, and it opens contact 1 for the first time. The closed contacts provide a complete path for current flow to the main drive motor, and they set up the phasing of the windings so that the motor starts in a direction that shifts the transmission for its spin operation. And as the motor approaches its normal running speed, the centrifugal switches change state to remove the start winding from the motor circuit and feed power to the motor through contact CS1B again.

The machine is now running in a spin operation, and water is being pumped out into the home's sewage system. Opening timer contact 1 during this operation makes it possible to shut down all motor operations if anyone should open the lid on the washer. Of course this is an important safety feature that has doubtless saved many sprained wrists or more costly and painful accidents. Note that the timer motor stops running if anyone opens the lid during a spin operation. This is an important feature in the case of unbalanced loads that make the machine jump around the floor during a spin cycle. The user, in other words, can open the lid to readjust the load without upsetting the length of time necessary to get an effective spin operation.

The spin operation runs through time increment 24 when the motor is turned off by opening timer contacts 7, 9A, and 9B. And as the motor slows down during increment 25, the centrifugal switches automatically reset for another motor start-up.

The pause step in time increment 25 is slightly different from the one that takes place in increment 19. At the onset of increment 25, the water solenoids are energized through the closing of timer contacts 6A and 6B. Rinse water thus begins running into the machine at increment 25, and the temperature of that water is determined by the setting of the water temperature selector switch, S3. If, for instance, the user has chosen a WARM RINSE, switch contacts S3B and S3C are both closed to energize both the hot and cold water solenoids.

Motor circuit timer contacts 7, 8A, and 8B close at increment 26 in the rinse fill operation; but since timer contact 4 and CS1B are open at the time, the motor does not start. The fill operation thus proceeds uninterrupted through time increment 29.

Another agitation operation begins at increment 30 when timer contact 4 closes to create a complete path for current flow to the motor circuit. The rinse water is turned off at the same time by the opening of contacts 3, 6A, and 6B.

The motor thus starts running in a direction that shifts the transmission to its agitate mode. By the time contact 4 opens again, the motor is running fast enough to close CS1B, thus keeping power applied to the motor circuit. The system is then allowed to operate without any change in switch contacts through the end of the rinse operation at increment 35.

The pause step and final spin operations between increments 36 and 41 are identical to those employed after the wash step between increments 19 and 24.

The EXTRA WASH cycle is essentially complete at the end of increment 41 where only timer contacts 1 and 2 are closed. Closing contact 1 makes it possible to open the lid on the machine without stopping the timer motor. This is a handy feature because a user will often want to remove the laundry the moment that the final spin operation is over. Closing contact 2 during this reset interval insures that the timer motor continues running, even after the on/off switch is either manually or automatically set to OFF.

At the end of increment 45, the timer motor opens contact 2 to turn itself off. The machine is then completely shut down and reset for the next washing cycle.

A NORMAL WASH cycle is initiated by manually rotating the timer knob to increment 9. Operations from that point follow the same general pattern as an EXTRA WASH. The RINSE ONLY cycle is, of course, started by rotating the timer knob to increment 25 before setting the on/off switch to its ON position.

It is quite likely that some clever appliance technician could design a washing machine that performs the same operations just described, but without using as many timer contacts and switches. The circuit design in Fig. 10-9, however, has an additional goof-proof feature that has not been discussed until this point. Consider what might happen if a user attempted to initiate a washing cycle at some time increment other than those specifically designated as starting points. The EXTRA WASH is supposed to be started at increment 1, the NORMAL WASH is started at increment 9, and the RINSE ONLY cycle is supposed to start at increment 25. But what would happen if the user started the machine with the timer dial rotated to another increment, increment 1 for example?

Under this abnormal start-up condition, there would be no water in the machine and the motor would not be running. According to the timing diagram, timer contacts 1, 7, 8A, and 8B are closed at the onset of interval 7. The motor cannot start because contact 4 and CS1B are both open. Contact 2 is closed, however, to start the timer motor; and as soon as the timer mechanism reached increment 9, contacts 5A and 5B would close to energize the wash water solenoids and start the NORMAL WASH cycle.

The only apparent problem associated with starting a cycle at some non-designated starting point is a long delay before the washer actually goes to work. The machine does nothing at all until the timer reaches the next major step in the overall cycle. Problems such as starting an agitation operation with no water in the machine are thus eliminated at the expense of a few extra switches and timer contacts.

10-3.2   Troubleshooting Guide

The following list of symptoms and troubleshooting procedures apply specifically to the automatic washer illustrated in Fig. 10-9. The symptoms and procedures, however, are representative of many similar kinds of washers on the market today, especially those having the following features:

1. Timed fill operations.
2. A transmission that is shifted according to the direction the main drive motor spins.
3. Drain and spin operations that always run at the same time.
4. A centrifugal start-up circuit for the main drive motor.

The boldface letters in the troubleshooting notes refer to test points in the machine that are normally exposed for ready access.

No water, motor does not start, appliance draws no current and seems dead at any cycle setting

1. No power to the appliance—check the voltage level at the washer by measuring the voltage across the line connections (between points **A** and **D**). The trouble is confirmed if no voltage is present at those points. Check the power cable, plug assembly, and the service branch leading to the washer.

2. On/off switch S1 open—this is a likely cause of these symptoms if full line voltage is reaching the machine. Check this diagnosis

by first unplugging the machine and connecting a jumper wire across the on/off switch terminals (between points **A** and **B**). This jumper "cheats" the switch; when the appliance is plugged in, it should start running as soon as the timer knob is set to the beginning of a washing cycle.

Remove the jumper while the machine is running. The trouble is definitely in the on/off switch if the whole operation shuts down.

Appliance draws excessive current or blows fuses; operations seem sluggish or fail altogether

These are the symptoms of a serious short-circuit condition somewhere in the appliance. A visual inspection of the components and wiring might offer some clues to the nature of the short. Whenever such clues are not obvious, however, it is necessary to eliminate sections of the circuitry by a systematic process. Disconnect the motor circuit, for example, by opening the wiring between timer contact 7 and the motor circuits (at point **H**). Try restarting the appliance. If the short circuit condition seems to be eliminated, the trouble is in the disconnected circuit. If, on the other hand, the excessive current condition persists, look for the short in another part of the appliance.

No agitation; other operations normal

The fact that the motor runs normally in some operations eliminates the possibility of a problem in the drive motor itself.

1. Timer contact 8A or 8B stuck or broken open—confirm this trouble by cheating the suspected contacts with jumper wires across them (one between points **M** and **N** and another between **Q** and **R**). Set the timer to the beginning of a wash cycle and turn on the machine. It is possible to eliminate the fill operation by connecting a jumper across timer contact 4 (between points **C** and **H**). If the agitation operation begins under these test conditions, the trouble is confirmed.

2. Timer contact 9A or 9B shorted or stuck closed—under this fault condition, the washer will most likely blow a fuse whenever it reaches an agitation operation. Other operations, including spin, will run without blowing a fuse, however. The reason for this set of conditions is that closing both contacts 8 and 9 at the same time creates a dead short across the power lines.

3. Transmission or clutch defective in the agitate gear—consult the manufacturer's service manual for specific troubleshooting and repair hints.

No spin or drain; other operations normal

1. Lid switch S2 open—cheat the lid switch with a jumper wire (between points **B** and **C**), rotate the timer knob to a spin operation, and turn on the machine. It is possible to eliminate the waiting time involved in this test by connecting a second jumper across timer contact 4 (between points **C** and **H**). If the spin operation takes place, the lid switch is indeed open and must be replaced.

2. Timer contact 9A or 9B stuck or broken open—confirm this trouble by cheating the suspected contacts with jumper wires (between points **R** and **N** and points **M** and **Q**). Set the timer to a spin operation and turn on the machine. An additional jumper across timer contact 4 will again eliminate any waiting time. If the spin operation begins, the trouble is confirmed.

3. Timer contact 8A or 8B shorted or stuck closed—under this fault condition, the washer will blow a fuse whenever it reaches a spin operation. The reason is that closing contacts 8 and 9 at the same time create a dead short across the power lines.

4. Transmission or spin clutch defective—consult the manufacturer's service manual for specific troubleshooting and repair hints.

Water does not drain out; other operations appear normal

1. Drain hose clogged or pinched—inspect the drain hose and plumbing for obstructions of any sort.

2. Defective linkage between the pump and transmission—inspect the operation of the pump assembly during a spin operation. Consult the manufacturer's manual for more details.

3. Defective water pump—check the water pump for loose parts or obstructions of any kind. Again, the manufacturer's service manual is the best source for specific details concerning the water pump.

No spin or agitate; fill and pause operations normal

1. Timer contact 4 stuck or broken open—connect a jumper wire across contact 4 (between points **H** and **M**), and start a washing cycle. The trouble is confirmed if the agitation operation begins immediately.

2. Timer contact 7 stuck or broken open—cheat this contact by connecting a jumper wire across it (between points **H** and **M**), and try starting an agitate operation. Leaving the jumper connected across contact 4 from the previous test can eliminate any waiting time. The trouble is confirmed if the agitation operation starts.

3. Centrifugal switch contact CS2 stuck or broken open—with the jumpers from the previous two tests still in place, cheat the centrifugal switch contact with another jumper (between points **N** and **P**). The trouble is confirmed if the motor starts.

4. Defective motor windings—if the motor does not start with all the jumpers in place from the previous three tests, there can be little doubt that either the motor or the transmission is at fault. The jumpers actually complete a circuit from the on/off switch directly to the motor. As it is easier to test the motor than it is to check out the transmission, it is a good idea to remove the motor from the washer and test it on the bench. If the motor does not run when connected directly to a power outlet or if the windings do not have resistances specified in the manufacturer's test data, it must be replaced.

5. Transmission defective—if the motor checks normal according to the previous test, the logical process of elimination leaves only the transmission as the cause of the trouble. Consult the manufacturer's service manual for transmission testing and repair information.

No water at all, but agitation and spin actions normal

Carefully distinguish this symptom from one where the machine can be filled with either hot or cold water during the wash or rinse steps. In this case, there is no water at all.

1. No water supply to the washer—make certain that both water faucets are turned on full and that water is reaching the faucets from the home's water supply system.

2. Centrifugal switch contact CS1A stuck or broken open—cheat this switch contact with a jumper wire across it (between points **C** and **L**), and attempt a fill operation. If water runs into the machine as it should, the trouble is confirmed and the switch must be replaced.

3. Temperature selector switch assembly defective—start the machine at the beginning of a wash cycle and connect one end of a jumper wire to the common terminal on the water temperature selector switch (at point **L**). Set the selector switch for WARM WASH and touch the loose end of the jumper wire to the three other contacts on the selector switch one at a time (to point **F**, then **I**, and finally point **J**). This test jumper cheats the selector switch, so that if water runs into the machine while touching the jumper to any one of these points, the trouble is indeed in the selector switch assembly. Replace the entire water temperature selector.

    Note: Timer contacts 6 and 5 and the water valves could cause this symptom, but it is unlikely that such troubles will ever occur in practice because both sets of contacts or both water valves would have to fail at the same time.

Agitation begins before fill operation is completed

1. Centrifugal switch SC1B shorted or stuck closed—disconnect the wiring to centrifugal switch CS1B and check the continuity of that contact with a continuity tester or ohmmeter. A good switch of this type shows a reading of infinity or a complete lack of continuity. The trouble is confirmed, however, if the test shows zero resistance or good circuit continuity.

2. Timer contact 4 shorted or stuck closed—unplug the washer, set the timer to the beginning of any wash cycle, and check the continuity or resistance of that contact (between points **H** and **C**). If this test shows zero resistance or good continuity, contact 4 is indeed shorted. Replace the entire timer assembly.

Water does not stop running; other operations appear normal

1. Water valve stuck open—this trouble is a likely candidate if water continues running into the machine, even when it is unplugged. Inspect the water valves for obstructions or damage.

If it appears impossible or impractical to service the defective valve, replace it with a new one.

2. Centrifugal switch CS1A shorted—the symptoms in this case will appear only as long as the washer is turned on and set for a washing cycle. Connect a voltmeter across the contacts of CS1A (between points **C** and **L**), and short out timer contact 4 with a jumper wire (between points **C** and **H**) to start the drive motor. If the motor runs, the meter shows zero volts, and water continues flowing into the machine, the centrifugal switch contact is the likely cause of this trouble.

**Wash and spin start, but run only for a moment;
fill operations normal**

The centrifugal switch contact CS1B is probably stuck open or broken. Cheat the switch by connecting a jumper wire across it (between points **C** and **H**) and turning on the washer. If the motor starts immediately and seems to run indefinitely, the trouble is indeed in that centrifugal switch.

10-4 A THREE-CYCLE WASHER USING NONTIMED FILL OPERATIONS

The automatic washer circuit described in this section and illustrated in Fig. 10-10 is a rather simple model, but it differs from the machine featured in the previous section in several important respects. First, this washer uses a pressure switch to sense the water level in the laundry drum, making the fill operations nontimed—the agitation operation starts the moment the water level is right, regardless of how long it takes to do the job.

The circuit in Fig. 10-10 also uses more than the usual number of solenoids. This model, for instance, has a warm water solenoid in addition to the usual hot and cold water solenoid valves. And finally, this model uses solenoids to shift the transmission between the agitate and spin operations. The neutral gear in this instance operates a water pump for drain operations. The primary advantage of the solenoid-shift transmission, by the way, is that the main drive motor always spins in the same direction, eliminating the need for motor-reversing switches.

10-4.1 Theory of Operation

As shown in the timing diagram in Fig. 10-10, the wash cycle begins with a nontimed WASH FILL step. In this step, timer switches 2, 3, 4, and 5 are closed; but because there is no water in the machine at the outset, the water level switch S2 is in its EMPTY position and only contacts 5A and 5B receive any power from the supply lines. The timer and main drive motors

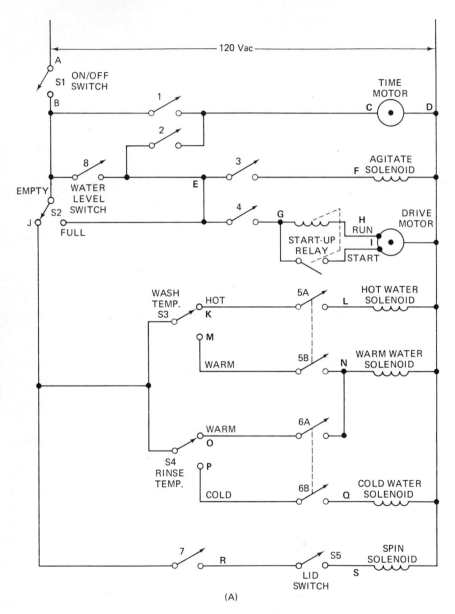

Fig. 10-10   A typical washing machine featuring nontimed fill operations: (A) Schematic diagram, (B) Timing diagram.

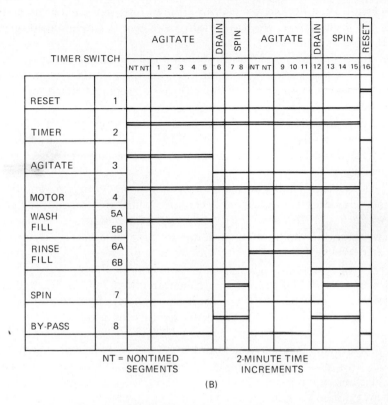

TIMER SWITCH		AGITATE						DRAIN	SPIN	AGITATE				DRAIN	SPIN	RESET
		NT NT	1 2 3 4 5				6	7 8	NT NT	9 10 11		12		13 14 15	16
RESET	1															
TIMER	2															
AGITATE	3															
MOTOR	4															
WASH FILL	5A 5B															
RINSE FILL	6A 6B															
SPIN	7															
BY-PASS	8															

NT = NONTIMED   2-MINUTE TIME
SEGMENTS   INCREMENTS

(B)

Fig. 10-10   (Continued)

are thus de-energized while the tub is being filled with either hot or warm water, depending on the setting of the wash temperature control switch, S3. If S3 is set to HOT, the hot water valve is activated; but if S3 is set to WARM, the warm water valve is energized.

The agitation operation begins the moment the water level switch changes to its FULL position. This switch thus removes power from the water valves, stopping the flow of fresh water into the machine. At the same instant, the water level switch energizes contacts 2, 3, and 4 so that the timer motor starts, the transmission shifts to its agitate gear, and the main drive motor turns on.

As shown in the timing diagram in Fig. 10-10, this agitation operation takes place through the fifth time increment—about ten minutes. At increment 6, timer contacts 3 and 5 drop open and contact 8 closes to start the drain operation.

During this drain operation, line power is still applied to the timer motor through contact 2 and to the main drive motor via contact 4. The main drive motor is still running, but the agitate solenoid has been de-energized. This places the transmission into its neutral gear where it is allowed to operate only the drain pump.

As the drain pump removes the water from the laundry tub, the water level switch changes from FULL to EMPTY. The timer and drive motors continue running, however, because timer contact 8 remains closed during the drain operation.

The spin operation is started at increment 7 as timer contact 7 closes to energize the spin solenoid. As long as the lid switch S5 remains closed and the laundry tub is not full of water, the spin solenoid remains energized through time increment 8.

The RINSE FILL step begins at increment 9 as timer contacts 3 and 6 close and contacts 7 and 8 open. Opening contact 7 shifts the transmission out of the spin gear and closing contact 3 shifts it to the agitate gear. The motor cannot run during the fill interval, however, because contact 8 is open and the water level switch is still in its EMPTY position.

The only contacts that are closed *and* energized during RINSE FILL are contacts 6A and 6B. These contacts are energized through the rinse temperature selector switch, S4. If that switch is at WARM, the laundry drum begins filling with warm water. Of course the machine fills with cold water if the user has selected the COLD RINSE setting on S4.

The RINSE FILL step continues until the water level switch changes over to FULL. This action removes power from the water valves and applies it to the motor and agitate solenoid circuits. The agitation operation thus begins and runs through time increment 11.

The electrical operations involved in the drain step of increment 12 are identical to those of the same operation in increment 6: the agitate solenoid and water valves are de-energized, but the motor remains running in its neutral gear to pump out the water.

The second spin operation takes over at time increment 13 when the spin solenoid is activated through timer contact 7. And at the end of this spin operation, all the timer contacts open except the timer reset contact, contact 1.

Contact 1 provides power to the timer motor for one time increment. The purpose of this step is to rotate the timer assembly to the starting point of the next wash cycle. Contact 1 drops open at the end of increment 16 to turn off the timer motor, and a cam on the timer shaft forces the on/off switch S1 open.

10-4.2 Troubleshooting Guide

The following list of symptoms and troubleshooting notes apply to the washer circuit in Fig. 10-10. Many washers on the market today use similar features, however, and the notes apply in a general way. This information is especially helpful in the case of machines that have:

1. Nontimed fill operations.
2. A solenoid-shifted transmission.
3. Separate spin and drain operations.
4. A relay start-up circuit for the main drive motor.

The boldface letters in the troubleshooting notes refer to convenient test points indicated on the schematic in Fig. 10-10.

Appliance does not run; seems dead at all cycle settings

1. No power to the washer—check the voltage at the main washer connections (between points **A** and **D**) with a voltmeter. The trouble is confirmed if the voltage is low or absent altogether. Inspect the condition of the power cable, plug assembly and the service branch leading to the washer.

2. On/off switch S1 open—set the timer knob to OFF, and connect a jumper wire across the terminals of the on/off switch (between points **A** and **B**). Set the timer to start a washing cycle. If the cycle starts normally with the jumper connected across the on/off switch, the trouble is confirmed. Replace the entire switch assembly.

3. Water level switch S3 sticking or broken open—set the timer knob to OFF, and connect a jumper wire between the common and EMPTY terminal of the water level switch. This jumper effectively shorts out the switch; if the switch is indeed open, the jumper will bypass it. Set the timer to begin a washing cycle and note the machine's response. The trouble is in this switch if water begins flowing into the machine. Replace the switch assembly.

No agitation action, other operations normal

1. Water level switch S2 broken or stuck open—set the timer knob to OFF and connect a jumper wire between the common and FULL connection on the water level switch (between points **B** and **E**). This jumper bypasses the water level switch and applies power directly to the drive motor circuitry. The trouble is indeed in this switch assembly, then, if the agitation action

begins the moment the timer control is set to start a washing cycle.

2. Timer contact 3 broken or stuck open—if the agitation does not start under the test conditions described under the first trouble, chances are quite good that the real trouble is in timer contact 3. Turn off the machine and add a second jumper across the timer contact in question (between points **E** and **F**). Set the timer control knob to the beginning of a wash operation and note the machine's response. The trouble is narrowed down to the timer contact if the agitation operation starts under this test condition. Replace the timer assembly.

3. Agitate solenoid defective—assuming that the agitation operation did *not* start under the first two test conditions, check the agitate solenoid by connecting a voltmeter across it (between points **F** and **D**) and starting a wash operation. The agitate solenoid is at fault if full line voltage appears across it, but it does not appear to be energizing or shifting the transmission.

4. Agitate transmission clutch too tight or too loose—This trouble is best diagnosed by the process of elimination and visual inspection. If the three component tests described thus far for this symptom prove that there are no defective components, that leaves only a mechanical problem in the motor-to-transmission assembly. Consult the manufacturer's specifications and maintenance manual for details concerning the agitate clutch assembly.

Motor does not operate, water fill operations normal

1. Motor circuit breaker open—locate and reset the motor circuit breaker located on or near the main drive motor assembly. Keep in mind the fact that such breakers seldom pop open for no real reason at all; something causes the overcurrent condition. If the motor seems to run normally after resetting the circuit breaker, allow the machine to operate through at least one complete cycle before deciding that the problem was a "fluke."

2. Timer contact 4 stuck or broken open—turn off the machine and set the timer control knob to an AGITATE position. Make a direct jumper connection across timer contact 8 (between points **B** and **E**), and turn on the appliance. The motor will *not* start if contact 4 is sticking open. To confirm the diagnosis of a faulty

contact 4, connect a second jumper wire across it (between points **E** and **G**). The contact is indeed at fault if the motor does start under these test conditions.

3. Motor start-up circuit defective—if the motor fails to start under the test conditions just described, chances are good that the real trouble is in the motor start-up circuit. To check this circuit, turn off the machine and connect a third jumper wire across the start relay contacts (between points **G** and **I**) and yet another jumper between the motor's start and run windings (between **H** and **I**). These jumpers short out all contacts and the relay coil that stand between the power line and drive motor. Turn on the machine and note the response. The trouble is in the start-up assembly if the motor begins running immediately. Do not allow the motor to run for more than a few moments under this set of test conditions.

4. Defective motor winding—if the motor does not run under the test conditions described in the previous trouble, there can be little doubt that the motor itself is at fault. Disconnect the motor shaft from the transmission assembly and test the windings as described in Sec. 5-4.

5. Transmission bound up or frozen—the process of elimination leads to a transmission problem if the machine passes the first four tests described under this set of symptoms. Consult the manufacturer's specifications and maintenance notes for specific details concerning the transmission assembly.

No spin action, other operations normal

1. Door safety switch stuck or broken open—make certain that the machine is completely emptied of water and set the timer control knob for a spin operation. Do not apply power to the machine at this time. Connect a jumper wire across the door safety switch (between points **R** and **S**), and turn on the washer. The switch is defective if the spin operation starts and runs normally with this jumper in place.

    Doublecheck the diagnosis by removing the suspected switch assembly from the machine and testing its continuity with a continuity tester or ohmmeter. The trouble is doubly confirmed if the switch shows no continuity or infinite resistance whether or not the pushbutton is depressed.

2. Timer contact 7 broken or stuck open—turn off the machine and

connect a second jumper into the circuit; this one across timer contact 7 (between points **J** and **R**). Set the timer control knob for a spin operation, and turn on the machine. The trouble is confirmed if the spin action starts.

3. Spin solenoid defective—assuming that the spin operation did *not* start under the first two test conditions, check the spin solenoid by connecting a voltmeter across it (between points **S** and **D**), and starting a spin operation. The spin solenoid is at fault if full line voltage appears across it, but it does not seem to be energizing or shifting the transmission.

4. Spin transmission clutch out of adjustment—this trouble is best diagnosed by the process of elimination. If the three electrical tests described for these symptoms prove that there are no electrical problems, the evidence points to a mechanical trouble in the motor-to-transmission linkage. Consult the manufacturer's specifications and maintenance manual for details concerning the spin clutch assembly.

Agitate starts before tub is filled

1. Water level switch S2 shorted—disconnect the wiring to the FULL connection on the water level switch and start a normal washing cycle. The trouble is confirmed if the agitation *does not* begin at all, even after the water flow stops.

    Doublecheck the diagnosis after removing the water level switch assembly from the washer. If the switch is actually shorted as indicated, an ohmmeter or continuity test on the switch's terminals will show good continuity or zero resistance between any two terminals whenever the switch is not activated.

2. Timer contact 8 stuck closed—turn off the machine, reconnect the wires disconnected in trouble 1, and disconnect the common connection to the water level switch (at point **B**). Start a washing cycle and note the machine's response. If the agitation operation still starts before the water is finished running into the tub, the trouble is most likely in the timer assembly.

No water for wash operations; rinse fill and other operations normal

The symptoms in this instance should be observed rather carefully. If the water is not running into the machine at the beginning of a wash cycle, the timer and agitation operation never start, and that response can mislead the troubleshooter into thinking something is wrong elsewhere in the washer—in the drive motor circuit, for example.

To confirm that the symptoms stated here, set the timer control to the RINSE operation, and start the machine. The symptoms are confirmed if the machine fills normally during this part of the washing cycle. If the machine *does not* fill in wash or rinse, see "No water in wash or rinse."

1. Wash temperature selector switch S3 open—set the wash temperature selector switch to HOT, and connect a jumper wire across the HOT connections on that switch (between points **J** and **K**). Start a normal wash cycle and note the machine's response. The trouble is in the wash temperature selector switch if the machine begins filling with hot water under this test condition.

2. Timer contact 5A stuck or broken open—turn off the machine and reconnect the jumper wire from the previous test so that it bypasses both the selector switch and timer contact 5A (between points **J** and **L**). Start a normal wash cycle. This timer contact is at fault if the hot water now begins running into the machine.

3. Hot water solenoid defective—assuming that hot water *does not* run into the washer under the test conditions just described, connect a voltmeter across the solenoid contacts (between points **L** and **D**). If the meter shows full line voltage, but there is no evidence that the solenoid valve is being energized, the trouble is indeed in that assembly. Replace the hot water solenoid.

No water for rinse operations; wash fill and other operations normal

The cycle in this instance seems to stall out at the beginning of the rinse phase of the wash cycle. The reason for this observation is that the timer is stopped until the laundry tub is filled with rinse water; and whenever there is a fill problem, the cycle stalls indefinitely.

1. Rinse temperature selector switch S4 open—set the rinse temperature selector switch to COLD, and connect a jumper wire across the COLD terminal and common connection on that switch (between points **J** and **P**). Start the machine at a RINSE phase and note the response. The trouble is in the rinse temperature selector if the machine begins filling with cold water.

2. Timer contact 6B stuck or broken open—turn off the washer and reconnect the jumper wire from the previous test so that it

shorts out both the selector switch and timer contact 6B (between points **J** and **Q**). Start the machine at the beginning of a RINSE phase of the cycle. This timer contact is at fault if cold water now begins running into the machine.

3.   Cold water solenoid defective—assuming that cold water *does not* run into the machine under the test conditions described under trouble 2, connect a voltmeter across the cold water solenoid contacts (between points **Q** and **D**). Note the meter's response when the machine is started at the beginning of a RINSE phase. The cold water solenoid is at fault if the meter shows full line voltage, but water does not run into the machine. Replace the cold water solenoid.

No water in wash or rinse

Confirm this symptom by trying the cycle under the following conditions:

(A)   Set the timer knob to the beginning of a WASH operation, and switch the wash water temperature selector back and forth between HOT and WARM.

(B)   Set the timer knob to the beginning of a RINSE operation, and switch the rinse water temperature selector back and forth between WARM and COLD.

The symptoms are confirmed if water does not flow into the machine under either of these test conditions. If it happens that water does indeed flow into the machine under one or more of the conditions A or B, carefully redefine the symptoms and use the appropriate troubleshooting procedures described elsewhere in this section.

Confirming the symptoms leads to the possibility of a defective water level switch. To check this switch, set the timer knob to OFF, and connect a jumper wire between the common and EMPTY terminals on the water level switch S2 (between points **B** and **J**). This jumper bypasses the water level switch; if there is a broken contact in it, the jumper wire will provide a path for current flow that lets the fill operations begin.

Improper water temperature

1.   Low water temperature from the home's hot water supply—check the temperature of water from a different faucet in the

home. The hot water temperature should be between 140°F and 160°F. If the maximum water temperature is below this range, suggest that the homeowner set up the thermostat on the hot water tank.

2. Water supply hoses to the washer reversed, pinched or clogged—inspect the hoses for proper installation and any sort of obstruction. Also make certain that both water taps are turned on fully.

3. Wash water temperature selector switch defective—perform the following tests with the water hoses disconnected from the home's water supply system.

   Turn off the washer, set the timer control knob to the middle of the WASH phase, and connect one jumper across timer contact 5A (between points **K** and **L**) and a second jumper across timer contact 5B (between points **M** and **N**). Turn on the machine and check the voltage across the hot water solenoid with a voltmeter. Switch the wash temperature selector switch back and forth between HOT and WARM, noting the response on the voltmeter. Under normal conditions, full line voltage should appear across the hot water solenoid (between points **L** and **D**) whenever the selector switch is set to HOT. There should be no voltage across the warm water solenoid (between points **N** and **D**) at that setting, however. Setting the switch to WARM normally reverses these readings: full line voltage on the warm water solenoid and zero volts on the hot solenoid. Any departure from these test results indicates a defective wash temperature selector switch.

4. Rinse temperature selector switch defective—perform the following tests with the water hoses disconnected from the home's water supply system.

   Test the rinse temperature switch in a manner similar to that used for the wash temperature selector switch in the previous trouble. Connect the jumpers across 6A and 6B, however, and run the tests with the timer control knob set to the middle of a RINSE phase. Check the voltage across the warm and cold water solenoids while switching the cold water temperature selector back and forth between WARM and COLD. Under normal conditions, full line voltage should appear across the WARM solenoid whenever the selector switch is set to WARM, and there should be no voltage across the cold water solenoid at that setting. The readings are then reversed whenever the selector switch is set to COLD—full line voltage on the cold valve and none on the warm valve. If the voltage readings do not follow this pattern while the timer contacts are shorted out, the rinse water temperature selector switch is at fault.

5.   Timer switch contact 5A, 5B, 6A, or 6B defective—check the condition of these timer switches by repeating the tests recommended for the wash and rinse temperature selector switches in troubles 3 and 4. Run the tests in this instance, however, after removing all the jumper wires. Any lack of correspondence between the settings on the temperature selector switch and the water solenoids that are supposed to be energized with full line voltage indicates a defective timer contact. Of course this test assumes that the temperature selector switches are in good working order.

6.   Water valve solenoid mechanically defective—if any of the water solenoids receive full line voltage, but do not appear to be opening, they should be replaced.

Fill water does not stop flowing

1.   Water valve stuck open—this trouble is clearly present in instances where water can be stopped only by turning off the water supply to the machine. The water, in other words, cannot be stopped by simply setting the on/off switch to OFF. Remove the water valve assemblies and inspect them for some obvious cause of the trouble such as foreign objects jammed into the valves. Replace the entire valve assembly if a "quick fix" is impossible or impractical.

2.   Water level control switch S2 shorted—in this case, water does stop flowing whenever the on/off switch is set to OFF. To confirm the trouble, disconnect the wiring to the valve side of the water level switch (at point **J**), and start a washing cycle. The trouble is confirmed if water *does not* flow into the machine.

Water does not drain from machine; other operations normal

1.   Defective water control valve—the valve assembly responsible for rerouting the water from the washer's recirculation system to the drain system can fail mechanically. Remove this valve assembly from the machine and visually inspect it for obvious troubles, for example, broken parts or foreign objects jammed into the flapper valve. Replace the entire valve assembly if a repair seems impossible or impractical.

2. Transmission linkage to the water pump defective—visually inspect the linkage between the main drive transmission and the water pump. Look for obvious problems and consult the manufacturer's maintenance manual for additional troubleshooting and repair hints.

Timer does not run

It is important to confirm this symptom before starting a troubleshooting procedure in the timer motor circuit. The problem is that several troubles elsewhere in the washer can mimic this particular symptom.

To confirm the symptom, set the machine to start a normal washing cycle. If the water fill starts and ends normally, and if the agitation operation begins as it should, the symptom is confirmed— provided, of course, that the timer knob does not rotate out of the WASH phase.

1. Defective timer motor—turn off the washer and short out the fill operations by connecting a jumper wire across the water level control switch (between points **B** and **E**). Eliminate the possibility of an open timer contact by connecting a second jumper across timer contact 2 (between points **B** and **C**). Connect a voltmeter across the timer motor (between points **C** and **D**), and start the machine at the beginning of a WASH phase. The timer is at fault if full line voltage appears on the meter, but the timer knob does not turn under its own power.

2. Timer contact 2 stuck or broken open—if the timer motor runs normally under the test condition just described, remove the jumper across the timer contact (the one previously connected between points **B** and **C**), and note the response of the timer motor assembly. If the timer motor stops, the diagnosis of a faulty timer switch contact is confirmed.

Appliance blows fuses whenever it is started

The first step is to visually inspect the appliance for obvious signs of a short-circuit condition: burned wiring or signs of "flashing" between the wiring and the metal frame. If no such signs are apparent, eliminate major sections of the circuitry one at a time by disconnecting some of the wiring and applying power. Whenever the fuse or circuit breaker holds after a section has been disconnected, there can be little doubt that the trouble is in that particular section.

A closer visual inspection of the wiring and components in that section often uncovers the real trouble. Electrical continuity tests on each of the components in the suspected section might be necessary.

10-5 QUESTIONS

1. What are the four basic operations that make up any washing cycle?

2. Which of the two operations listed in question 1 are sometimes combined into one?

3. What is the basic advantage of a washer with nontimed fill operations compared to one with timed operations?

4. What determines the temperature of the water that fills the washing machine?

5. What is the purpose of a suds return feature?

6. What is the purpose of a door interlock switch on an automatic washer?

11

Electric Clothes Dryers

Automatic clothes dryers have made backyard clotheslines obsolete. The sight of a family's laundry flapping in the breeze on a sunny day is now a thing of the past, and although clothesline rope and wire and wooden clothespins are still available in many stores, the demand for them is slight.

Automatic clothes dryers have two main advantages over the old clothesline process. First, the laundry drying job is much faster with the automatic dryer: the user doesn't spend as much time setting up the process and the actual drying operation takes less time. The other advantage of an automatic drying scheme is that it can be used at any time of the day, in any season of the year, and under any sort of weather conditions.

11-1 GENERAL OPERATING PRINCIPLES

Figure 11-1 shows the basic sections of a typical automatic clothes dryer. The purpose of the forced-air blower is to draw in fresh air, force it through a heating assembly, and then channel it into the rotating hamper.

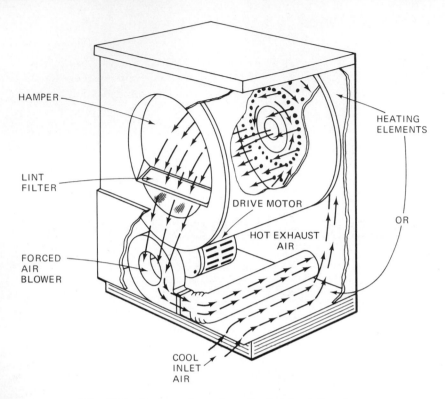

Fig. 11-1   Basic sections of an all-electric clothes dryer.

The warmed air picks up moisture from the laundry as it passes through the hamper; and the blower finally directs the moisture-laden air through a lint filter and out of the machine.

The heating assembly in an all-electric dryer consists of a set of nichrome heating elements situated in the force-air steam. The heating assembly in a gas dryer performs exactly the same function, but it uses gas flame heat.

The lint filter, located near the output end of the air stream, traps most of the dry, lightweight particles of lint and other foreign materials picked up by the moving air.

The electrical sections of modern clothes dryers can be rather simple compared to some other kinds of modern appliances. The basic electrical units of a dryer include heating controls that maintain a fairly constant drying temperature and a timer mechanism that turns off the machine at the end of a user-selected drying interval. The essential differences between the simpler dryer models and the top-of-the-line versions can be found in the number and types of heat and timer controls.

11-1.1 Typical Dryer Cycles

Most modern clothes dryers have at least two kinds of drying cycles, and some have as many as four. The following paragraphs describe these cycles in rather general terms. A more complete technical analysis of the cycles can be found in descriptions of specific dryers presented in Secs. 11-3 and 11-4.

THE BASIC TIMED DRYING CYCLE. All automatic dryers include a basic drying cycle that is normally labeled a TIMED cycle on the user's timer control knob. When operating in this mode, the machine tumbles the laundry continuously and regulates the heat level of the forced air throughout the entire drying interval. The tumbling and heating actions both stop at the end of the selected drying time. The user can set the drying interval to any point between zero and about 180 minutes, depending on the amount and wetness of the load.

A DELICATE CYCLE. The DELICATE cycle is intended for drying only delicate and permanent press fabrics. It so happens that modern artificial fabrics dry "wrinkle free" only if they are first dried with moderate heat, then tumbled for a short time without heat. The DELICATE cycle performs this sequence of operations through an interval selected by the user, tumbling the load without heat for about ten or twenty minutes before shutting off.

MOST DELICATE cycles completely shut down after the tumble-without-heat step is over. A few models, however, have a special feature that tumbles the laundry without heat for about one minute every five minutes or so. This on-off tumbling action takes place indefinitely, or until the user has a chance to turn off the machine and remove the laundry. The whole point of this special on-off tumbling action is to prevent creasing of the permanent press fabrics once the main drying sequence is over.

THE FLUFF CYCLE. A FLUFF cycle found on some machines simply tumbles the laundry without heat for a selected period of time. This cycle is especially useful in instances where the laundry has been lying dry in the machine, getting wrinkled or "stale" for some time.

AN AUTOMATIC CYCLE. This rather new drying cycle is reserved for better machines. The basic idea of the AUTOMATIC cycle is to run the tumbling and heating actions only long enough to dry the laundry. When using the normal TIMED cycle, for instance, the user has to reckon the drying time that is needed. If the timer interval is set too short, the laundry will still be damp when it is removed from the machine; setting the timed interval too long simply wastes electrical energy by heating laundry that is already dry.

The AUTOMATIC cycle does away with the need for reckoning the drying time because it automatically ends all operations the moment the laundry is dry—regardless of how long it takes to do the job. And furthermore, most machines equipped with this AUTOMATIC cycle also allow the user to select the level of dryness. The cycle, in other words, can be preset to turn off while the laundry is still slightly damp, or it can be set to run until the fabrics are bone dry.

11-1.2 User Controls

The type and number of user controls on an automatic dryer depend largely on the number of cycles the machine is capable of performing. In general, the greater the number of possible operating cycles, the more controls the user has at his or her disposal. (Figure 11-2 shows a typical AUTOMATIC clothes dryer.)

TIMER CONTROL KNOB. The timer control knob performs two important functions: it lets the user select the appropriate drying cycle and it lets her set the drying time (or dryness level in the case of an AUTOMATIC cycle.) See Fig. 11-3.

START SWITCH. The user initiates a drying cycle by depressing the start switch. This switch usually pops back out the moment the user releases it, but a latching circuit in the machine effectively holds the switch on.

The start switch can be located either in the center of the timer control knob or situated elsewhere on the control panel as a separate switch.

HEAT SELECTOR SWITCH. A heat selector switch lets the user choose a heating level appropriate for the kinds of fabrics in the machine. The idea is to lower the drying heat for delicate and permanent press fabrics.

TUMBLING SPEED SWITCH. A few dryers have a switch that sets the tumbling speed at either NORMAL or LOW. Lowering the tumbling rate makes the laundry dry more slowly, producing much the same effect as lowering the heat level.

11-2 GENERAL THEORY OF OPERATION

Modern clothes dryers include some scheme for timing the drying cycle, a main drive motor, a heater assembly, and a host of control switches and thermostats. The top-of-the-line models generally differ from the simpler models only in the complexity of the automatic controls.

11-2.1 The Main Drive Motor System

Electric clothes dryers use 120 V, split-phase drive motors having power ratings on the order of 1/3 hp (See Sec. 5-2.1 for operating details).

Fig. 11-2 This clothes dryer includes two AUTOMATIC cycles and a normal TIMED cycle. A wide selection of pushbutton controls let the user adjust the cycles and temperatures for different load and fabric conditions. (Courtesy of General Electric Major Appliance Group)

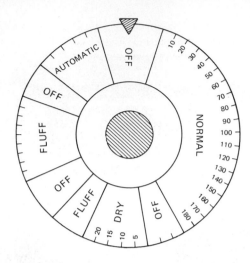

Fig. 11-3 A timer control dial for a typical automatic clothes dryer.

Even all-electric dryers having a nameplate rating of 240 V use a 120 V drive motor connected between one hot line and neutral.

The main drive motor normally runs the blower assembly directly at a speed of 1100–1700 rpm. The hamper is driven by the same motor, but a belt drive mechanism lowers the tumbling rate to 55–60 rpm.

The drive motor is self-lubricating thus requiring no routine maintenance. In fact the trend today is toward using more "throw-away" motors in dryers —motors that are built and priced in such a way that it is easier and cheaper to replace them than it is to fix them.

The start-up circuits for dryer motors are rather straightforward. Some use relay start-up circuits, but most have a centrifugal switch start-up mechanism. See Sec. 5-3.1. Modern dryers seldom have electrical motor speed controls; and even the machines that do allow the user to adjust the tumbling speed use a mechanical gearing arrangement. Automatic dryers equipped with an adjustable speed control have a fixed-speed motor with a tapered shaft. A mechanical linkage slides the drive belt up and down along the motor shaft to change the motor-to-drum pulley ratio.

Motor direction controls do not apply at all to automatic clothes dryers.

11-2.2 Timer Motor Assembly

A standard timing assembly for automatic dryers consists of a 120 V shaded-pole motor, a reducing gear, and a set of leaf-type switch contacts, which open and close the appropriate electrical circuits.

Actually there is no essential difference between the timing mechanism in a clothes dryer and that found in automatic dishwashers and clothes washers. See details in Sec. 9-2.1. The timing cams in dryer units are generally simpler, however, because a drying cycle often amounts to little more than turning off the motor and heating coils after a selected time interval has passed.

11-2.3   Cycle Start and Stop Circuit

Figure 11-4 illustrates a typical start-up and stop circuit for an electric dryer. Line power is fed to the motor circuit via a door interlock safety switch and a timer switch. The purpose of the interlock switch is to shut down all dryer operations whenever the hamper door is opened during an ongoing cycle. The timer switch opens at the end of the drying cycle to stop all operations.

Setting the timer switch to start a drying cycle closes the timer contact, and closing the hamper door closes the interlock switch. When the user depresses the normally open START pushbutton, it completes a circuit through both the timer motor and the main drive motor's start and run windings. Both motors begin running, and as the drive motor approaches its normal operating speed, its centrifugal switch contact swings out to its RUN position.

Two things happen whenever the centrifugal switch moves to its RUN position. First, it cuts the motor's start winding out of the circuit to provide more efficient running. More important, it bypasses the user's START pushbutton so that it can be released without interrupting ongoing operations. The user has to hold down the START button only long enough for the centrifugal switch to close—and that is normally a matter of one second or less.

Resetting this start-up circuit is accomplished by interrupting power to the main drive motor long enough to let the centrifugal switch fall back to its

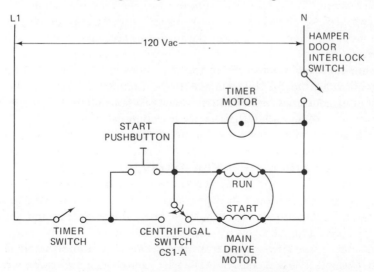

Fig. 11-4   Start-up and stop circuit for an electric dryer.

START position. Opening the hamper door, for instance, cuts off power to the drive motor and resets the circuit. The motor does not start the moment the door is closed again because the centrifugal switch is in its START position and no longer bypasses the user's START pushbutton. The machine has to be restarted by depressing the START button once again.

Of course the timer automatically resets the circuit when it opens the timer contact.

11-2.4   Heat Control Circuits

The term *speed control* can be confusing to a repairman studying clothes dryers for the first time. The problem is that the term can have two entirely different meanings. One would normally think that *speed control* has something to do with the rate of rotation of the hamper drum. This can be the case, but it rarely is.

As the term is used most often in connection with automatic clothes dryers, *speed control* refers to the rate at which the clothes are dried. And since the rate of drying is directly related to the amount of heat generated in the heating assembly, changing the speed control setting actually changes the amount of heat applied to the laundry. Delicate and permanent press fabrics should be dried much more slowly (at a lower temperature) than normal fabrics; and it is the dryer's heat control that determines the amount of heat to be applied and, hence, the drying speed.

Figure 11-5 shows a simplified electrical diagram of a typical two-heat control circuit. The two heating elements, H1 and H2, are connected in series across the 240 V lines. Whenever the heat selector switch is set to LOW, both heating elements are in the circuit; and as they divide the line voltage between them, their total power consumption is on the order of 4000 W.

Setting the heat selector switch to HIGH, however, shorts H1 out of the circuit, allowing the full line voltage to be applied to H2. This heating element thus consumes its full rated power of about 6000 W, producing a greater amount of heat than the series connection can.

The B section of the heat selector switch determines which one of two control thermostats will operate the heater circuit. Setting the heat selector switch to HIGH shorts out H1 as just described; but at the same time, it connects the high heat thermostat (TH2) in series with the heater circuit.

TH2 is factory calibrated to open at a temperature between 140° and 160°F. As the temperature of the hamper rises, then, the contacts of TH2 bend in a direction that eventually opens them. When the thermostat contacts open, power is removed from the heater circuit and the air flow is allowed to cool. The contacts of TH2 ease closed again as the operating temperature falls, and they eventually close to reapply power to the heater circuit.

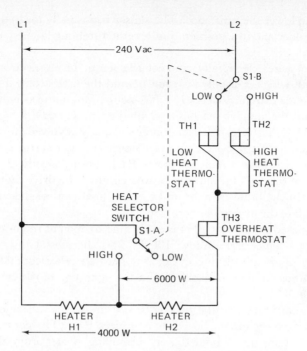

Fig. 11-5 A typical heat selector circuit for electric dryers.

Whenever the temperature control switch is set to HIGH, then, TH2 controls the operating temperature by switching heating power on and off at the appropriate times.

Setting the temperature selector switch to LOW places both heating elements in series across the 240 V line and connects the low heat thermostat TH1 into the circuit. TH1 thus controls the operating temperature, usually in the range of 110°–120°F.

Note that TH3 is connected in series with the heating circuit, regardless of the setting of the heat selector switch. This thermostat is calibrated to open only at temperatures on the order of 170°–200°—a temperature level that is well above the trip point of either control thermostat. TH3 thus opens only in the event of a serious overheating condition. Many dryer models have a similar kind of overheat thermostat connected in series with the entire appliance feed line. An overheating condition in this case completely shuts down the machine.

11-2.5   Electronic Dryness Control

An electronic dryness control is used only in machines featuring an AUTOMATIC drying cycle (see Sec. 11-1.1). This circuit uses a sensor that changes resistance according to the wetness of the laundry; the wetter the clothing, the lower the resistance. The sensor is normally located just inside the hamper door and in a position that lets the tumbling laundry wipe across it.

A pair of wires electrically connect the sensor to an electronic printed circuit board, which is usually fastened behind the user's control panel. The electronic control circuit is actually a fast-acting automatic switch that turns off the instant the laundry reaches a selected dryness level.

Figure 11-6 illustrates the components directly involved in one type of automatic moisture control circuit. Whenever the user starts a load of wet laundry, the electronic circuit energizes RL1, closing electrical contacts to both the main drive motor and the heater circuit. The drive motor tumbles the laundry in the usual manner and a set of heat control thermostats (not shown) regulate the drying temperature.

An additional thermostat TH4 is calibrated to open at room temperature and close at a temperature above 100°F. This thermostat thus closes very early in the automatic drying cycle, but because relay contact RL1-A is closed, TH4 has no direct influence upon the operation of the circuit at that time.

As the laundry dries to the selected level, the sensor resistance increases to a point where the circuit board de-energizes RL1. The contacts of RL1 respond by falling open, immediately removing power from the heating circuit. The operating temperature of the hamper, however, is still high enough to hold TH4 closed and keep the main drive motor running.

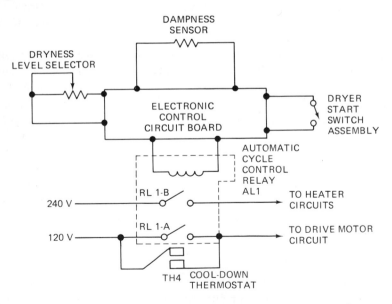

Fig. 11-6 Diagram of an automatic dryness control system.

The drive motor continues tumbling the laundry without heat until the load is cooled enough to allow TH4 to open. And once that thermostat opens, all operations cease and the automatic cycle is complete.

If a piece of wet laundry should pass across the sensor during the cool-down interval, the circuit is completely reset—the relay closes to reapply heat to the circuit. A moment later the circuit will de-energize again to restart the cool-down phase.

All machines equipped with this electronic drying cycle work in a similar fashion. Some use the electronic circuit to control the operation of the timer motor, however. The circuit board in these models short out the timer motor until the selected drying level is reached. At that time, the electronic circuit turns off the heat and allows the timer motor to start. The timer motor then controls the length of the cool-down interval.

11-3 A SIMPLE TWO-CYCLE AUTOMATIC DRYER

The dryer circuit shown in Fig. 11-7 features NORMAL and PERMA-NENT PRESS cycles and a HIGH/LOW heat selector switch. This is a rather simple circuit, but it is representative of most automatic dryers on the market today.

11-3.1 Theory of Operation

Figure 11-7(B) shows the timing diagram for this dryer. The NORMAL drying cycle can occupy up to 180 minutes, or ninety two-minute increments. During the drying time, the main drive motor tumbles the clothes continuously, and the heater circuit regulates the temperature level in the hamper. The PERMANENT PRESS cycle occupies a total of thirty minutes, or fifteen two-minute increments. When using the PERMANENT PRESS cycle, the user can adjust the first drying phase to run as long as twenty minutes. The fluff or cool-down phase, however, always runs ten minutes at the end of the cycle.

Referring to the schematic and timing diagram in Fig. 11-7(B), suppose that the user wants to run a NORMAL cycle at HIGH for thirty minutes. The user loads the laundry into the hamper, closes the door, sets the timer knob to "30" on the NORMAL cycle, sets the heat selector switch to HIGH, and momentarily depresses the START pushbutton. The user notes that the dryer starts running, and can walk away from the machine for thirty minutes, returning to find the machine completely turned off and the laundry dry.

Retracing these steps from an electrical point of view, closing the hamper door closes the door interlock switch S1, and rotating the timer knob away from its OFF position closes timer contacts 1 and 2. Setting the heat selector switch S3 to HIGH shorts out heating element H1 and connects the high heat

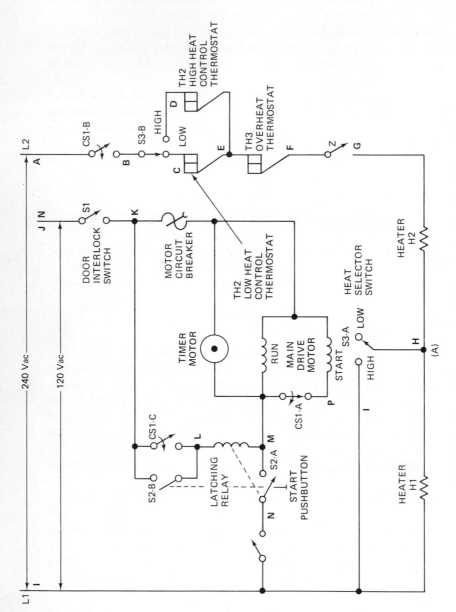

Fig. 11-7 A typical two-cycle all-electric dryer: (A) Schematic diagram, (B) Timing diagram.

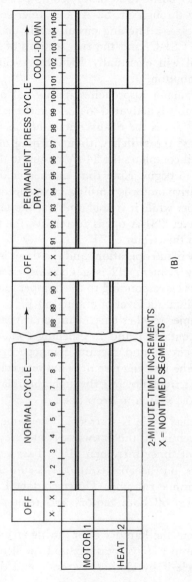

Fig. 11-7 (Continued)

control thermostat TH1 into the heater circuit. There are, however, no complete circuits to either the motors or heaters at this time.

Depressing the START pushbutton finally completes a 120 V circuit to the timer and drive motors through S1, S2-A, and timer contact 1. Closing the START switch also energizes a latching circuit made up of a relay coil, centrifugal switch contact CS1-C, and the two sections of S2. Current flowing through the relay coil will eventually hold S2-A closed when the user releases the START pushbutton.

As the main drive motor approaches its normal operating speed, the centrifugal switch assembly is activated to perform three important functions. First, closing CS1-C bypasses the S2-B contact of the START pushbutton so that the user can release the switch without turning off the machine. The moment CS1-B closes, it completes the 240 V circuit to the heater and allows the heating operation to begin. Note that the heater does not receive any power until the main drive motor is running up to speed—heat should never be applied to the hamper while it is not tumbling the laundry. And finally, centrifugal switch contact CS1-A opens to remove the start winding of the main drive motor from the circuit.

The machine is now in full operation, and the timer is running through its NORMAL cycle. Heating element H2 is generating an equivalent of about 6000 W of heat, and TH2 is responding to the hamper temperature by cycling open and closed to maintain a level of about 150°F.

The moment the timer reaches OFF, at increment 90 on the timing diagram, it opens timer contacts 1 and 2. Opening contact 2 removes 240 V power from the heater circuit, and opening contact 1 breaks open the 120 V circuit to the motors. The latching circuit is automatically reset at the same instant because current stops flowing through the relay coil, allowing the S2-A section of the START switch to drop open.

The PERMANENT PRESS cycle is started in the same way as the NORMAL cycle, but it ends differently. In the PERMANENT PRESS cycle, the timer opens contact 2 at the end of timer increment 100. This action removes 240 V power from the heaters, but because contact 1 is still closed, the timer and main drive motors continue running. Timer contact 1 finally opens at the end of the cycle to turn off both motors and reset the start-up latching circuit.

If the user ever opens the hamper door during an ongoing drying cycle, the timer stops, the hamper stops rotating, and the heat goes off. The only way to resume the cycle is by closing the door and depressing the START pushbutton again.

Electrically speaking, opening the hamper door during a drying cycle interrupts the 120 V circuit to the main drive motor. The drive motor thus slows down and allows the centrifugal switches to fall to their off positions. CS1-B in the 240 V heater circuit, for instance, opens to remove power from the heater circuit. Likewise, CS1-C opens to turn off the latching relay and reset that circuit. The electrical condition of the dryer during an interrupted cycle is exactly the same as the original start-up condition.

11-3.2 Troubleshooting Guide

The following troubleshooting notes apply to the automatic dryer circuit illustrated in Fig. 11-7.

Machine does not start at all

Carefully distinguish this symptom from one where the machine starts, but stops the moment the START pushbutton is released.

1. No power to the dryer—check the voltage applied to the motor circuit (between points **I** and **J**) with a voltmeter. The trouble is confirmed if no voltage is present. Inspect the power cable and service branch for poor connections.

2. Drive motor circuit breaker open—the dryer most likely has a pushbutton circuit breaker mounted on or near the motor housing. Make certain that this button is depressed and held in.

3. Door interlock switch S1 stuck or broken open—set the timer knob to OFF, and connect a jumper wire across the terminals on the door interlock switch (between points **J** and **K**). Attempt to start a drying cycle. If the cycle starts normally, the trouble is confirmed. Replace S1.

4. Start pushbutton S2 open—set the timer knob to OFF, and disconnect the jumper wire connected across S1 in the previous test. Connect the jumper across the start pushbutton (between points **M** and **N**), and attempt to start a drying cycle—with the hamper door closed, of course. If the cycle starts with this jumper in place, but stops again when it is disconnected, the trouble is confirmed. Replace the start switch assembly.

5. Timer contact 1 stuck or broken open—assuming that the dryer cannot be started under the first four test conditions described here, set the timer knob to OFF, and remove any jumper wires. Bypass the suspected timer contact with a jumper wire (between points **N** and **I**). If the machine can be started with this jumper in place, the trouble is indeed in that timer contact. Replace the entire timer contact assembly.

6. Centrifugal switch contact CS1-A stuck or broken open—the purpose of this switch contact is to place the start winding of the

main drive motor into the motor circuit. If this switch is stuck open, the main drive motor might "buzz" and draw current, but it cannot start. To confirm this diagnosis, connect a jumper wire across the CS1-A contacts (between points **M** and **P**), and attempt to start a drying cycle. The trouble is confirmed if the motor starts and the drying cycle begins normally. Replace the entire centrifugal switch assembly.

7.   Main drive motor defective—if the dryer fails to start under any of the previous six tests just described, there can be little doubt that the trouble is in the main drive motor system. The process of elimination is responsible for this logical conclusion.

Remove the main drive motor from the machine and test its windings according to the procedures outlined in Sec. 5-4. Consult the manufacturer's specifications for further motor-testing details.

Cycle begins before the start button is depressed

In this instance the drying cycle begins the moment the hamper door is closed and the timer is set for any drying interval—the machine starts *before* the start pushbutton is depressed.

The most likely cause of this trouble is a set of shorted contacts in the start switch S2. Set the timer knob to OFF, and disconnect the wires fastened to the A-section terminals of S2 (at points **M** and **N**). Check the continuity of the switch contacts with a continuity tester or ohmmeter. Under normal circumstances, this switch shows infinite resistance when it is not depressed and zero resistance or good continuity whenever it is depressed. The switch is causing the start-up trouble, however, if it shows zero resistance or good continuity, whether it is depressed or not.

Machine starts and runs, but timer does not cycle

There can be little doubt that the timer motor is at fault. Remove the timer motor from the circuit and try running it "on the bench." The trouble is confirmed if the motor does not run. If it turns out that the timer motor does run when disconnected from the circuit, look for foreign objects or broken parts in the timer switch assembly that might be binding the motor.

Note: The timer motor is rated at 120 V, even in instances where the dryer is rated at 240 V. Bench-test the motor at 120 V.

Machine runs only while the start button is depressed

1. Centrifugal switch contact CS1-C stuck or broken open—set the timer control knob to OFF, and bypass the suspected switch contact with a jumper wire (between points **L** and **K**). Attempt to start a drying cycle. If the machine starts and continues to run after releasing the start pushbutton, the trouble is confirmed. Replace the entire centrifugal switch assembly.

2. Latching relay coil defective—turn off the machine and remove the latching relay assembly from the circuit. Test the resistance of the relay coil with an ohmmeter and compare the result with the manufacturer's specifications. Replace the relay assembly if the figures do not match.

Drying operation does not stop at the end of a cycle

Shorting out timer contact 1 causes this particular set of symptoms. To check this diagnosis, set the timer knob to OFF, and disconnect the wiring to timer contact 1 (at points **N** and **I**). With the timer still set to OFF, test the continuity of the suspected timer contact with a continuity tester or ohmmeter. If this test shows good continuity or zero resistance, the contact is either stuck or internally shorted. Replace the entire timer switch assembly.

Machine starts, but heat goes off during the cycle

Carefully distinguish this trouble from one where the heat does not go on at all.

1. Blower defective or air duct clogged—an automatic dryer runs properly only when there is a free flow of air through the system. The most common cause of this trouble is a build-up of lint in the air duct leading out of the machine. Make certain that the air duct is cleared and that the blower is running properly.

2. Thermostat TH1 or TH2 shorted or stuck closed—the first step is to determine which one of the two control thermostats is at fault. It turns out that the trouble is in TH1 if the symptom appears only when the machine is operating at LOW heat, and that it is in TH2 if the symptom shows up only when operating at HIGH.

The next step is to make certain that the heat is turning off because of an overheat condition that is tripping open the overheat thermostat TH3. Connect a 240 V voltmeter across the contacts of the overheat thermostat (between points **E** and **F**), set the heat selector switch for the troubled heat level, and start a drying cycle. If the overheat thermostat trips open at some time during the cycle, as indicated by the sudden appearance of 240 V on the meter, the suspected control thermostat is indeed sticking closed. Replace the defective control thermostat assembly.

If, on the other hand, the heat goes off during the drying cycle, but 240 V does not appear on the meter, reconnect the meter across the suspected control thermostat (between points **C** and **E** for the LOW heat control or between points **D** and **E** for the HIGH heat thermostat). If the voltage across the suspected control thermostat is 240 V, and if that voltage level remains for five minutes or more, the contacts are now sticking open.

Whether these tests show that the control thermostat is sticking open or closed, it must be replaced.

Motor runs, but no heat at either heat setting

1. Heating element H2 open—set the timer knob to OFF, and set the heat selector switch to LOW. Connect an ohmmeter across heating element H2 (between points **G** and **H**), and note the resistance. The trouble is confirmed if this test shows infinite resistance. Replace the heater assembly.

2. Timer contact 2 open—connect a 240 V voltmeter across timer contact 2 (between points **F** and **G**), and set the timer knob to start a drying cycle. The contact is stuck open if the meter shows 240 V.

3. Overheat thermostat TH3 open—connect a 240 V voltmeter across the overheat thermostat contacts (between points **F** and **G**), and start a drying cycle. This thermostat contact is stuck open if the meter shows 240 V the moment the main drive motor starts.

4. Centrifugal switch contact CS1-B stuck or broken open—set the timer to OFF, and connect a jumper wire across the contacts of CS1-B (between points **A** and **B**). Attempt to start a drying cycle, and note the machine's response. The trouble is confirmed if the heat goes on.

This diagnosis can be doubly confirmed by removing the jumper wire across CS1-B and replacing it with a voltmeter. The centrifugal switch is indeed at fault if the meter shows 240 V while the main drive motor is running.

5. Heat selector switch S3-B stuck or broken open—connect a voltmeter across the B-section contacts of the heat selector switch S3 (between points **B** and **C**), and start a drying cycle. A reading of 240 V on the meter indicates an open switch that must be replaced.

No heat at low heat setting; motor runs normally, high heat normal

1. Heating element H1 open—set the timer knob to OFF, and set the heat selector switch to LOW. Connect an ohmmeter across heating element H1 (between points **H** and **I**), and note the resistance. A reading of infinity is a clear indication of an open heating element. Compare any other resistance reading with the manufacturer's specifications.

2. LOW heat control thermostat TH1 stuck or broken open—set the timer knob to OFF, and set the heat selector switch to HIGH. Connect a continuity tester or ohmmeter across the contacts of TH1 (between points **C** and **E**), and note the reading. The trouble is confirmed if the test shows no continuity or infinite resistance. Under normal circuit conditions, the contact should be closed at room temperature, and the test should show good continuity or zero resistance.

Low heat at high setting; low heat operation normal and motor runs normally

The most likely trouble is open or broken contacts in the heat selector switch S3-A. To check this diagnosis, connect a voltmeter across heating element H1 (between points **H** and **I**), set the heat control selector to HIGH, and start a drying cycle. The trouble is confirmed if the meter shows any voltage above three or four volts.

No heat at high setting; low heat setting normal

The high heat control thermostat TH2 is most likely stuck or broken open. Set the timer control knob to OFF, and set the heat selector switch to LOW. Connect a continuity tester or ohmmeter across the contacts of TH2 (between points **D** and **E**), and note the result. The trouble is confirmed if this test shows no continuity or infinite resistance.

Motor does not stop when door is opened during a cycle

The door interlock switch S1 is most likely shorted out or stuck closed to create this symptom. Inspect the door switch to make certain it operates freely. To check this switch electrically, set the timer knob to OFF, and disconnect the wiring to one of the terminals on the door interlock switch (at either point **B** or **C**). Check the continuity of the switch with a continuity tester or ohmmeter. If this test shows good continuity or zero resistance while the hamper door is open, the trouble is confirmed. Replace the interlock switch assembly.

Heat does not go off during cool-down phase of the permanent press cycle

Timer switch 2 is the most likely cause of this trouble. The simplest way to check this contact is by unplugging the dryer, setting the timer control knob to the cool-down phase of the PERMANENT PRESS cycle, and checking the contacts of timer switch 2 with an ohmmeter or continuity tester. Under these test conditions, the check should show a complete lack of continuity or infinite resistance. Any other reading indicates a shorted timer contact, and the timer contact assembly must be replaced.

11-4 A "DELUXE" FOUR-CYCLE AUTOMATIC DRYER

The automatic dryer illustrated in Fig. 11-8(A) is representative of the top-of-the-line models on the market today. As shown on the timing diagram in Fig. 11-8(B), the machine features four basic drying cycles: TIMED, WASH-AND-WEAR, FLUFF, and AUTOMATIC. These cycles are described completely in Sec. 11-1.1.

The user's controls include the usual timer knob, start pushbutton, a drying temperature selector switch, and a dryness selector knob for the AUTOMATIC cycle. Other features not shown on the diagram could include a fluorescent or incandescent lamp over the control panel, an interior light that goes on whenever the hamper door is opened, an indicator light that goes on

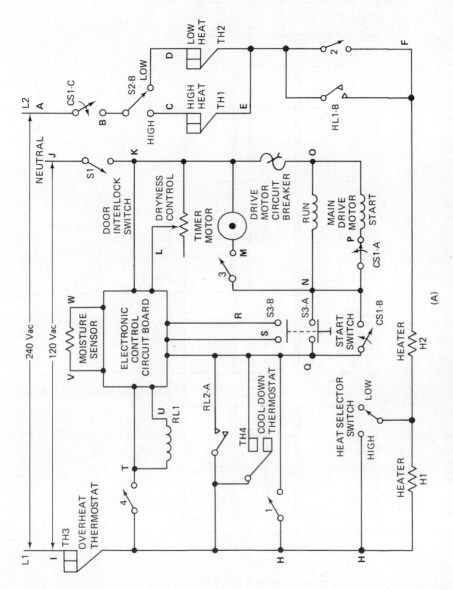

Fig. 11-8 A four-cycle dryer: (A) Schematic diagram, (B) Timing diagram.

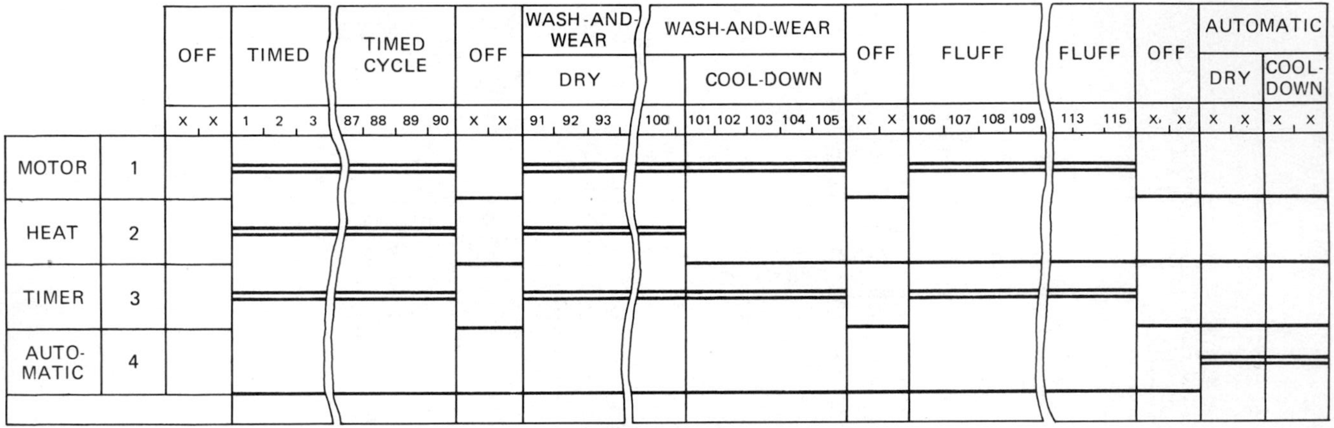

TIMED — OFF

TIMED CYCLE — 87 88 89 90

OFF

WASH-AND-WEAR — DRY — 91 92 93

WASH-AND-WEAR — COOL-DOWN — 100 101 102 103 104 105

OFF

FLUFF — 106 107 108 109

FLUFF — 113 115

OFF

AUTOMATIC — DRY

AUTOMATIC — COOL-DOWN

TIMED — 1 2 3

		OFF	TIMED
MOTOR	1	X	X
HEAT	2		
TIMER	3		
AUTO-MATIC	4		

2-MINUTE TIME INCREMENTS
X = NONTIMED SEGMENTS

(B)

Fig. 11-8 (Continued)

while a cycle is in progress, and a buzzer that sounds the moment a drying cycle is completed.

11-4.1 Theory of Operation

Suppose that the user wants to set up a normal TIMED drying operation at HIGH heat. The user loads the hamper, closes the hamper door, sets the timer to a desired drying time on the TIMED cycle, sets the heat selector switch to HIGH, and momentarily depresses the START pushbutton.

Closing the hamper door closes S1 to the neutral line, rotating the timer knob to any portion of the TIMED cycle, closes timer contacts 1, 2, and 3. Depressing the START pushbutton can then complete a 120 V circuit to the main drive motor through S1, the run and start windings of the main drive motor, the A-section of S3 and timer contact 1. The main drive motor thus begins running, throwing closed centrifugal switch contact CS1-B to latch the start circuit. The timer begins running at the same instant because of its complete circuit through timer contact 3.

Setting the heat selector switch S2 to HIGH both shorts out heater H1 and connects the high temperature control thermostat TH2 into the 240 V heater circuit. As the main drive motor reaches its normal operating speed, CS1-C in the heater circuit closes to apply full line power to H2 through timer contact 2.

The motors run continuously through all ninety possible increments of the TIMED drying cycle. The heater circuit, however, cycles on and off as TH2 maintains the high heat level in the hamper.

At the end of the TIMED cycle, at timer increment 90, all timer switches drop open. Opening timer contact 1 breaks the 120 V circuit to the motors, letting both motors stop running; as a result, the timing cycle ends, and all centrifugal switches fall to their off states. For all practical purposes, then, the machine is completely reset for the start of another cycle.

If the user should ever open the hamper door during an ongoing TIMED cycle, S1 in the motor circuit opens to remove power to the timer and main drive motors. And whenever the main drive motor stops running, its centrifugal switches turn off the heat and reset the start-up circuit. The cycle can be resumed from the point of interruption by closing the hamper door and depressing the START pushbutton.

The WASH-AND-WEAR cycle, sometimes called the DELICATE or PERMANENT PRESS cycle, operates in much the same fashion as the TIMED cycle described above. The only real differences are that the WASH-AND-WEAR cycle is shorter, and that it runs through the final ten minutes (increments 101–105) without heat. Note on the timing diagram that timer contact 2 in the 240 V heater circuit opens through the fluff phase of the WASH-AND-WEAR cycle.

The FLUFF cycle runs between timer increments 106 and 115 with timer contacts 1 and 3 closed. The timer motor and main drive motor are thus allowed to run throughout the FLUFF cycle; but because timer contact 2 is open during this particular cycle, there is never any heat applied to the hamper.

The user sets up the AUTOMATIC cycle by loading the hamper, closing the hamper door, selecting a heating level, setting the timer knob to AUTOMATIC, and selecting a level on the DRYNESS control. The machine then starts the moment the START pushbutton is depressed. The AUTOMATIC cycle runs with tumbling and heat until the laundry reaches the desired level of dryness. At that time the heat is turned off, but the tumbling action continues until the laundry is cooled.

According to the timing diagram in Fig. 11-8(B), timer switch 4 is the only timer contact that is closed during the AUTOMATIC cycle—all operations are under the control of the electronic control circuit board.

Closing timer contact 4 applies 120 V power to the electronic control board, and whenever that board is energized with wet laundry in the hamper, it activates relay RL1. Activating RL1 closes contact RL1-A in the motor circuit so that the main drive motor starts the moment the user depresses the START pushbutton. RL1 also closes contact RL1-B in the 240 V heater circuit; and as soon as the main drive motor closes CS1-C, the heater circuit is completed.

The main drive motor continues running and the chosen heat control thermostat, TH1 or TH2, regulates the heating level as long as the electronic control board keeps RL1 activated. The cool-down thermostat TH4 closes early in the heating phase of the AUTOMATIC cycle, but it has no real effect on operations at that point.

The dampness sensor eventually signals the desired dryness level has been reached, and the circuit board responds by de-energizing RL1. Both relay contacts, RL1-A and -B thus drop open to initiate the cool-down phase. Opening RL1-B turns off the heater circuit, but the main drive motor continues running because the cool-down thermostat contacts are still closed. The main drive motor runs until the contacts of TH4 open at cool-down level of 90°–100°F.

11-4.2   Troubleshooting Guide

Although the following troubleshooting notes apply specifically to the automatic dryer illustrated in Fig. 11-8, the general principles can be extended to similar machines on the market today. The boldface letters indicate circuit test points that commonly appear in dryer circuits of this type.

Note: The electronic control board should be serviced only by an individual who is fully qualified to troubleshoot, test, and repair modern semiconductor electronic circuits. Most dryer manufacturers recommend replacing the board whenever symptoms and preliminary tests indicate an electronic trouble.

Machine does not start at all in any cycle

Carefully distinguish this symptom from one where the machine starts, but stops the moment the START pushbutton is released.

1. No power to the dryer—check the voltage applied to the motor circuit (between points **I** and **J**) with a voltmeter. This trouble is confirmed if no voltage is present. Inspect the power cable, service branch, and circuit breaker panel for bad connections or a blown circuit breaker.

2. Drive motor circuit breaker open—the dryer most likely has a red pushbutton circuit breaker mounted on or near the main drive motor housing. Make certain that this button is depressed and held in. To check for a defective circuit breaker, connect a voltmeter across it (between points **K** and **O**), and attempt to start a TIMED drying cycle. If 120 V appears across the circuit breaker whenever the START pushbutton is depressed, the breaker is defective and should be replaced.
    Note: Be prepared to look for a motor circuit trouble that caused the circuit breaker to fail.

3. Overheat thermostat contacts open—the overheat thermostat in this circuit opens at about 200°F and holds open until the hamper temperature drops to about 100°F. In the event of any overheating condition, this thermostat completely shuts down the machine until it is cool. This thermostat is one likely candidate for a trouble where the machine cannot be started, even when it is cool.
    To check the condition of TH3, set the timer to OFF, and bypass the thermostat contacts with a jumper wire (between points **H** and **L**). Attempt to start a TIMED drying cycle, and note the machine's response. The overheat thermostat is indeed defective if the cycle starts under this test condition. CAUTION: Do not allow the machine to run more than a few moments with a jumper wire bypassing the overheat thermostat.

4. Door interlock switch S1 stuck or broken open—set the timer knob to OFF, and connect a jumper wire across the terminals of the door interlock switch (between points **J** and **K**). Attempt to

start a TIMED drying cycle. The trouble is confirmed if the machine now starts and runs normally. Replace S1.

5. Start pushbutton S3 open—set the timer knob to OFF, and disconnect any jumper wires connected for previous tests. Clip a jumper wire across the START pushbutton (between points **N** and **Q**), and attempt to start a TIMED drying cycle. If the cycle starts, but stops again when the jumper is removed, the trouble is confirmed. Of course this test must be carried out with the hamper door closed.

6. Centrifugal switch contact CS1-A stuck or broken open—connect a jumper wire across the contacts of this centrifugal switch (between points **N** and **P**), and attempt to start a drying cycle. The trouble is confirmed if the motor starts and the cycle begins normally. Replace the entire centrifugal switch assembly.

7. Main drive motor defective—if the dryer fails to start under any of the previous six tests just described, there can be little doubt that the trouble is in the main drive motor system.

   Remove the main drive motor from the machine and test its windings according to the procedures outlined in Sec. 5-4. Consult the manufacturer's specifications for further details concerning motor tests.

Machine starts only in the automatic cycle

The most likely cause of this symptom is a set of open or broken contacts in timer switch 1. Set the timer knob to OFF, and bypass timer switch 1 with a jumper wire (between points **H** and **Q**). Attempt to start a TIMED cycle, and note the machine's response. The trouble is in that timer contact if the cycle starts immediately and stops the instant the jumper is disconnected. Replace the timer switch assembly.

Machine does not start in the automatic cycle; other cycles normal

1. Moisture sensor open—disconnect the wires to the moisture sensor (at points **V** and **W**), and measure the resistance of the sensor with an ohmmeter. The trouble is confirmed if this test shows infinite resistance. Consult the manufacturer's specifications for the proper resistance reading.

2. Timer contact 4 stuck or broken open—assuming that the moisture sensor checks good according to the test in the previous

trouble, test the timer contact by setting the timer control knob to OFF and connecting a jumper wire across timer contact 4 (between points **H** and **T**). Connect a second jumper wire across the sensor contacts (between points **V** and **W**), and attempt to start an AUTOMATIC cycle. The trouble is in the timer contact if this cycle starts under these test conditions.

Note: It is important to short-circuit the moisture sensor when testing the AUTOMATIC cycle without loading the hamper with wet clothing. Otherwise, the electronic control will "read" a dry load and immediately shut down.

3. Relay RL1 defective—remove the jumper wire connected across timer contact 4 during the previous test, but do not disconnect the jumper across the moisture sensor. Connect a voltmeter across the relay coil (between points **T** and **U**), and attempt to start the AUTOMATIC cycle. If 120 V appears on the meter, but the machine does not start, the trouble is in the relay assembly.

It is possible to doublecheck this diagnosis by observing the voltage across the contacts of RL1-A while depressing the START pushbutton in the AUTOMATIC mode. If 120 V appears on the meter, even when the START button is depressed, the trouble is doubly confirmed. Replace the relay assembly, RL1.

4. Electronic control board defective—if the machine fails to start under the previous three test conditions, the process of elimination leads to a trouble in the electronic control circuit. Replace the electronic control circuit board with a new one.

Timed cycles start, but timer does not advance

1. Timer contact 3 open—set the timer control to OFF, and clip a jumper wire across timer contact 3 (between points **M** and **N**). Start a TIMED cycle, and note the timer's response. The trouble is confirmed if the timer now advances normally. Replace the timer switch assembly.

2. Timer motor defective—remove the timer motor from the machine, and try running it on the bench. The trouble is confirmed if the motor does not run.

Machine runs only while the start button is depressed

The most likely cause of this symptom is an open contact in the centrifugal switch section, CS1-B. Set the timer control knob to OFF, and bypass the suspected centrifugal switch contact with a jumper wire (between points **N** and **Q**). Start a TIMED cycle. If the machine starts and continues running after releasing the START pushbutton, the centrifugal switch is the cause of the trouble. Replace the entire centrifugal switch assembly.

Tumbling action does not stop at the end of timed cycles

1. Timer contact 1 shorted—set the timer control knob to OFF, and disconnect the wiring to timer contact 1 (at point **Q** or **H**). Check the continuity of the timer contact with an ohmmeter or continuity tester. The switch is indeed shorted if this test shows zero resistance or good continuity.

2. Cool-down thermostat TH4 contacts shorted or stuck closed— set the timer control knob to OFF, and disconnect the wiring to one terminal on the cool-down thermostat (at point **Q** or **H**). Check the continuity of the contacts with an ohmmeter or continuity tester. The thermostat is shorted if the test shows zero resistance or good continuity.

3. Relay contacts RL1-A shorted or stuck closed—with the timer control knob still set to OFF, disconnect the wiring to one terminal of contact RL1-A (at point **Q** or **H**). Check the continuity of the contacts with an ohmmeter or continuity tester. As in the case of the timer contact and thermostat, a reading of zero resistance or good continuity indicates a shorted relay contact. Replace the entire relay assembly.

Timer motor runs during automatic cycle

This symptom is a clear indication that timer contact 3 is shorted or stuck closed. Replace the timer switch assembly.

Automatic cycle does not end; other cycles normal

1. Start switch contacts S3-B shorted—closing S3-B at the beginning of an AUTOMATIC cycle simulates a "perfectly wet" load of laundry, thus resetting the electronic control board to its proper starting point. If this switch contact is shorted, however, the control circuit is fooled into reading a wet load at all times, and it never cycles off.

To check the switch contacts, remove the wiring leading to them (at points **R** and **S**), and test the switch contacts with an ohmmeter or continuity tester. If the test shows zero resistance or good continuity whenever the START button is *not* depressed, the trouble is confirmed. Replace the START switch assembly.

2. Moisture sensor shorted—set the timer control knob to OFF, disconnect the wires to the moisture sensor (at points **V** and **W**), and attempt to start an AUTOMATIC cycle. The trouble is confirmed if the cycle does not start or runs for a very short time.

    Doublecheck this diagnosis by measuring the resistance of the moisture sensing element and comparing the result with the manufacturer's specifications.

3. Dryness selector control open—disconnect the wiring to this control (at points **K** and **L**), and connect an ohmmeter across the control's terminals. Rotate the control knob between the two extremes and record the high and low resistance levels. The control is indeed open if the test shows infinite resistance at any point in the adjustment. Compare other readings with those listed in the manufacturer's specifications.

Machine shuts down before a cycle is completed

This symptom is probably caused by the overheat thermostat TH3 opening. The question is, why? The overheat thermostat opens whenever the air temperature exceeds about 200°F—it is a safety feature which prevents a hazardous overheating condition. Any trouble resulting in an overheating condition can make TH3 open, and the real problem is to determine why it is happening.

1. Exhaust duct clogged—check the lint filter and exhaust duct for an excessive build-up of lint. Small children sometimes stuff a strange assortment of objects into an outside exhaust port for automatic dryers; and anything that impedes the normal flow of air can create the overheating condition.

2. Control thermostat TH1 or TH2 shorted or stuck closed—to check the high heat thermostat TH1, connect a voltmeter across its terminals (between points **C** and **E**), and start a TIMED drying cycle. The contacts should trip open, as indicated by the sudden appearance of 240 V on the meter, before the overheat thermostat turns off the machine. The control thermostat is at fault if the meter shows a steady 0 V up to the time the overheat thermostat opens.

Test the LOW heat thermostat in a similar fashion with the meter connected between points **D** and **E**.

Every cycle begins before start button is depressed

In this instance the drying operation begins the moment the hamper door is closed and the timer is set to start any one of the drying cycles.

1. START switch S3-A shorted or stuck closed—set the timer knob to OFF, disconnect the wiring to one of the terminals on the START switch (at either point **N** or **Q**), and check the resistance of the switch contacts with an ohmmeter or continuity tester. If the test shows zero resistance or good continuity, the switch is shorted and must be replaced.

2. Centrifugal switch contact CS1-B shorted or stuck closed—carry out the same test described for the START switch, but disconnect the wiring to the centrifugal switch (at point **N** or **Q**), and make the continuity test across that switch.

Machine does not turn off when door is opened during any cycle

The hamper door interlock switch S1 is the most likely candidate for this particular symptom. Inspect the door switch to make certain that it operates freely. Check it electrically by setting the timer control knob to OFF and disconnecting the wiring to one of the terminals on that switch (at point **J** or **K**). Check the continuity of the switch with an ohmmeter or continuity tester. If the test shows zero resistance or good continuity when the hamper door is open, or the switch is *not* depressed, the trouble is confirmed.

No heat at all, but motor runs normally

1. Heating element H2 open—set the timer knob to OFF, set the heat selector switch to LOW, and connect an ohmmeter across heating element H2 (between points **F** and **G**). A reading of infinity indicates an open heating element. Replace the heating assembly if it appears a repair job is not feasible.

2. Heat selector switch S2-B open—set the timer knob to OFF, set the heat selector switch to HIGH, and connect a jumper across the

S2-B contact. Start a TIMED drying cycle, and note any heating effects. The trouble is confirmed if the heat goes on with the jumper in place (between points **B** and **C**) and off again when the jumper is removed.

3. Centrifugal switch contact CS1-C stuck or broken open—set the timer to OFF remove any jumpers connected during previous tests, and connect a voltmeter across the terminals of CS1-C (between points **A** and **B**). Start a TIMED drying cycle, and note the reading on the meter. The switch contact is indeed open if the meter shows 240 V the moment the motor starts running.

No heat during timed cycles; heating normal in automatic cycle, and motor runs normally in all cycles

There can be little doubt in this case that timer contact 2 is stuck or broken open. Confirm the diagnosis by setting the timer control to OFF, connecting a jumper wire across timer contact 2 (between points **E** and **F**), and starting a TIMED drying cycle. The diagnosis of a defective timer contact is confirmed if the heat goes on while this jumper wire is in place.

Low heat (slow drying) at high heat setting

The most likely cause of this trouble is a set of broken or stuck contacts in the heat selector switch S2-A. Test this switch for a possible open-circuit condition by connecting a voltmeter across heating element H1 (between points **H** and **I**), setting the heat selector switch to HIGH, and starting a TIMED cycle. The trouble is confirmed if the meter shows any voltage greater than three or four volts.

Automatic cycle stops before laundry is dry

1. S3-B section of the START switch broken or stuck open— disconnect the wiring to the B-section of the START switch, and check the continuity between the switch terminals (between points **S** and **R**) with an ohmmeter or continuity tester. The trouble is confirmed if this test shows infinite resistance or no continuity whenever the switch is depressed. Replace the entire START switch assembly.

2. Dryness selector control shorted—disconnect the wiring to the dryness control (at points **K** and **L**), and connect an ohmmeter across the control's terminals. Rotate the control knob between its two extremes and record the resistance readings at those points. Compare the readings with those listed in the manufacturer's specifications. A shorted control is clearly indicated, however, if this test shows zero resistance at all settings.

3. Electronic control board defective—if the START switch and dryness control check good according to the previous two tests, the process of elimination leads to a trouble in the electronic control circuit. Replace the electronic control circuit board with a new one.

No heat at low setting; high heat normal

1. Heating element H1 open—set the timer knob to OFF, and set the heat selector switch to LOW. Connect an ohmmeter across heating element H1 (between points **H** and **G**), and note the resistance. A reading of infinity is a clear indication of an open heating element. Compare any other resistance reading with the manufacturer's specifications.

2. LOW heat control thermostat TH2 stuck or broken open—set the timer knob to OFF, and set the heat selector switch to HIGH. Connect a continuity tester or ohmmeter across the contacts of TH2 (between points **D** and **E**), and note the reading. The trouble is confirmed if this test shows no continuity or infinite resistance.

No heat at high setting; low heat normal

The most likely cause of this particular set of symptoms is open contacts in the high heat thermostat TH1. To confirm this diagnosis, set the timer knob to OFF, set the heat selector switch to LOW, and connect a continuity tester or ohmmeter across the contacts of TH1 (between points **C** and **E**). The trouble is confirmed if this test shows no continuity or zero resistance.

Low heat setting produces high heat; high setting normal

1. Heat selector switch contact S2-A or S2-B shorted or stuck closed—remove the heat selector switch assembly from the

machine, and test the operation of the contacts with an ohm-meter or continuity tester. Both sets of contacts should show infinity or a complete lack of continuity when the switch is set to one position, and the readings should change to zero resistance or good continuity at the opposite switch setting. The trouble is confirmed if either set of contacts shows zero resistance or good continuity, regardless of the switch setting.

2. Heating element H1 shorted—set the timer control knob to OFF, set the heat selector switch to LOW, and check the resistance heating element H1 (between points **G** and **H**). A reading of zero resistance is a clear indication of a shorted heater. Consult the manufacturer's specifications for the proper resistance reading. Replace the heating element if the element's resistance is substantially below the specified figure.

Heat remains on during fluff operations; no cool-down phase in the automatic cycle

1. Timer contact 2 shorted or stuck closed—set the timer control knob to the middle of the FLUFF cycle, but do not start the machine. Disconnect the wiring to one terminal on relay contact RL1-B (at point **E** or **F**), and connect an ohmmeter or continuity tester across timer contact 2 (between points **E** and **F**). Removing RL1-B from the circuit eliminates it as a possible path for short-circuit current; therefore, if this continuity test shows zero resistance or good continuity, timer contact 2 is indeed closed when it should not be. Replace the timer contact assembly if this is the case.

2. Relay contact RL1-B—set up the test conditions described in the previous step, but connect the ohmmeter or continuity tester across the terminals of RL1-B. An indication of zero resistance or good continuity indicates that the trouble is confirmed. Replace the entire RL1 relay assembly.

11-5 QUESTIONS

1. What are the basic differences between a gas and an all-electric automatic dryer?

2. What are two different definitions for the term *speed control*?

3. What is the difference between a TIMED cycle and an AUTOMATIC cycle?

4. What is the purpose of a latching circuit in the start-up circuitry for an automatic dryer?

5. What drying cycle most likely operates with the timer motor turned off?

12

Electric Ranges

Electric cooking ranges produce the heat needed to carry out most cooking chores in the home. Today's electric ranges are equipped with a variety of extra features and optional conveniences; but once the "extras" are removed, a rather simple heating appliance remains.

Electric ranges are supposed to cook things, and they have two basic sections for doing the job: the surface units and the ovens. Surface units are the range-top "burners" that are commonly used for frying, boiling, and warming operations. Of course the ovens are used mainly for baking and broiling. (See Fig. 12-1 for typical four-burner electric range.)

Most electric ranges have four separate surface units—usually two on the order of six inches in diameter and two others about eight inches across. A six-inch surface unit is normally rated at 250–500 W, and the larger units are rated anywhere from 700–1250 W each.

Ranges having two ovens are becoming popular today. There is normally a larger, 5200–7200 W oven section for taking care of the bigger, heavy-duty baking jobs, and there is a smaller (4500–6100 W) oven for the lighter work.

Fig. 12-1 This electric range has the usual four surface heating units and features a self-cleaning oven. (Courtesy of General Electric Major Appliance group)

Most modern electric ranges operate on a three-wire, 240 V system. A few economy models operate from 120 V sources, but the appliance industry is anxious to respond to consumers' demands for the wider range of heat control and self-cleaning features, which 240 V models can offer.

Microwave ovens are not considered in this book because the technology of microwave heating is vastly different from anything else found in the appliance industry.

12-1 SURFACE UNITS

Surface units and ovens in a modern electric range produce their heat by means of resistive heating. *Calrod* heating elements are by far the most common type of element in use today, although a few newer ranges have *flat-surface* heaters for surface units. See Chapter 3 for detailed discussions of resistive heating and heating elements.

The basic heater circuits are quite simple, and they follow the principles already outlined in Sec. 3-1. Adding independent heat selector switches, heat controls, and timers, however, lends an impression of great complexity. A novice serviceman should not be intimidated by his first view of the wiring in a modern electric range. As demonstrated in this chapter, the individual circuits are rather simple, and the "spaghetti" impression comes about because there are so many individual circuits.

Each surface unit, for instance, has its own heat selector switch; and since each of the four selector switches has about five wires attached to it, it is not unusual to find bundles of fifteen or twenty wires running between the surface units and control console. The same basic idea applies to the oven sections.

12-1.1   Theory of Surface Units

As described in the introduction to this section, the heating elements for range surface units can be made of calrod elements, flat-surface heaters, or coiled-wire heaters. The calrod elements are most popular today, and a serviceman encounters one flat-surface unit for every fifty or so calrod models he sees.

Surface units can be classified according to the type of elements they use to produce the heat, but they can also be classified according to the type of circuit used to select and control their heating. This section describes the theory of operation of three basic heat selection and control circuits for surface units: switched-heat selectors, infinite heat selectors, and thermostatic controls. These circuits can be applied to both calrod and flat-surface heating elements.

The switched-heat selector scheme is the most popular of the three selector and control circuits. The user has access to a set of pushbuttons that provides a selection from among three and seven different heating levels. The popularity of this circuit is largely due to its simplicity, reliability, and relatively low cost.

Infinite heat selector circuits have a smooth-turning dial that lets the user select a heating level anywhere between OFF and full heat. The user, in other words, is not restricted to a small number of discrete heating levels as in the case of switched-heat circuits.

Although infinite heat selectors are more desirable from a user's point of view, they are less popular than the switched-heat version because (a) the infinite controls are more complex in a mechanical sense, (b) they cost more, and (c) they are more likely to develop troubles over the years.

The third type of circuit for surface units, a thermostatic control circuit, is quite different in principle from the other two. Like an infinite heat selector circuit, a thermostatic control circuit has a dial that lets the user select any heating level between OFF and full heat. The difference is that the thermostatic control circuit also controls the actual cooking temperature—the switched-heat and infinite heat selector circuits operate independently of the actual cooking temperature.

The cost and complexity of thermostatic control circuits make them the least popular of the three basic kinds of circuits for surface units. Many electric ranges, however, have one surface unit that is thermostatically controlled, leaving the other three to operate from the less sophisticated switched-heat or infinite heat selector schemes.

SWITCHED-HEAT SURFACE UNITS.   A switched-heat surface unit uses a set of switch contacts to vary the amount of heating power the unit generates. Closing different combinations of switch contacts changes the circuit configuration of the heating elements, making them produce some desired amount of heat. The switching combinations can be rather elaborate, but the user is not aware of the electrical sophistication of the switch. All the user does is set a dial or depress a pushbutton labeled with titles such as OFF, LOW, MED, HIGH, and so on. The internal arrangement of switches takes care of setting up the proper circuitry.

One of the primary characteristics of a modern switched-heat surface unit is that it uses a set of two heating elements wound in a double spiral shape as shown in Fig. 12-2. The two elements can have the same power rating, but the inner element normally has a smaller power rating than the outer one. The switch circuit interconnects the two heating elements in series, parallel, or one at a time to the main power source.

Another important feature of a switched-heat surface unit is the fact that it provides only a certain number of different heat settings. The number of

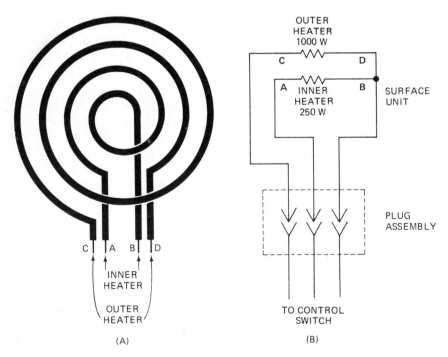

Fig. 12-2 A typical two-element surface unit heater: (A) Outline drawing, (B) Electrical schematic.

heat settings generally increases with the quality and cost of the range. Economy ranges, for instance, might have surface units with only three heat settings. Moderately-priced ranges have five heat settings for each surface unit, whereas the more expensive models can have up to seven different heat settings.

A third characteristic of switched-heat surface units is that they do not have any kind of temperature control mechanism. The units tend to produce the same amount of heat for a given heat setting, regardless of the cooking conditions.

Figure 12-3 shows an equivalent schematic for a simple three-heat surface unit. The table accompanying the schematic shows the switches that must be closed to produce a given heat level. It is important to note that the user does not actually have to punch out the specified switch combinations; all that is necessary is to depress a button or set a rotary switch to one particular position such as OFF, LOW, MED, or HIGH. The internal mechanical workings of the switch assembly take care of setting up the appropriate switch combinations.

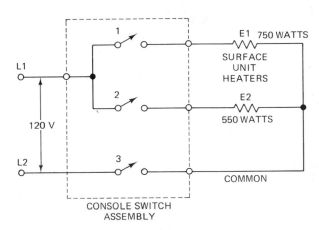

Fig. 12-3 A three-heat surface unit selector switch assembly.

Setting the console switch for OFF, for instance, automatically opens all three internal switch contacts, removing all power from the heating elements. Setting the console switch for LOW heat, however, closes internal contacts 2 and 3; and when contacts 2 and 3 are closed, heating element E2 is connected directly between the 120 V power lines. Since E2 is rated at 550 W when 120 V is applied to it, the surface unit consumes about 550 W when the console switch is set to LOW.

Setting the console switch to MED closes internal contacts 1 and 3, connecting heating element E2 between the 120 V lines and making the surface unit consume about 750 W. Whenever the console switch is set to HIGH, the internal mechanism closes contacts 1, 2, and 3. With all three switches closed, both heating elements are connected to the 120 V line in a parallel configuration. The total power consumption at HIGH heat is thus 550 W + 750 W, or 1300 W.

Electric ranges having three-heat surface units normally operate from a 120 V service line. Ranges featuring five- and seven-heat surface unit controls, however, must operate from a three-wire, 240 V system. Note the connections shown on the block diagram in Fig. 12-4.

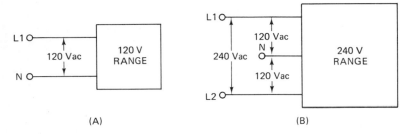

(A)   (B)

Fig. 12-4 Typical electrical connections to electric ranges: (A) 120 V models, (B) 240 V models.

Figure 12-5 shows an equivalent schematic for a five-heat surface unit. With the console switch set to OFF, all internal switch contacts are open, and no power reaches the heating elements. As shown in the switch diagram accompanying the schematic, setting the console switch to WARM closes internal contacts 1 and 3, effectively connecting the two heating elements in series with a 120 V source between L1 and neutral. Since the two elements are connected in series, the 120 V is divided between them, making them produce much less than their rated power output. In fact the sum of the two power levels is less than that found by connecting either one directly to 120 V.

Whenever the user sets the console switch on a five-heat control to LOW, contacts 1 and 4 close to place heating element E1 across a 120 V source between L1 and neutral. E2 is not in the circuit at all in this case, but the total power dissipation is greater than it is when the elements are connected in series to 120 V.

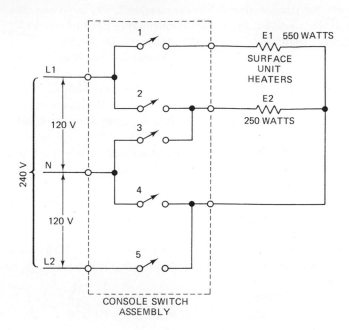

Fig. 12-5 A five-heat surface unit selector switch assembly.

Heat level 2 occurs when contacts 1, 2, and 4 are closed. This particular switch combination places heating elements E1 and E1 in parallel across a 120 V source (L1 to neutral).

The heating can be further increased by setting the console switch to heat level 1. In that setting, internal contacts 1 and 5 close to connect heating element E1 directly across the 240 V source. Element 1 thus produces its maximum heating power which is greater than any 120 V combination.

Finally the HIGH setting closes contacts 1, 2, and 5. When these switches are closed, elements E1 and E2 are connected in parallel to 240 V. This condition makes both elements produce their maximum heat.

It is important to note that the five-heat surface unit in Fig. 12-5 takes advantage of the 120–0–120 V nature of a three-wire, 240 V wiring system. The switch combinations vary the circuit configuration of the heating elements as in a three-heat model; but the 120/240 V feature of the three-wire system makes it possible to get more heating ranges on the five-heat surface unit.

Actually, the five-heat surface unit illustrated in Fig. 12-5 does not take advantage of all the possible circuit combinations between a 120–0–120 V input and a two-element heating assembly. In fact there is a total of eight possible switch combinations, not including an OFF position. The circuit in Fig. 12-6 shows the most elaborate kind of switched-heat surface unit in use today. The circuit has seven discrete heat settings.

Referring to the schematic and switch table in Fig. 12-6, the switch settings and resulting circuit configurations can be summarized as follows:

OFF—no switches closed.

WARM—switches 1 and 4 closed to connect E1 and E2 in series across 120 V (L1 and neutral).

LOW—switches 4 and 5 closed to connect only E2 to 120 V (L1 and neutral).

MED—switches 2 and 5 closed to connect only E1 to 120 V (L2 and neutral).

3—switches 2, 4, and 5 closed to connect E1 and E2 in parallel with 120 V (L1 and neutral).

2—switches 3 and 5 closed to connect only E2 to 240 V (L1 and L2).

1—switches 1 and 5 closed to connect only E1 to 240 V (L1 and L2).

HIGH—switches 1, 3, and 5 closed to connect E1 and E2 in parallel across 240 V (L1 and L2).

Note that E1 is the only element connected in the circuit when the console switch is set to MED and 1. The voltages are different in these two cases, however, making the element produce about four times as much heat in setting 1 then it does in the MED setting. The same idea holds for E2 in settings LOW and 2. It turns out that E2 has a lower power rating than E1; thus, E2 always produces less heat than E1 when they are connected to the same voltage source.

The two elements are connected in parallel at settings 3 and HIGH. The power consumption is about four times greater in the HIGH setting because the applied voltage is twice as high.

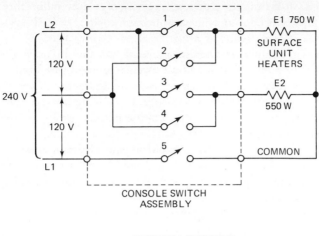

Fig. 12-6 A seven-heat surface unit selector switch assembly.

The only condition that places the two elements in series is the WARM setting. The elements are connected in series with a 120 V source in that case, and they produce their smallest amount of heat because the line voltage is divided between them.

The only other heating element arrangement that could be used is one that places both elements in series across 240 V. This paticular arrangement is not used, however, because the overall heating effect would not be significantly different from the 3 setting where both elements are connected to 120 V.

INFINITE HEAT SURFACE UNITS. An infinite heat selector circuit lets the user smoothly adjust the element's power dissipation anywhere between

OFF and full heat. Infinite heat selectors effectively have an "infinite" number of different heat settings—they are not limited to 3, 5, or 7 different levels as switched-heat selector switches are.

Although an infinite heat selector circuit uses one or more thermostats, it is important to realize that such units are *not* temperature-controlled units. Infinite heat circuits make no attempt to correlate the heat from the heating element with the temperature of the substance being heated. Thermostatic controls—circuits that *do* control the cooking temperature—are described in the last part of this section.

Figure 12-7 illustrates a typical infinite heat selector circuit. The circuit consists of a double-pole on/off switch, a set of bimetal thermostat contacts, a warp or bias heater, and the main surface heating element. All these com-

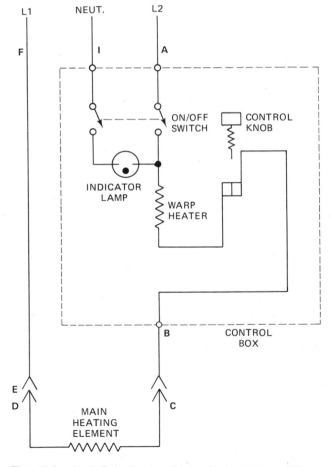

Fig. 12-7 An infinite heat surface unit selector assembly.

ponents, with the notable exception of the main heating element, are enclosed in a box behind the control console.

Note that an infinite heat selector circuit requires only one surface heating element. This situation is quite different from a switched-heat circuit that requires two separate surface heating elements.

When the user turns on the on/off switch, the 240 V between L1 and L2 is applied to a series circuit made up of the main surface unit heater, the warp heater, and a set of normally-closed thermostat contacts. The supply voltage divides between the surface unit and warp heaters, but the circuit is designed in such a way that the surface element drops about 230 V, leaving only about 10 V to operate the warp heater.

With full line power applied to the heaters, they begin to warm up. The warp heater is situated very close to the bimetal thermostat; thus, it is the heat from the warp heater—and not the main surface unit—that influences the thermostat. As the warp heater warms the thermostat, the contacts begin to ease open; and when the contacts pop open, power is removed from both heaters.

The thermostat contacts remain open until the warp heater cools off a little bit. The contacts then close to reapply full power to the circuit again. The thermostat contacts continue to cycle open and closed until the user turns off the on/off switch.

An infinite heat selector circuit is thus either full on or full off. The heating effect of the surface unit is determined by the *average* power dissipation over a period of time. If, for instance, the circuit spends more time on than off, the overall heating effect of the surface unit will be rather high. On the other hand, the surface unit will run rather cool if the circuit is turned off most of the time.

The user adjusts the heating level of an infinite heat selector circuit by varying the amount of mechanical spring pressure on the bimetal contacts. Setting the control knob for a high operating temperature places a rather large amount of spring pressure on the bimetal contacts, making it more difficult for them to open. The warp heater then has to generate a relatively large amount of heat before it can open the thermostat contacts. By the same token, the warp heater does not have to be off very long before the spring tension forces the contacts closed again. Full line power is thus applied to the surface unit about 90 percent of the time.

Whenever the user sets the control for less heat, the spring tension on the bimetal contacts is lowered, and full power is applied to the surface heater a smaller percentage of the time.

The infinite heat selector circuit in Fig. 12-7 is used in many electric ranges today. There are some models, however, that have the warp heater connected in parallel with the surface unit heater instead of in series with it. There are no differences in the basic theory of operation between the series-

and parallel-connected warp heaters; there is, however, one important practical difference.

Electric ranges employing parallel-connected warp heaters can use identical control units for all four surface units, regardless of their respective power ratings. A series-connected warp heater, on the other hand, must be used with surface units of one particular power rating. Replacing a series-connected warp heater designed for a 500 W surface unit with one designed for 1250 W application, for instance, would throw the entire heating cycle out of kilter.

THERMOSTATIC SURFACE UNITS.   A thermostatic control circuit is more than a selector switch. The switched-heat and infinite heat controls described thus far in this section are selector switches. In a manner of speaking, thermostatic surface units are also selector switches, but they are also *control* circuits. These circuits actually control the cooking temperature.

The differences between heat selector circuits and heat control circuits can be stated another way: A selector circuit operates dumbly at one particular power level without regard to the actual cooking temperature. A heat control circuit, on the other hand, generates only enough heat to warm up the cooking vessel and maintain its temperature at some preset level.

Figure 12-8 illustrates one kind of thermostatic control scheme for surface units. This particular model uses a diaphragm thermostat assembly. (See Sec. 4-1.2 for further details about the operation of diaphragm thermostat controls.) The thermostat bulb in this instance is a hollow metal wafer situated in the center of the main heating coil. The wafer is fairly well insulated from the unit's direct heat, but it is spring loaded so that it makes firm contact with the bottom of any heating vessel placed on the surface unit.

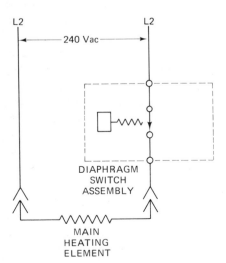

MAIN
HEATING
ELEMENT

Fig. 12-8 A single-element thermostat control using a diaphragm (Robertshaw) control sensor.

The diaphragm part of the control is located on the control console, behind the heat control knob for that particular surface unit. The wafer and diaphragm are both filled with an oily fluid and interconnected with a long capillary tube.

As shown in Fig. 12-8, the diaphragm switch is normally closed. When the user turns on the "burner," full line voltage is immediately applied to the surface unit. As the temperature of the surface unit and cooking vessel rises, the fluid in the wafer expands to stretch the diaphragm and open the thermostat switch contacts. Opening the thermostat contacts removes 240 V power from the main surface heating element until the fluid cools enough to allow the thermostat contacts to close again. The unit then continues cycling on and off, maintaining an average cooking temperature close to that selected by the user.

The temperature control dial on the console is calibrated in actual degrees Fahrenheit. To cook at 200°F, for example, the user rotates the control dial to that position. Setting the control dial adjusts the spring tension on the diaphragm switch, keeping the contacts closed until the wafer senses a temperature of about 200°F.

A simple heat control circuit such as the one shown in Fig. 12-8 has one disadvantage, however, that limits its use to lower-priced electric ranges. The problem is that a calrod heating element holds its heat for some time after its electrical power is cut off. As a result, the cooking temperature tends to overshoot the preset level, creating uneven and rather unpredictable heating situations.

Of course some sort of heat control is better than none at all, but it is possible to reduce the temperature overshoot by using a two-element surface heater and a special diaphragm thermostat assembly that has two switch contacts.

Referring to the schematic in Fig. 12-9, both thermostat contacts are closed during the initial heating phase. Full line power is applied to both heating elements, and the surface unit produces its maximum heating power.

The thermostat switch connected in series with the high-power heating element is calibrated to open about 30°F *below* the preset cooking temperature. When the cooking temperature rises to a point about 30°F below the selected cooking level, the high-power heater is turned off, letting the smaller heater ease the cooking temperature toward the designated level rather slowly.

The thermostat switch connected in series with the low-power heating element opens as the preset temperature is reached. There is very little temperature overshoot because the brute-force heating power was removed about 30°F below the preset temperature. The thermostat contact in series with the smaller heater then maintains the cooking temperature by adding a little bit of heat as it is needed.

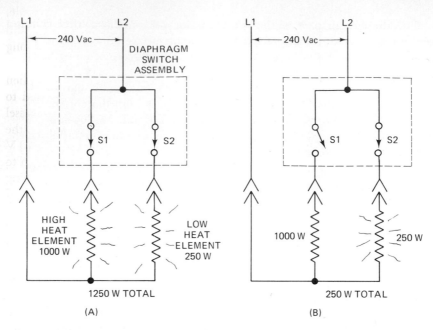

Fig. 12-9 A two-element version of a diaphragm surface-unit thermostat control. (A) Surface unit temperature below selected operating temperature. (B) Surface unit temperature at or slightly below the selected operating temperature.

The main idea behind this improved, two-element thermostatic control is to apply maximum heating power only as long as large temperature increases are necessary. The smaller element then takes over, peaking up the cooking temperature and maintaining it without a great deal of temperature overshoot. The overall result, as far as the user is concerned, is more even heating under a wider variety of cooking conditions.

Section 4-3.3 describes the most sophisticated surface-unit thermostatic control presently used in consumer electric ranges—the King Seeley heat control system. The cost and complexity of this circuit generally limits its use to only one surface unit out of the four that are normally available. The remaining units employ one of the simpler heat selector circuits described earlier in this section.

The primary advantage of the King Seeley control is that it eliminates the need for a mechanical diaphragm and a long capillary tube. The King Seeley circuit also has four features that are seldom found elsewhere in consumer heating appliances:

1. The main control system operates from a 12 V source supplied by a step-down power transformer.

2. The temperature sensing element is a special resistor that changes resistance as the applied temperature changes.

3. The control knob on the user's console operates a variable resistor, rather than a switch or mechanical thermostat assembly.

4. The bimetal thermostat assembly is actually a differential thermostat —one that operates according to the difference between two temperatures, rather than the temperature of a single heat source. See Sec. 4-1.3.

12-1.2 Troubleshooting and Servicing Surface Units

This section deals with general troubleshooting procedures for electric range surface units. The circuits and suggested test points are representative of those appearing in most electric ranges today.

SWITCHED-HEAT SURFACE UNITS. Switched-heat surface units are relatively simple to troubleshoot and repair. They are easy to troubleshoot because so few things can go wrong with them and because their troubles generally exhibit very clear-cut symptoms. Switched-heat surface units are rather easy to service because there are so few components (heating elements, switch assembly, plug assembly, and interconnecting wiring), and because the parts are generally of the plug-in variety.

Figure 12-10 shows a wiring diagram for a typical four-unit range top assembly. Note that all four switch and heating units are fed by the same three-wire, 240 V service line. The important point here is that any trouble that affects all four surface units has to be located in a portion of the feed line that is common to all of them. A trouble that affects only one surface unit, on the other hand, must be in the switch assembly or heaters for that particular unit.

Figure 12-11(A) shows a general circuit for five- and seven-heat surface units. The only real difference between the two kinds of circuits is in the complexity of the selector switch assembly. They both work from the same three-wire, 240 V source, and they both have the same set of two heater coils.

The tables in Figs. 12-11(B) and 12-11(C) show the voltages that should appear at the indicated test points as the selector switch is set to various heating levels. Any departure from this pattern indicates a trouble in the circuitry.

The following symptoms and test procedures apply only to those troubles that affect only one of the four surface units. Recall that any trouble affecting all of them has to be in the common wiring leading to the surface-unit control section.

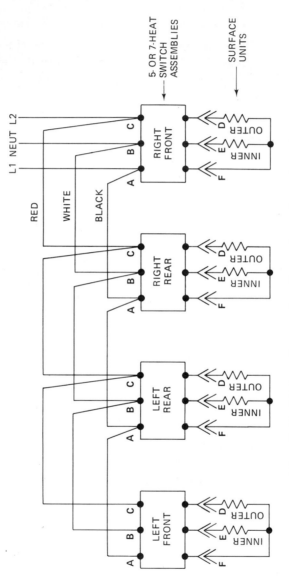

Fig. 12-10 Wiring diagram for the surface-unit section of an electric range using only switched-heat selectors.

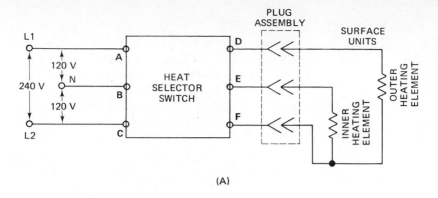

(A)

5-HEAT SELECTOR	TEST POINT VOLTAGES					
FUNCTION	A-B	B-C	A-C	D-E	E-F	D-F
OFF	120	120	240	0	0	0
WARM	120	120	240	120	72*	48*
LOW	120	120	240	120	0	120
2	120	120	240	0	120	120
1	120	120	240	240	0	240
HIGH	120	120	240	0	240	240

(B)

7-HEAT SELECTOR	TEST POINT VOLTAGES					
FUNCTION	A-B	B-C	A-C	D-E	E-F	D-F
OFF	120	120	240	0	0	0
WARM	120	120	240	120	72*	48*
LOW	120	120	240	120	120	0
MED	120	120	240	120	0	120
3	120	120	240	0	120	120
2	120	120	240	240	240	0
1	120	120	240	240	0	240
HIGH	120	120	240	0	240	240

(C)

*APPROXIMATE VOLTAGE READINGS

Fig. 12-11 General two-element heat selector circuit for surface units. (A) Electrical diagram. (B) Test-point voltages for a five-heat selector. (C) Test-point voltages for a seven-heat selector.

No heat at any heat setting

1. Feed line connection loose or broken open—check the voltages at the input side of the selector switch assembly (between points **A** and **B**, **B** and **C**, and **C** and **A**), and compare the results with the voltages indicated in Figs. 12-11(B) or 12-11(C). Visually inspect the wiring for signs of damage, and pull gently on the wires and connections to make certain that they are tightly secured.

2. Defective selector switch assembly—set the selector switch to any one of its heating positions and measure the voltages at the surface-unit plug assembly (between points **D** and **E**, **E** and **F**, and **D** and **F**). Compare the results with the figures shown on the appropriate table in Fig. 12-11. If the voltages are correct at the input of the switch, but no voltage is reaching the plug assembly, the trouble is confirmed and the heat selector switch must be replaced.

3. Both heating elements open—this is a possible, but unlikely, trouble. It is confirmed if the voltages are correct at the output end of the plug assembly, but the surface unit does not generate any heat. Replace the surface unit.

Improper heat level at one or more heat settings

1. Feed line connection loose or broken open—check the voltages at the input side of the selector switch assembly, and compare the results with the figures listed in Fig. 12-11. Any departure from the specified pattern of voltages confirms the trouble. Locate the trouble by a close visual inspection and make the appropriate repair.

2. Defective heat selector switch assembly—set the selector switch to each of its heat settings, measuring the pattern of output voltages at each setting. Compare the results with voltage tables in Fig. 12-11. Any departure indicates a defective selector switch that must be replaced.

3. Defective heating element—remove the heating element assembly from the range, and check the resistance of the elements. A reading of infinity for either element indicates an open circuit. Compare any other reading with the manufacturer's specifications. This trouble is doubly confirmed if the pattern of voltages at the output of the plug assembly is correct, but the surface unit still fails to generate the correct heating pattern.

INFINITE HEAT SURFACE UNITS.   Infinite heat surface units are somewhat more complex than their switched-heat counterparts, but they are
really no more difficult to troubleshoot and service. Figure 12-12 is a wiring
diagram of a typical range-top system that has four infinite heat surface units.
Note the similarities between this wiring diagram and the one for switched-
heat units shown in Fig. 12-10.

The theory of infinite heat surface units is described in Sec. 12-1.1.
Figure 12-7 in that section shows the complete schematic diagram, including
the components inside the control box. From a troubleshooter's point of
view, however, the control circuit either works or it does not—there is no
need to describe troubles within the "black box" on a part-by-part basis.

The following list of symptoms and test procedures applies only to those
affecting one of the four surface units. Any trouble affecting all of them has
to be in the feed-line system leading up to the infinite heat control assemblies.

No heat at any control setting, pilot lamp does not go on

1. Feed-line connection loose or broken open—check the voltages
   at the input side of the control box. The readings should be close
   to the following:
   Between L1 and neutral (points **F** and **I**)—120 V.
   Between L2 and neutral (points **A** and **I**)—120 V.
   Between L1 and L2 (points **F** and **A**)—240 V.
   Visually inspect the wiring for signs of damage, and pull
   gently on the wires and connections to make certain that they
   are tightly secured.

2. Control box defective—set the heat selector knob to the highest
   heat level, and measure the voltage at the output connections of
   the control box (between points **B** and **E**). The trouble is confirmed if the test shows a very low voltage or none at all. Doublecheck the diagnosis by connecting a jumper wire across the entire
   control box (between points **A** and **B**). The control box is then
   considered the cause of the trouble if the heating element suddenly operates at full heat. Note: Do not allow the heating
   element to operate under this test condition for more than a
   few minutes.
   Replace the control box.

No heat at any control setting, pilot lamp goes on

The fact that the pilot light goes on indicates that 120 V power is
reaching L2 and neutral (points **A** and **I**). The trouble, however,

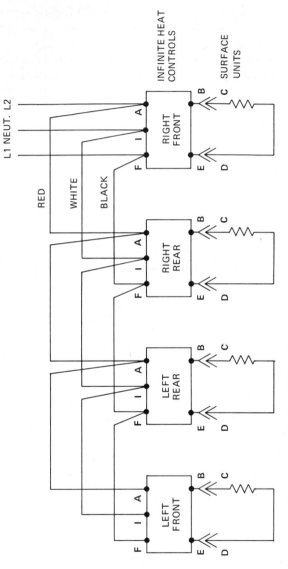

Fig. 12-12 Wiring diagram for the surface-unit section of an electric range using infinite heat controls.

could be in the remaining feed line L1 or the thermostat portion of the control box. Another likely trouble in this case is an open main heating element.

Test the voltage at L1 and the control box as described under "No heat at any control setting, pilot lamp does not go on." Check out the heating element by removing it from the range and testing its resistance. A resistance of infinity indicates an open heating element. Compare any other reading with the manufacturer's specifications.

Improper heating level at one or more control settings

1. Incorrect voltages at the input of the control box—measure the voltage distribution at the input terminals on the control box, and compare them with the diagram in Fig. 12-12.

2. Defective heating element—remove the heating element from the range, and measure its resistance with an ohmmeter. Readings of zero resistance or infinity indicate a trouble in the element. Compare any other reading with the manufacturer's specifications.

3. Control box circuit defective—the process of elimination leads to the control box. If the voltages to the box are correct and the main heating element checks good, there can be little room for doubt that the control box must be replaced.

DIAPHRAGM THERMOSTAT SURFACE UNITS. Figure 12-13 is a wiring diagram for a surface-unit section that uses a diaphragm thermostat control on one of the four units. The second heating element and neutral power connection to the thermostat unit are used on some models. Compare the control box schematics in Figs. 12-7 and 12-8.

The troubleshooting notes that follow apply only to the thermostatically controlled surface unit in Fig. 12-13. Treat the three switched-heat units as described in the opening paragraphs of this section.

No heat at any control setting

1. Feed-line connection loose or broken open—check the voltages at the input side of the control box (between points **A** and **C**). If this test shows a voltage level significantly less than 240 V, visually inspect the wiring for signs of damage and make certain that the contacts are secure.

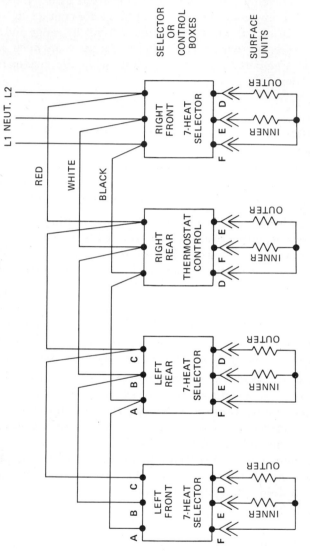

Fig. 12-13 Wiring diagram for the surface-unit section of an electric range using one thermostat control and three switched-heat selectors.

In instances where the neutral line is connected to the input side of the control box, check the voltage between neutral and the two hot lines (between points **A** and **B** and points **B** and **C**). These readings should be 120 V.

2. Control box defective—set the heat control knob to the highest heat level, and measure the voltage at the output of the control box (between points **D** and **E** for single-element units, and between points **D** and **E** and points **F** and **E** for two-element heaters). The trouble is confirmed if no voltage appears at these test points. Replace the control assembly, including the sensor wafer.

3. Open heating element (single-element model only)—remove the heating element from the range, and check its resistance with an ohmmeter. A reading of infinity confirms the trouble. Compare any other reading with the figures published in the manufacturer's specifications.

Improper heating level at one or more control settings

1. Incorrect voltages at the input of the control box—measure the voltages at the input terminals as described in trouble 1 under "No heat at any control setting."

2. Defective heating element—remove the suspected heating elements from the range, and measure their resistance with an ohmmeter. Readings of zero ohms or infinity indicate a trouble in the element. Compare any other readings with the manufacturer's specifications.

3. Control box defective—if the voltages at the input terminals of the control box are correct, and if the heating element(s) checks good, there can be little doubt that the real trouble is in the control assembly itself. Replace the entire control assembly with a new one.

Elements heat too slowly (two-element units only)

The trouble in this case is caused either by a defective high-heat element or the control assembly. Check out the heating element by removing the surface unit from the range and measuring the resistance of the high-heat element (between points **F** and **E**). This trouble is confirmed if the test shows infinite resistance.

If the high-heat element checks good, the trouble has to be in the control assembly. Replace that portion of the circuit.

KING SEELEY SURFACE UNITS.   It is possible to distinguish a King Seeley surface unit from the diaphragm versions by looking for a pair of wires, rather than a capillary tube, leading from the sensing wafer in the center of the surface unit to the control assembly.

Troubleshoot a King Seeley surface-unit control as described in Sec. 4-3.3.

12-2 OVEN UNITS

Ovens and surface units in electric ranges serve entirely different functions as far as the user is concerned, but there are some remarkable similarities as far as the theories of operation and troubleshooting procedures are concerned. Consider the following similarities:

1.   Most surface units and ovens have two separate heating elements.
2.   Most surface units and ovens operate from three-wire, 240 V service.
3.   Ovens use the same kinds of heat control thermostats as many thermostatically-controlled surface units do.

12-2.1 Theory of Oven Units

Most ovens for electric ranges have two calrod heating elements in them—one located at the top of the oven space and the other at the bottom. The lower heating element is used mainly for baking operations, while the upper one is used for broiling. Special operations, for example oven preheating and automatic cleaning, often take advantage of both elements.

Figure 12-14 shows two basic shapes for oven baking and broiling elements. Note that baking elements generally have a rectangular shape, whereas broiling elements are often bent into a semicoiled shape. Table 12-1 shows some typical outline dimensions, shapes, and power ratings for oven heating elements.

Broiling coils often have higher power ratings than the baking elements in the same oven unit. Also note from Table 12-1 that the elements in larger ovens tend to have higher power ratings than those found in the smaller versions.

The fact that most modern electric ranges operate from a three-wire, 240 V service line makes it possible to operate the two oven elements separately, in series or in parallel with either 120 V or 240 V. The advantage in this case is that the heat can be distributed in ways that are most appropriate for different kinds of baking and broiling tasks.

Thermostat assemblies used to control the oven temperature are identical to the thermostatic surface unit controls described in Sec. 12-1.1 and the general controls outlined in Sec. 4-1.

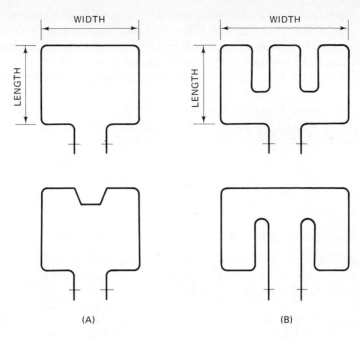

Fig. 12-14 Outline diagrams of oven heating elements. (A) Bake elements. (B) Broil elements.

TABLE 12-1 Dimensions of oven bake and broil heating elements

Function	Dimensions (Width × Length)	Outline	Power Rating (240 V Operation)
Smaller ovens:			
Bake	$8\frac{1}{4}'' \times 16''$	Rectangular	2000 W
	$13\frac{1}{2}'' \times 21\frac{1}{2}''$	Rectangular	2500 W
	$9\frac{1}{2}'' \times 15''$	Rectangular	1500 W
Broil	$12'' \times 17''$	Rectangular	3000 W
	$11\frac{1}{4}'' \times 15\frac{1}{4}''$	Semicoiled	3600 W
Larger ovens:			
Bake	$19'' \times 17''$	Rectangular	3000 W
	$18\frac{1}{2}'' \times 15''$	Rectangular	2500 W
	$20\frac{1}{4}'' \times 15''$	Rectangular	2200 W
	$22\frac{1}{2}'' \times 17\frac{1}{2}''$	Rectangular	3600 W
Broil	$16'' \times 15''$	Semicoiled	3000 W
	$19'' \times 12''$	Semicoiled	3600 W

BAKE AND BROIL CONTROL CIRCUITS.   Figure 12-15 shows a simple oven temperature control circuit. The bake and broil heating elements are connected to Ll through separate selector switches, but they are connected to L2 through the same set of thermostat contacts and switch contact 2.

Whenever the user selects a BAKE operation, switches 1 and 3 in the switch assembly close, thereby applying full 240 V power to the baking element. As the baking element heats up, it warms the inside of the oven space. A connection to the neutral line provides 120 V to operate the oven indicator light as long as the thermostat contacts remain closed.

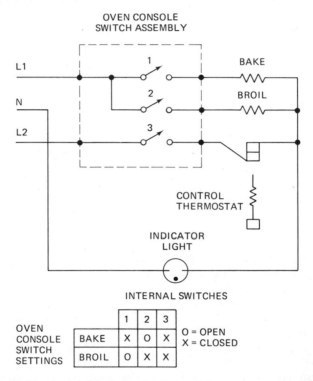

		1	2	3	
OVEN CONSOLE SWITCH SETTINGS	BAKE	X	O	X	O = OPEN X = CLOSED
	BROIL	O	X	X	

Fig. 12-15 A simplified circuit diagram for an oven selector and control.

The oven temperature eventually reaches a point at which the thermostat contacts pop open to remove 240 V power from the baking element and interrupt 120 V power to the indicator lamp. The oven temperature responds by gradually dropping to a point where the thermostat contacts close again. The oven heats again, and the thermostat contacts continue responding by opening and closing to maintain a fairly constant baking level—the level set on the user's temperature control knob.

The user sets up a broiling operation by rotating the temperature control knob for maximum heat and setting the oven selector knob to BROIL. Setting the selector switch to BROIL closes switch contacts 2 and 3, applying 240 V line power to the broil element at the top of the oven space and 120 V to the indicator lamp. The temperature of the oven rises rapidly toward the maximum level at which the thermostat switch opens (about 600°F). The thermostat then cycles open and closed to maintain that peak operating temperature.

To get a proper broiling effect, however, the broiling element should be turned on at all times. The actual oven temperature, in other words, is not as important as having full heat applied to the food at all times. Most manufacturers thus recommend performing broiling operations with the oven door slightly open. As long as the door is open a little bit, the oven temperature cannot reach the trip point for the thermostat, and the coil remains running at full heat throughout the entire broiling operation. If the door is closed for any reason, however, the 600°F thermostat acts as a safety device to prevent the oven temperature from rising to a dangerously high level.

The oven circuit just described is commonly found in low- to moderately-priced electric ranges. The circuit has a disadvantage that can be overcome by adding some extra components. The problem with the simpler oven circuit is in the BAKE operation where the oven space is to be heated from room temperature to the selected baking temperature by means of a single bake heating element. It can take some five or ten minutes for an oven to reach the selected baking temperature; and since many foods cannot (or should not) be placed into the oven until the specified temperature is reached, the delay can be something of a nuisance.

The oven circuit in Fig. 12-16 shows one way to get around the problem of slow preheating. In this instance, the bake and broil coils operate from separate thermostat switch contacts. The contacts, however, are ganged together to the same thermostat assembly. The really unique feature of this oven circuit is that the thermostat switch connected to the broiling element is calibrated to open at about 75°–80°F below the temperature set on the control knob. Whenever the oven is set to PREHEAT, all three switches are closed and full line power is applied to both heating elements.

Both elements produce their maximum heating power during the initial heat-up phase; but as soon as the oven temperature reaches a level that is 75°–80° below the selected temperature, the thermostat contact in series with the broil element pops open. With the broil element thermostat thus open, that element is completely removed from the circuit, and the baking coil is responsible for easing the operating temperature up to the selected level.

From the user's point of view, an oven using the circuit in Fig. 12-16 heats up to the operating temperature much faster in the PREHEAT mode

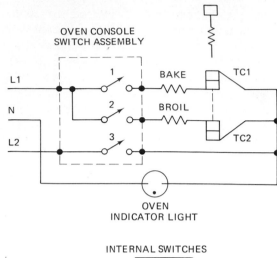

OVEN CONSOLE
SWITCH ASSEMBLY

OVEN
INDICATOR LIGHT

INTERNAL SWITCHES

	1	2	3	
BAKE	X	O	X	O = OPEN
BROIL	O	X	X	X = CLOSED
PREHEAT	X	X	X	

OVEN
CONSOLE SWITCH
SETTINGS

Fig. 12-16 A simplified circuit diagram for an oven that includes a
PREHEAT operation.

than is possible if the preheating is done by the bake element, alone. Other
techniques for rapid preheating are described later in this section.

The switch diagram accompanying Fig. 12-16 shows the contact closures
for nomal BAKE and BROIL operations. These modes operate in a fashion
similar to the simpler circuit illustrated in Fig. 12-15. The only real difference
is that the bake and broil heating elements are operated from separate contacts on the thermostat assembly.

The oven circuit in Fig. 12-17 is not really much different from that described in connection with Fig. 12-16. This expanded circuit includes a time-
bake feature in addition to the usual baking and broiling functions. The
circuit also includes a 120 V light bulb circuit for lighting the interior of the
oven, an indicator light that goes on whenever power is applied to the baking
element, and a clock.

The interior light circuit consists of a 40 W, 120 V incandescent light bulb
that is connected to L1 through one of two switch contacts. When either
switch is closed, the light bulb receives 120 V power between L1 and the
neutral connection on the service line.

The door switch in the light circuit is a normally closed pushbutton switch
located at the frame of the oven door. This switch contact is closed whenever

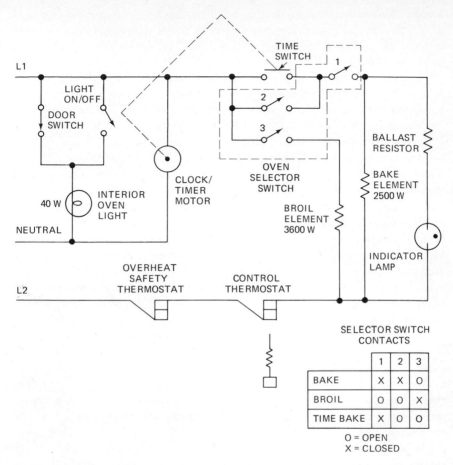

Fig. 12-17 Schematic of an oven unit that includes a TIME BAKE operation.

the oven door is open, thus completing the circuit to turn on the light. Closing the door opens the switch and breaks open that path for current to flow to the bulb.

An on/off toggle switch connected in parallel with the door switch lets the user turn on the oven light, even when the door is closed. This feature is used only with oven units that have a glass window in the door to let the user see the food being baked without having to upset the oven temperature by opening the door. This oven light switch is located either near the oven door or on the user's control panel.

The indicator lamp is connected in parallel with the baking element and thus goes on and off as 240 V power to that element is cycled on and off. The indicator lamp goes on the moment the oven is turned on, and the user knows the oven has reached the desired operating temperature when the light goes out. The ballast resistor connected in series with the indicator lamp reduces the voltage applied to the lamp from 240 V to whatever the lamp's operating voltage might be—generally 65 V.

The electric clock is actually an integral part of the oven timing control. It is simply a matter of convenience that the manufacturer puts a couple of hands on the clock so that it indicates the time of day. The clock motor is connected directly between L1 and the neutral line so that it operates continuously as long as power is applied to the range.

The true purpose of the clock is to operate a set of two mechanical timers. The timers, located on the user's control panel, are used to set the start and stop times for a baking operation in the TIME BAKE mode.

The user, for example, can set the START timer to begin a baking operation at three o'clock. If he or she wants to operate the oven at the preset bake temperature for two hours, the STOP timer is set to five o'clock—two hours later than the start time. When the clock shows three o'clock, the START time closes the timer switch contacts; and when the clock reads five o'clock, the STOP time opens the timer switch contacts. During the timed interval, the oven operates at whatever temperature the user dials on the temperature control knob.

Referring to the switch table accompanying Fig. 12-17, setting the oven for a BAKE operation closes switch contacts 1 and 2. The baking element is then connected to L1 through contacts 1 and 2, and the other side of the element is connected to L2 through the thermostat contacts. Full power is thus applied to the baking element as it begins warming the oven to the preset operating temperature. The control thermostat begins cycling open and closed at the selected operating temperature.

It is necessary to close switch contact 2 during BAKE so that the timer switch cannot play any part in the operation. Note that switch 2 bypasses the timer switch contacts in the BAKE mode.

The oven is set up for BROIL whenever switch contact 3 is closed and the thermostat control is set for BROIL or maximum heat. The timer switch assembly and indicator light are not included in this broil circuit.

Setting the oven for TIME BAKE closes contact 1. The only path for current to the bake element is through the timer switch contacts; and those contacts operate under the control of the clock and timers as described earlier in this section. The control thermostat regulates the baking temperature in the usual fashion as long as the timer contacts are closed.

Some ovens that have the TIME BAKE feature have a slightly different circuit arrangement, which keeps a small amount of heating power applied to the bake element before and after the selected baking interval. The idea is to gently preheat the oven before the actual baking operation is to begin and to keep the food warm after the timed interval is over. This particular circuit is incorporated in the oven circuit shown in Fig. 12-18.

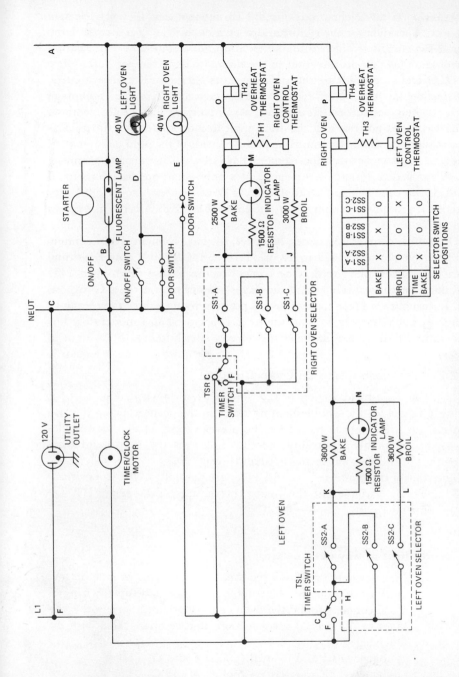

Fig. 12-18 Complete schematic of a double-oven section.

	SS1-A SS2-A	SS1-B SS2-B	SS1-C SS2-C
BAKE	X	X	O
BROIL	O	O	X
TIME BAKE	X	O	O

SELECTOR SWITCH POSITIONS

Referring to the schematic in Fig. 12-18, suppose that the user selects a TIME BAKE operation for the right-hand oven section. The user sets the oven selector switch SS1 to the TIME BAKE position and rotates the temperature control knob for that oven section to the desired baking temperature. Once the START and STOP times are set, the TIME BAKE operation is underway.

Selecting the TIME BAKE cycle closes contact SS1-A in the right oven selector switch (see the switch diagram accompanying Fig. 12-18). As long as the clock has not reached the time indicated on the START timer, TS1 remains set to the **G–C** position, connecting one side of the right bake element to neutral. This means that the element has only half its normal operating voltage applied to it, and it thus generates only about one-fourth its rated power. If this bake element is rated at 2500 W when operating at 240 V, for example, it produces the equivalent of 625 W of heat when 120 V is applied to it.

Once timer contact TS1 closes, however, the bake element is immediately switched from the neutral line to L1, and it receives full 240 V power. Normal baking then takes place under the control of the baking thermostat TH1 until the time interval is over and the timer contact returns to its **G–C** position. Returning the timer contact to this position reduces the bake element's voltage to 120 V once again, and the oven is operated at a moderately low temperature until the user switches the selector switch to OFF.

12-2.2   Troubleshooting an Oven Circuit

The right-hand section of the double oven shown in Fig. 12-18 is used as a model for the troubleshooting notes in this section. Since the two oven circuits are identical except for the power ratings of the heating elements, the symptoms and troubleshooting notes for the right-hand oven section apply equally well to the left-hand oven.

The control thermostats, TH1 and TH3, are normally of the Robertshaw or King Seeley variety; but the safety thermostats, TH2 and TH4, are usually bimetal types.

No heat at any oven setting

1. Line power not reaching the oven section—if the oven lights and clock work properly, the trouble has to be some open wiring or a bad contact around the oven control circuit. Measure the voltages at the oven control section, and compare them with the following:

   Between L1 and neutral (points **F** and **C**)—120 V.
   Between L2 and neutral (points **A** and **C**)—120 V.
   Between L1 and L2 (points **A** and **F**)—240 V.

Visually inspect the wiring for signs of damage, and tug gently on the wires and connections to make certain they are tightly secured.

2. Control thermostat TH1 contacts stuck or broken open—set the oven selector knob to BAKE, and rotate the temperature control dial for maximum heat. Measure the voltage across the control thermostat contacts (between points **M** and **O**). The trouble is confirmed if full 240 V line voltage appears at that point. Replace the thermostat assembly.

3. Overheat safety thermostat TH2 contacts stuck or broken open —set up the test conditions described for the previous trouble, checking the voltage across the safety thermostat (between points **O** and **A**). An indication of 240 V confirms the trouble.

It is possible to doublecheck this diagnosis by connecting a temporary jumper wire across the thermostat contacts. The trouble is then doubly confirmed if the bake element grows hot.

No heat in bake or time bake; broil operation is normal

1. Bake heating element open—turn off the appliance, and remove the bake heating element from the circuit. Measure the resistance of the element with an ohmmeter. An indication of infinity confirms the trouble. Consult the manufacturer's specifications if there is any question about any other resistance reading.

2. Selector switch S1 defective—replace the bake heating element (assuming that it is in good condition), and set up the oven controls for a BAKE operation at maximum heat. Measure the voltage at the output side of the oven selector switch (between points **I** and **M**). Any reading less than full line voltage confirms the trouble. Replace the entire selector switch assembly.

No heat in broil; bake and time bake operations normal

1. Broil heating element open—turn off the power, and remove the broil heating element from the circuit. Check its resistance with an ohmmeter. A reading of infinity is a clear indication of an open heating element. Compare any other resistance reading with the figures published in the manufacturer's specifications.

2. Selector switch S1 defective—replace the broil heating element, and set up the oven controls for a BROIL operation. Measure the

voltage across the broil element (between points **J** and **M**). The trouble is confirmed if the meter shows any voltage less than the main supply voltage.

Time bake operation warms oven, but does not go to full heat

1. Clock/timer motor defective—this trouble is confirmed if the clock does not keep time properly. Make certain that the clock is receiving full 120 V line power before replacing it with a new one.

2. Timer switch mechanism defective—if the clock keeps proper time, set the oven START and STOP controls so that the oven begins running at full heat, and measure the voltage at the timer switch contact (between points **G** and **A**). The trouble is confirmed if the meter shows 120 V or less. Under normal conditions, this test shows 240 V.

Food burns in time bake; other operations normal

The real problem in this case is that the timer switch continues applying 240 V power to the bake element after the timer assembly has timed out. The trouble is doubly confirmed if the bake element goes to full heat before the START time is reached. Replace the timer switch assembly.

Uneven baking; foods burned on bottom, but undone on top

This complaint is most often caused by improper use of the oven racks. The user's manual should clearly specify the proper arrangement of racks and cooking utensils for various types of baking and broiling jobs.

Oven temperature incorrect

Carefully confirm this symptom by comparing the reading on an oven thermometer against the temperature settings on the oven's thermostat control knob. The manufacturer's servicing notes most likely spell out exact procedures for carrying out such a test.

If the thermostat can be calibrated, set up the test and calibration operations specified in the service manual. Replace the thermostat control if it cannot be calibrated or if it appears to be badly out of alignment.

12-3 CIRCUITS FOR SELF-CLEANING OVENS

Many modern electric ranges have self-cleaning ovens. The circuitry for self-cleaning operations is always an integral part of the normal oven controls; but for the sake of simplicity, this chapter deals with self-cleaning and normal oven circuits separately.

Self-cleaning ovens simply use brute-force heat to literally burn away any grease and food substances collected in the oven space. During this CLEAN cycle, both heating elements are allowed to produce their maximum heat and to raise the oven temperature to 850°–1000°F. Most food materials vaporize in this temperature range; and after running the self-cleaning operation for an hour or two, the user can expect to find the oven fairly clean. Larger oven units often have a special blower that forces the resulting vapors and smoke outside the house.

A normal oven unit operated in the range of 850°–1000°F would pose some serious safety hazards. The outside surfaces of the range, for instance, would get dangerously hot; and anyone opening the oven door at such operating temperatures might walk away with some serious burns on the hands and face.

Electric ranges designed for self-cleaning operations have extra-thick heat insulation around the oven spaces, and there is an oven door latch that is automatically engaged throughout the self-cleaning cycle.

From the user's point of view, a self-cleaning operation begins by setting the oven selector knob to CLEAN and adjusting the STOP timer (the same one used for TIME BAKE) to the desired cleaning interval. The self-cleaning circuitry then takes over all operations throughout the cleaning interval.

12-3.1 Theory of Self-Cleaning Ovens

Figure 12-19 shows a simplified schematic diagram for the self-cleaning portion of a modern electric range. The diagram is simplified in the sense that most switches used only for BAKE and TIME BAKE are not included. The timer motor is the same one used for the TIME BAKE operations described in Sec. 12-2. Selector switch contacts SS1 are operated by the same oven selector switch used for selecting other oven operations. The bake and broil heating elements are also the same ones used for normal oven operations. The

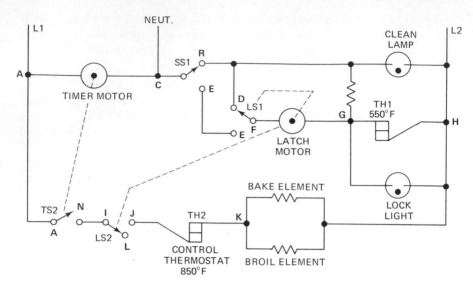

Fig. 12-19   Simplified schematic of a self-cleaning section.

remaining components that are normally used only during the CLEAN cycle are described in the following paragraphs.

CLEAN lamp—this 120 V neon lamp goes on the moment the user starts a self-cleaning cycle, and it remains lighted until the cycle is ended. This lamp actually confirms that the oven is set up for self-cleaning.

Latch motor—the latch motor is a small 120 V motor that performs two important functions: it drives a gear assembly that operates the oven latch and it operates a set of two limit switches, LS1 and LS2, which prevent the cleaning operations from starting until the door is indeed properly latched closed.

LOCK light—this 120 V neon lamp goes on as soon as the oven door is latched and heat is applied to the oven space. The LOCK light goes out when the heating cycle is over and the oven is cooling off. Its main purpose is to inform the user that the cleaning cycle is progressing as it should and that the oven door is latched closed.

TH1 thermostat—TH1 is a normally closed thermostat contact that opens at about 550°F. This thermostat operates the LOCK light and prevents the latch motor from running while the oven temperature is above 550°. The user, in other words, cannot stop a self-cleaning operation mid-cycle and expect to be able to open the oven door.

TH2 thermostat—TH2 is the main heat control thermostat for self-cleaning operations. The thermostat might be calibrated to open at 850°F as shown in the schematic in Fig. 12-19, but some models use control thermostats rated as high as 1000°F.

The oven CLEAN cycle can be broken down into six distinct phases: start, preheat, clean, cool down, automatic reset, and manual reset. The contact configurations for each of these phases are shown in Table 12-2.

The start phase begins the moment the user sets the oven selector knob to CLEAN and sets the STOP timer to a selected cleaning interval—normally a time interval on the order of two hours. As shown in Table 12-2a, this start phase provides a 120 V circuit for the CLEAN lamp through SS1 and a second 120 V path for the latch motor through TH1, LS1, and SS1. The CLEAN lamp thus goes on and the latch and timer motors begin running.

The start phase ends and the preheat phase begins the moment the latch motor activates limit switches LS1 and LS2. At that moment, the latch motor is turned off by LS1, and the heating elements both receive full 240 V power through TS2, LS2, and the closed contacts of TH2. The oven door is now latched closed and heat is being applied to the oven.

The third phase, the actual cleaning phase, begins the moment the oven temperature reaches 550°F and TH1 contacts open. Opening these contacts turns on the LOCK lamp and, more importantly, makes it impossible for the user to stop the cycle and immediately open the oven door.

The oven temperature eventually rises to a point where it trips open the contacts of TH2, which is the clean temperature control thermostat. This thermostat regulates the oven temperature throughout the cleaning phase by cycling open and closed.

The cleaning phase ends and the cool-down phase begins as soon as the timer reaches the end of its timing interval. The STOP timer then opens TS2 to remove all 240 V power to the heating elements. The oven temperature thus begins falling toward room temperature.

As the oven temperature cools below 550°F, the contacts of TH1 close to extinguish the LOCK light and make it possible to unlatch the door during the final phase of the cycle.

The moment the LOCK light goes out, the user knows the oven cleaning operation is over, and that the cycle can be ended by setting the oven selector switch to any position other than CLEAN. Setting the oven selector switch away from CLEAN allows the latch motor to run through a 120 V path provided by the closed contacts of TH1, LS1, and the C–E connection of SS1. See Table 12-2f. The latch motor thus begins running, pulling open the door latch and resetting LS1 and LS2 to their normal off positions.

12-3.2 Troubleshooting Self-Cleaning Oven Circuits

The following symptoms and troubleshooting notes apply to the self-cleaning oven circuit shown in Fig. 12-19. The systematic test procedures illustrated here, however, can be extended to any other version of the same system on the market today.

TABLE 12-2   Contact configurations and actions for a self-cleaning oven operation

	Phase	Contacts Closed†		Ongoing Action
a.	**Start**	TS2	A–I	Latch motor running
		SS1	C–D	CLEAN lamp on
		LS1	D–F	LOCK light off
		LS2	I–L	No heat
		TH1	G–H	
		TH2	J–K	
b.	**Preheat**	TS2	A–I	Latch motor not running,
		SS1	C–D	door latched closed
		LS1	E–F*	CLEAN lamp on
		LS2	I–J*	LOCK light off
		TH1	G–H	Heat applied
		TH2	J–K	
c.	**Clean**	TS2	A–I	Latch motor not running,
		SS1	C–D	door latched closed
		LS1	E–F	CLEAN lamp on
		LS2	I–J	LOCK light on
		TH1	open*	Heat at 850°F
		TH2	cycling open and closed	
d.	**Cool-Down**	TS2	A–N*	Latch motor not running,
		SS1	C–D	door latched closed
		LS1	E–F	CLEAN lamp on
		LS2	I–J	LOCK light on
		TH1	open	Oven temperature falling
		TH2	J–K*	
e.	**Automatic Reset**	TS2	A–N	Latch motor not running,
		SS1	C–D	door latched closed
		LS1	E–F	CLEAN lamp on
		LS2	I–J	LOCK light on
		TH1	G–H*	Oven cool
		TH2	J–K	
f.	**Manual Reset**	TS2	A–N	Latch motor runs until LS1
		SS1	C–E*	and LS2 change state; door
		LS1	D–F	unlatched
		LS2	I–L	CLEAN lamp off
		TH1	G–H	LOCK light off
		TH2	J–K	Oven cool

†Asterisks (*) indicate a contact closure that is different from the previous phase.

Clean cycle does not start, but clean lamp goes on

1. Limit switch LS1 stuck or broken open—set the oven to start a CLEAN cycle, and connect a voltmeter across the latch motor (between points **F** and **G**). The trouble is confirmed if the meter shows zero volts and the LOCK light *does not* go on. Replace the limit switch assembly.

2. Latch motor defective—if the previous test shows 120 V across the motor terminals, but it still does not run, the trouble is in the motor or its linkage to the door latch. Remove the motor from the circuit and bench-test it by applying 120 V to it. The trouble is confirmed if the motor does not run when disconnected from the latch assembly. The trouble is in the latch assembly itself, however, if the motor runs properly on the bench. Replace the latch motor or latch assembly as appropriate.

3. Thermostat contacts TH1 stuck or broken open—this particular trouble is confirmed if the LOCK light goes on the moment the oven is set up for a CLEAN cycle. Replace the thermostat assembly.

Cycle does not start, clean lamp does not go on

1. Line voltage not reaching the cleaning circuitry—check the voltages at the lines feeding the cleaning circuitry (between points **A** and **C**, **C** and **H**, and **A** and **H**). These voltages should be 120 V, 120 V, and 240 V, respectively.

2. SS1 open—the process of elimination leaves little doubt that the selector switch contacts are stuck or broken open. If proper line voltages are reaching the cleaning circuit as confirmed by the previous voltage checks, replace the oven selector switch assembly.

Cycle starts, but door latch cycles open and closed

1. Selector switch SS1 shorted or stuck closed—this trouble is confirmed if the door latch continues cycling open and closed whenever the oven selector switch is set to some other oven function such as BAKE or BROIL. Replace the entire oven selector switch assembly.

2. LS1 shorted—this limit switch is at fault if the cycling action of the door latch stops the moment the oven selector switch is set to BAKE or BROIL. Replace the entire limit switch assembly on the latch motor shaft.

Cycle starts, but no heat is applied (lock light never goes on)

1. Timer switch contact TS2 stuck or broken open—connect a jumper wire across LS2 (between points **I** and **J**), connect a voltmeter across the suspected timer switch contacts (between points **A** and **I**), and connect a second jumper across the main heat control thermostat TH2 (between points **J** and **K**). Set up the oven for a CLEAN cycle, and note the voltage across the timer switch. The trouble is confirmed if the voltage goes immediately to 240 V. Replace the timer switch assembly.

2. Limit switch LS2 contacts LS2 stuck or broken open—if the test in the previous paragraph shows zero volts and the heating elements begin warming up, remove the jumper wire connected across LS2 (between points **I** and **J**). If the heat immediately goes off, the trouble is confirmed.

3. Control thermostat contacts TH2 stuck or broken open—assuming that the heat does not go off in the previous test, remove the jumper wire connected across TH2. If the heat immediately goes off, the trouble is confirmed. This diagnosis can be double-checked by letting the oven cool and connecting a jumper across both the timer switch contact and limit switch (between points **A** and **J**). The diagnosis is doubly confirmed if a voltmeter shows full 240 V power across the thermostat contacts (between points **J** and **K**) the instant the CLEAN cycle is initiated.

    Replace the control thermostat assembly.

Cycle runs normally, but lock light does not go on

The most likely cause of this complaint is a set of shorted contacts in TH1. This trouble is confirmed if the LOCK light goes on when the CLEAN cycle is operated with a jumper wire across the contacts of TH1 (between points **G** and **H**).

If the light does not go on under this test condition, the light itself is at fault and should be replaced.

Door cannot be unlatched at the end of a cycle

1. LS1 contacts stuck or broken open—assuming that the door is still latched closed and the cleaning cycle has ended, set the oven selector switch to a BAKE or BROIL operation, and carefully connect a jumper wire across the **E–F** contacts of LS1. The trouble is confirmed if the latch motor begins running.

2. Selector switch SS1 contacts stuck or broken open—set up the test conditions just described, however connect the jumper wire across the **C–E** contacts of the selector switch assembly. This trouble is confirmed if the latch motor begins running.

Heat phase of the cycle never ends

The trouble in this instance is most likely in the timer switch assembly. Attempt to open TS2 by setting the STOP timer so that the oven operation should stop, and set the oven selector switch to BAKE or BROIL. The timer switch assembly is at fault if the heating phase continues.

Oven shuts down during main cleaning phase

The main cleaning control thermostat is probably stuck closed, allowing the oven temperature to rise far enough to trip open the overheat safety thermostat (not shown in Fig. 12-19). The trouble can be confirmed by setting up a cleaning cycle and monitoring the voltage across the control thermostat contacts TH2 (between points **J** and **K**). If full 240 V power never appears across this thermostat up until the time the oven shuts down, the trouble is confirmed. Replace the control thermostat assembly.

Inadequate cleaning

This complaint is caused either by not following the instructions in the user's manual or by an open heating element. Check the elements by observing the operation of the oven in BAKE and BROIL. If the heating elements are at fault, they should display symptoms in these oven modes. See the appropriate troubleshooting notes in Sec. 12-2.2.

12-4 QUESTIONS

1. What is the main difference between a switched-heat and an infinite heat surface-unit control?

2. How is an infinite heat control different from a thermostatically controlled surface unit? How are they both different from a switched-heat control?

3. Name one simple and reliable way to distinguish a surface unit that is

controlled by a King Seeley system from one that is controlled by a Robertshaw circuit.

4. What is the purpose of a PREHEAT setting on an oven selector switch?

5. What is the typical temperature range for self-cleaning operations?

6. How is the design of an oven unit using self-cleaning circuits different from a normal oven unit?

13

Refrigerators and Freezers

The primary purpose of a refrigerator system—a refrigerator or freezer chest—is to lower the temperature of stored foods to near or below the point where bacteria can cause rapid spoilage. Most domestic refrigerators have two separate compartments: a freezer cabinet and a provisions cabinet. The freezer cabinet operates in a temperature range anywhere between 0°F and 20°F. The provisions cabinet runs at temperatures on the order of 35°–40°F.

A freezer chest, on the other hand, is used only for storing foods at very low temperatures. Freezers often operate at temperatures as low as −20°F.

Modern refrigerators and freezers are relatively simple and highly reliable appliances. It is no longer unusual for one of these appliances to serve continuously for five years or more without developing any significant troubles. Refrigerators and freezers do eventually develop troubles, however, and a serviceman must be prepared to service them with the same skill and competence that he exhibits for more trouble-prone appliances.

This chapter describes the general principles, theory of operation, and troubleshooting techniques appropriate for home refrigerators and freezers.

The emphasis is on the electrical features of these appliances. Chapter 6 describes the principles of cooling systems in greater detail.

13-1   GENERAL OPERATING PRINCIPLES

Older home refrigerators have a small freezer compartment located at the top of the provisions section. Cooling coils wound around the outside of the freezer compartment lower the freezer temperature to about 20°F. The same coils are exposed to air in the provisions space, but because the provisions space is much larger than the freezer cabinet, the temperature in the larger space normally remains at about 35°F. The temperature in the refrigerator space, in other words, is mainly determined by the temperature of the freezer—the colder the freezer, the cooler the provisions compartment.

13-1.1   Cabinet Temperature Control

Modern home refrigerators also have separate freezing and provisions compartments, but independent temperature controls. The main cooling operation still takes place in the freezer in most instances, but the freezer compartment no longer must be located at the top of the provisions cabinet (as shown in Fig. 13-1) if a small fan is used to circulate air between the two. Using one or more fans and appropriate air ducts between the cabinets makes it possible to locate the freezer compartment at the side or bottom of the refrigerator.

The temperatures in the two cabinets can be controlled by a set of thermostats. A thermostat located in the freezer compartment controls the temperature in that part of the refrigerator by cycling the compressor on and off. A mechanical thermostat, located in an air duct between the freezer and provisions cabinet, directly operates a set of louvers or baffles which, in turn, regulate the amount of chilled air flowing from the freezer to the provisions part of the refrigerator. See Fig. 13-2.

Some refrigerator systems have separate sets of evaporator coils for the freezer and provisions cabinets, and independent temperature control is made possible by thermostatically regulating the flow of refrigerant through the two sections. A few deluxe refrigerator models have completely independent cooling systems for the two cabinets.

13-1.2   Automatic Defrosting

Frosting is a perennial problem associated with refrigerators and freezers. As the cooling coils chill the air inside the unit, moisture condenses and freezes on them, and if the inside temperature is low enough, frost also gathers on the foods and packages.

Fig. 13-1 The freezer compartment of this refrigerator is located at the top of the unit. The user's controls are situated at the top of the provisions cabinet. (Courtesy of General Electric Major Appliance Group)

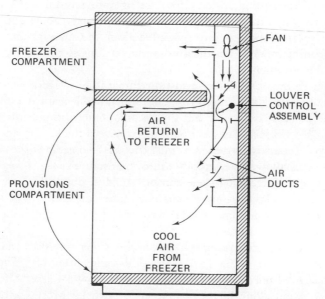

Fig. 13-2 Airflow between the freezer and provisions cabinets in a typical refrigerator.

If the refrigerator door is not opened very often, frosting can be held to a minimum because of a limited supply of warmer, damp air from the surrounding atmosphere. The more often a door is opened (or the longer it is held open), however, the more critical the frosting problem can become. In the case of "standard" refrigerators, the user has to defrost the unit at fairly regular intervals.

The simplest kinds of refrigerators and freezers are defrosted by manually turning off the cooling system, opening the doors, and allowing the warmer room air to thaw the frost. The user has to make some preparations for temporarily keeping the foods cold and has to contend with a dripping-water mess.

Some refrigerator and freezer appliances have low-power electric heating coils attached to the cooling coils to speed up the defrosting job. When using this type of semiautomatic defrosting system, the user must initiate the defrosting cycle by setting a control knob to DEFROST or by depressing a special pushbutton. The defrosting cycle is ended either manually (by resetting the control knob to COOL) or automatically by a defrost timer or thermostat control.

A few domestic refrigerators and freezers have defrosting systems that shunt some of the warm refrigerant from the condenser into the evaporator coils. The effect is the same as applying heat by means of electric heating elements.

Automatic defrosting or "frost-free" refrigerators and freezers are rapidly becoming the unanimous choice for busy homeowners. These appliances are somewhat more elaborate and expensive than the manual and semiautomatic defrosting models, but the automatic versions eliminate the defrosting mess and inconvenience.

The key to the operation of a so-called frost-free refrigerator or freezer is actually automatic defrosting. Frost does indeed collect on the cooling coils every time the door is opened, but the automatic defrosting feature melts off the layer of frost before it has a chance to grow very thick. The small amount of water that results is carried to a small tray at the bottom of the refrigerator unit where it is allowed to evaporate into the room air.

An automatic defrosting cycle can be ended in much the same way that semiautomatic cycles are—by means of a timer assembly or a thermostat control. Starting an automatic defrosting cycle at the right time, however, can be a more involved task.

Some automatic defrosting systems have a timer assembly that activates the defrosting cycle at regular twenty-four-hour intervals. The timer is actually a shaded-pole motor that drives a reducing gear assembly that turns once every twenty-four hours to activate a switch. Most of these timer-controlled units have a dial that allows the user to set the time of day when the defrosting cycle will take place.

A second kind of motor timing scheme for the defrost cycle keeps track of the compressor's running time. The timer motor, connected in parallel with the compressor circuit, activates the defrosting mechanism after a total running time of eight to twelve hours. This system is slightly more efficient than the regular-interval timer because its operation is based on the refrigerator's actual work load.

The most efficient timer defrosting system takes advantage of the fact that frost accumulates only after the refrigerator door has been opened to moist air from the outside for a while. The timer motor in this case is connected to a door switch and thus runs only while the door is open. After running for a total of about fifteen minutes, the timer activates the defrosting system. The less often the door is opened (or the more brief the openings), the less often the defrosting cycle runs.

Other schemes for initiating the defrosting cycle eliminate the need for a special electric timer motor. In one instance, the refrigerator has a mechanical counter that keeps track of the number of times the door is opened. After the door has been opened fifty or sixty times, the defrost cycle begins. Another nontimed defrost circuit starts the defrost cycle each time the compressor is turned off.

Automatic defrosting refrigerators and freezers must have a forced-air system that circulates inside air while the door is closed. Moving the air continuously in this fashion insures that all frost collects on the cooling coils, and not on stored foods and packages. Unfortunately, this same forced-air feature can create a dehydrating effect in the unit.

Foods stored in the main airstream of a frost-free refrigerator are likely to dry out after a short time if they are not packaged or tightly wrapped. An open container of ice cream in the freezer compartment, for instance, gradually turns into a sticky mess as the water is drawn from it. But note that fresh fruits and vegetables do not have to be wrapped. Will they not dry out? Not if they are stored in the special compartments provided for them. The fruit and vegetable bins in the provisions cabinet are not mere conveniences —they prevent dehydration by keeping the foods out of the main airstream inside the unit.

Frost-free refrigerators and freezers also have low-power electric heating elements that prevent defrosting water from freezing on its way to the evaporation tray at the bottom of the unit. Some refrigerators even have a separate heating coil for warming the drip pan, thereby preventing a build-up of water from the defrosting cycles.

13-1.3   Automatic Ice Cube Makers

Several popular refrigerator models include an automatic ice cube making feature, like the one displayed in Fig. 13-3. This system requires

Fig. 13-3 This refrigerator model has a side-by-side freezer/provisions cabinet arrangement and features an automatic ice cube maker. (Courtesy of General Electric Major Appliance Group)

a connection to the home's fresh water supply, and it uses a set of automatic controls to (a) inject the proper amount of fresh water into an ice cube mold, (b) control the freezing operation, (c) dump the cubes into a storage bin, and (d) stop the operation the moment the bin is filled.

One type of ice cube system uses a single plastic mold that has small holes running into each cube compartment. Whenever a cycle is started, a solenoid valve opens to let fresh water run through the holes into each of the ice cube compartments. This filling operation is timed by a master timer motor assembly.

A thermostat located near the front of the mold tray senses the temperature of the water and halts the freezing operation when the ice is cooled to a temperature of 15°–20°F. And when the thermostat contacts close, the motor engages a set of fingers at the bottom of each cube compartment; and these fingers lift the cubes out of the mold. Gravity then carries the cubes into a storage bin.

The storage bin is equipped with a lever switch that closes when the bin is full. The automatic ice cube cycle thus continues until the lever switch turns off the timer/control motor.

13-1.4   Freezer Thaw Alarms

Some freezer chests include an alarm system that is triggered whenever the inside temperature rises above about 15°F. The alarm can be a buzzer or a small red lamp on the outside of the appliance. Various types of thaw and power-failure alarms are also available as separate units from appliance dealers.

13-2   GENERAL THEORY OF OPERATION

Refrigerators and freezers operate according to the same general principles. Generally speaking, the only real difference between the two kinds of appliances is that a refrigerator has two main compartments, and a freezer has only one. The operating temperatures are also different, but any discussion of a freezer compartment for a refrigerator applies rather well to a freezer chest.

13-2.1   The Basic Cooling System

Home refrigerators and freezers use the basic sealed cooling system described in detail in Chapter 6. They all include sets of condenser and evaporator coils, a combination motor and compressor, and thermostats for controlling the operating temperatures and on-off times of the cooling system. Figures 13-4(A) and (B) illustrate two common layouts for the basic cooling components and cabinets.

In Fig. 13-4(A) the freezer cabinet is located at the top of the appliance. The evaporator coils are located at the back of this cabinet, but a small blower circulates air from both compartments across the coils. The compressor and condenser coils are both located at the bottom of the refrigerator unit. As the condenser coils are located in a rather confined space, it is necessary to cool them by means of a separate forced-air blower.

The freezer compartment of the refrigerator illustrated in Fig. 13-4(B) is located at the bottom of the unit. Again, the evaporator coils are located behind this compartment, and a blower circulates air from both compartments across these coils. The compressor in Fig. 13-4(B) is at the bottom of the appliance, but the condenser coils are situated over the rear surface of the refrigerator. Placing the condenser coils on the back of the refrigerator allows natural air currents to cool them, and there is no need for a condenser cooling fan. The disadvantage of condenser coils situated along the back of the refrigerator is that the unit has to be spaced four to six inches away from a wall. A condenser that uses convection-current cooling is called a *static condenser*.

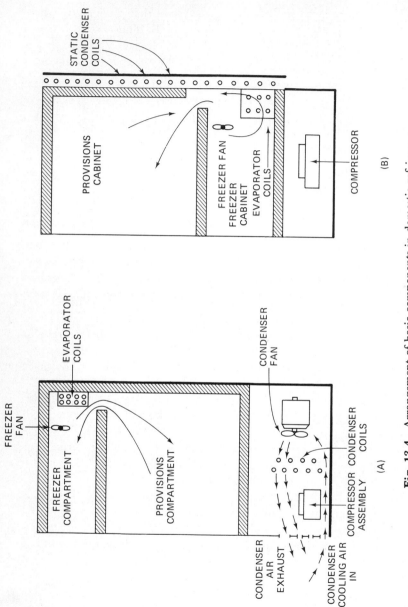

Fig. 13-4 Arrangement of basic components in domestic refrigerators. (A) Freezer cabinet at the top of the unit, forced-air fan for condenser cooling. (B) Freezer cabinet at the bottom of the unit, static condenser cooling.

Figure 13-4 merely illustrates two possible layouts for the compartments, evaporator and condenser coils, and compressor unit. The evaporator coils, for example, are usually located behind the freezer compartment, but they can also be fixed at the top, side, bottom, or some combination of these positions. The only rule about the placement of the evaporator coils is that they must be adjacent to the freezer compartment.

The motor/compressor assembly is rarely found anywhere but at the bottom of the refrigerator or freezer. The condenser coils, however, can be located at the bottom or on the back of the appliance, depending on whether or not they are to be cooled by a separate condenser fan. In the very early days of home refrigerator technology, the condenser coils were exposed at the top of the appliance.

A few deluxe refrigerator models have entirely independent cooling systems for the freezer and provisions compartments. Such appliances have two compressors, two evaporators, two condensers, and completely independent thermostat controls. (These models are obviously rather expensive.)

As in the case of most refrigeration and air-conditioning systems, the compressor and its motor are housed in the same sealed unit. The motor is normally a split-phase induction motor that can have built-in start capacitors and relays. Virtually all motor/compressor units have built-in thermal overload circuit breakers that automatically reset after a current overload condition has occurred. See Secs. 5-2.1 and 5-3.1 for further details about such motors and their start-up circuits.

13-2.2 Thermostat Controls

The compressor motor in domestic refrigerators and freezers is cycled on and off by means of a thermostat control. The thermostat is usually a bulb-and-diaphragm control that is quite similar to the Robertshaw heating control described in Chapter 4. In the case of this refrigeration control, however, the capillary is filled with a sample of the refrigerant rather than a hydraulic fluid.

The motor control thermostat bulb is fastened to the evaporator coils, causing the compressor motor to respond directly to the temperature of those coils. As the temperature around the evaporator coils rises, for instance, the fluid in the sensing bulb and capillary expands to force a set of motor-control contacts closed. The compressor thus begins running to lower the evaporator temperature; and when the preset cooling temperature is reached, the bulb's fluid contracts enough to allow the motor contacts to open again.

A second type of compressor motor control uses a diaphragm assembly but does away with the sensing bulb. This type of control responds to changes in the actual refrigerant pressure in the evaporator. A capillary tube leads a sample of the working refrigerant from the evaporator coils to the diaphragm. As the evaporator temperature rises because of an increasing temperature inside the refrigerator, the refrigerant expands and activates the diaphragm switch assembly. The compressor thus turns on to start a cooling cycle. The evaporator pressure gradually declines as it cools, eventually releasing the diaphragm pressure on the control switch and ending the cycle.

Refrigerator units that have a baffle or louver between the freezer and provisions compartments must use a mechanical thermostat to open and close the louvers. A capillary-and-diaphragm control is located at the exhaust duct between the two compartments; and as the temperature in the provisions cabinet rises, the fluid in the capillary expands to force open the louvers. Colder air from the freezer compartment then flows through the duct, across the louver control, and into the provisions cabinet. As soon as the temperature in the provisions cabinet falls to the level set on the control, the fluid in the capillary contracts to force the louvers closed.

Because the air flowing through the duct and louvers is always much colder than the air in the provisions section, a small electric heater is often used to delay the closing of the louvers. The need for this louver (or baffle) heater is explained in greater detail in Sec. 13-2.3.

Other thermostat controls may play secondary roles in some of the better refrigerator models. Thermostats, for instance, can be used to slow down or stop fan motors in the freezer and provisions cabinets whenever the temperature falls below a certain level. Overheat thermostats are sometimes used to control the upper heating level of defrost heaters during automatic defrosting cycles.

13-2.3   Heating Elements

Modern refrigerators and freezers have at least one low-power heating element. This particular heating element is a long, strip-type element that runs along the inside of the cabinet, directly behind the surface where the doors and cabinet meet. The stationary part of the cabinet behind or between the refrigerator doors is commonly called the mullion, and the electric heater located behind that surface is known as the *mullion heater*.

The main purpose of the mullion heater is to prevent condensation from forming around the doors or on the mullion. This condensation would create a messy and unsightly "sweating" effect on the outside of the appliance.

The mullion heater, normally rated somewhere between 10 W and 25 W, is often connected directly across the 120 V power terminals. The mullion heater is thus energized the moment the appliance is plugged in, and it remains energized as long as the appliance is in use. Other models have the mullion heater connected to the door switch in such a way that the heater is energized only as long as the door is closed.

Some refrigerators have additional heating elements that perform the same function as the mullion heater—preventing condensation from forming on outside surfaces of the appliance. And like the mullion heater, these extra heaters are generally named after the particular surface they warm.

A second type of heater is used to prevent the louvers or baffles between the freezer and provisions compartments from closing prematurely and operating too frequently. These louvers control the temperature of the provisions compartment by adjusting the flow of colder air from the freezer. The heater actually makes the louver thermostat less sensitive to the sudden temperature drops, which always occur at the air duct the moment the louvers are first opened.

This louver or baffle heater has a power rating of about 1 W, and it is usually connected directly across the 120 V supply line so that it is energized at all times.

Automatic defrosting systems call for additional electric heating elements. The defrost heating element is the "hottest" element used in any refrigerator or freezer. The element is attached or built into the evaporator coils, and it is energized at 120 V whenever the system calls for an automatic defrosting cycle. This heater is supposed to raise the temperature of the evaporator coils rather rapidly, thus clearing off any frost before the temperature inside the freezer compartment rises significantly. Defrost heating elements are rated anywhere between 200 W and 500 W.

Many freezers and refrigerators with an automatic defrosting feature also have drain-tube and drip-pan heaters. The drain-tube heater prevents the formation of ice in the tube that removes water from the defrosting cycle. The drip-pan heater is then used to warm the water as it accumulates in the pan, thus speeding up evaporation. The drain-tube heater has a relatively low power rating on the order of 5 W, and the drip-pan heater is rated at about 50 W. Both heaters are operated only during an automatic defrosting cycle.

13-3   A SIMPLE REFRIGERATOR OR FREEZER

The electrical schematics for simple refrigerators and freezers differ very little. In fact the schematic diagram in Fig. 13-5 could apply to either type of appliance. Of course the mechanical layouts for refrigerators and freezers are different, and freezers run about 10°–20°F colder than the freezer compartments in refrigerators.

13-3.1   Theory of Operation

The compressor assembly in Fig. 13-5 contains the compressor motor, start-up components, and an overload circuit breaker. Including all these components in the same sealed assembly makes the troubleshooting job easier, but servicing any part of the start-up circuit can be rather difficult.

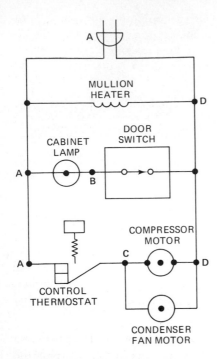

Fig. 13-5   Schematic diagram of a simple refrigerator or freezer.

The compressor motor starts whenever the control thermostat contacts snap closed, and it continues running until the unit is cooled enough to allow the contacts to pop open again.

The condenser fan is connected in parallel with the compressor assembly, and thus runs whenever the compressor does. Since the condenser motor is a rather low-power, shaded-pole motor, there is no need for any start-up or overload protection circuits.

There are not provisions for automatic or semiautomatic defrosting in this particular appliance.

13-3.2   Troubleshooting and Servicing Guide

The following troubleshooting notes apply to the circuit and test points in Fig. 13-5.

**Compressor and condenser fan do not start;
interior light does not go on**

Because it is unlikely that all three of these components will ever fail at the same time, chances are quite good that these symptoms are caused by a lack of 120 V power to them.

1. No 120 V power to the appliance—check for 120 V power at the service outlet. If no voltage is present at that point, check for a blown fuse or open circuit breaker in the service line.

2. Open wiring or broken connection at the input terminals of the appliance—check for 120 V power at various connections throughout the appliance. Visually inspect the wiring for loose or broken connections.

Compressor and condenser fan do not start; interior light goes on

1. Control thermostat stuck or broken open—locate the electrical contacts for the control thermostat, set the control for the coldest temperature, and measure the voltage across the contacts. The trouble is confirmed if the test shows full line voltage. Double-check this diagnosis by connecting a jumper wire across the thermostat contacts (between points **B** and **D**). If the compressor and condenser fan start running, the control thermostat must be replaced.

2. Loose electrical connection to the compressor and condenser fan motors—inspect the wiring between the control thermostat and the motors. Make any necessary repairs.

Compressor runs normally, but condenser fan does not; appliance smells hot

The most likely cause of these symptoms is an open condenser fan motor. Disconnect the wiring to the fan motor and check the continuity of the windings with an ohmmeter. A reading of infinity certainly confirms the diagnosis.

Also make certain that the fan blades turn freely on the motor shaft when the appliance is not running.

Unit does not cool; compressor short-cycles

These symptoms can be caused by a low service-line voltage, but they are the classic symptoms of a defective compressor unit. If the service-line voltage is greater than about 108 V when the compressor is attempting to start, the trouble must be in the compressor/motor assembly. Check the individual motor start-up components if they are readily accessible. Otherwise, replace the entire compressor assembly.

Compressor runs continuously; unit overcools

The user might have the thermostat control set too low, or the control knob might be loose on the shaft. Make certain that the knob is secured to the shaft, and set the control for the least cooling level.

If the compressor continues running, unplug the appliance, and disconnect one of the wires to the thermostat control. Plug in the appliance and note the response. The control thermostat is internally shorted if the compressor *does not* run under this test condition.

There is always an outside chance that the compressor will start after the thermostat has been disconnected. The trouble in this case is caused by a short circuit around the thermostat control. Inspect the wiring and electrical terminals for a short-circuit condition between points **C** and **A**.

Compressor and condenser fan run continuously, but unit does not cool

These are the classic symptoms of a leaky or plugged refrigerant system. Check the refrigerant system, including the compressor valves and seals, as recommended by the manufacturer.

Appliance blows service-line fuses as the compressor starts

The most likely cause of this trouble is a shorted condenser fan motor. The compressor should not blow service-line fuses if it is defective because it has its own built-in overload circuit breaker. To check this diagnosis, unplug the appliance and disconnect at least one of the wires to the condenser fan motor. Reapply power to the appliance. If the compressor runs normally and the unit does not blow a service-line fuse, the condenser fan motor must be replaced.

The compressor's overload circuit breaker is failing if the unit still blows fuses when the compressor starts and the condenser fan motor is disconnected.

Cabinet lamp does not go on

The owner will normally replace a burned-out cabinet lamp before calling a serviceman. Assuming that the lamp itself is in good order, check the operation of the door switch. Connect a voltmeter across the terminals of the door switch (between points **B** and **D**), and manually work the switch open and closed. The switch must be replaced if full line voltage appears across it, even when the button is not depressed.

Look for a loose or broken connection if no voltage appears at the door switch.

Excessive condensation around the door

The mullion heater is most likely open in this instance. Locate the wiring to the heater, and disconnect it from the circuit. Check the resistance of the heater with an ohmmeter. An indication of infinite resistance confirms the diagnosis and the mullion heater should be replaced. Compare any other resistance reading against the figures specified in the manufacturer's service manual.

13-4   A REFRIGERATOR WITH AUTOMATIC DEFROSTING

The circuit in Fig. 13-6 is representative of a two-cabinet refrigerator that has an automatic defrosting feature. The defrosting mechanism in this instance is one that uses a solenoid valve to bypass hot compressor gasses into the evaporator coils. A similar unit using electrical defrosting would have a defrost heating coil in place of the solenoid valve.

13-4.1   Theory of Operation

The compressor motor assembly and condenser fan motor are connected in parallel so that the two motors always run at the same time. The control thermostat assembly is connected in series with one of the supply lines for the motor circuit so that the motors run whenever the thermostat switch is closed. The thermostat, then, is set to pop open whenever the evaporator temperature drops to some preset level.

The defrost timer assembly consists of a small shaded-pole timer motor that runs whenever the compressor does. This defrosting system thus keeps track of the total running time of the compressor unit; and after a running time of eight to twelve hours, the timer mechanism moves the defrost control switch from COOL to DEFROST. The timer motor continues running through the defrosting cycle, and it sets the defrost switch to COOL again after a period of ten minutes or so. The manufacturer's service notes specify the exact timing intervals for the defrost cycle.

The defrost solenoid and FC (freezer cabinet) heater are both energized throughout the defrost cycle. The solenoid is responsible for running hot

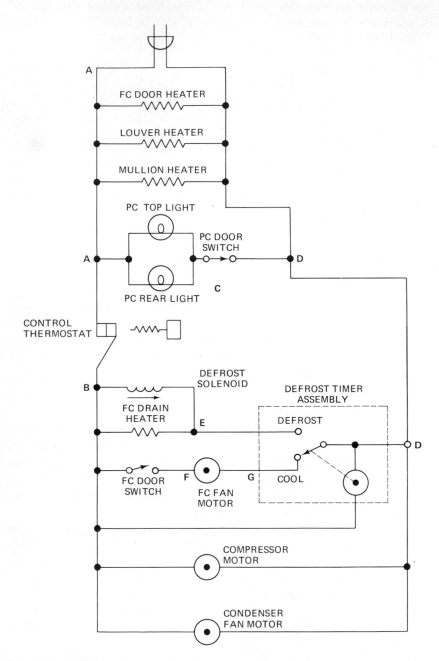

Fig. 13-6 Schematic diagram of a refrigerator that has an automatic defrost feature.

gasses from the condenser through the evaporator coils. This gas warms the coils and melts off any accumulated frost. The drain heater makes certain that the resulting water does not freeze on its way to the drip pan at the bottom of the appliance.

Note that the compressor runs throughout the defrosting cycle in this machine. Although the compressor is turned off during the defrost cycle in some machines (especially those using electrical defrost coils), it must run through the defrosting interval in this instance to provide the source of hot gasses.

This particular refrigerator has a single-speed fan motor in the freezer compartment that runs except when the freezer door is open or the system is running a defrost cycle. The temperature of the provisions cabinet (PC) is controlled by a louver thermostat. As this particular thermostat is a purely mechanical one, is does not appear on the electrical schematic. The louver control heater does appear on the schematic in Fig. 13-6, however.

13-4.2　Troubleshooting and Servicing Guide

The following troubleshooting and servicing notes apply to the circuit and test points for the refrigerator circuit in Fig. 13-6.

Motors do not start; interior lights do not go on

1. No power to the appliance—check for 120 V power at the service outlet. If no voltage is present, check for a blown fuse or circuit breaker in the service line.

2. Open wiring at the input terminals of the appliance—check for 120 V power at various test points throughout the appliance, and visually inspect the wiring for loose or broken connections.

Compressor and condenser fans do not start; interior lights go on

1. Control thermostat stuck or broken open—locate the electrical contacts for the control thermostat, set the control for the coldest operating temperature, and measure the voltage across the thermostat contacts. The trouble is confirmed if this test shows full line voltage.

    It is possible to doublecheck this diagnosis by connecting a temporary jumper wire across the thermostat contacts (between points **A** and **B**). If the compressor starts and runs normally, the trouble is doubly confirmed. Replace the entire control thermostat assembly.

2. Loose or broken electrical connection in the compressor circuit —check voltages, and inspect the wiring around the compressor and condenser fan motors. Make any necessary repairs.

Compressor runs normally, but condenser fan does not; appliance smells hot when running

The trouble in this instance is most likely due to an open fan motor winding. Disconnect the condenser fan motor from the circuit, and check the resistance of the windings with an ohmmeter. A reading of infinity confirms the trouble. Check any other resistance reading against the manufacturer's specifications before replacing the condenser fan motor.

Make certain that the fan is not jammed against another part of the frame.

Refrigerator does not cool; compressor short-cycles

1. Low supply voltage—check the voltage at the input terminals (between points **A** and **D**) while the compressor is attempting to start. If the voltage is less than about 108 V, the trouble is confirmed.

    The only appropriate repair in this case is to replace the service-line wiring with a heavier gauge wire. Of course a refrigerator should never be operated through an extension cord— a situation that invites low-voltage start-up problems.

2. Control thermostat operating erratically—connect a temporary jumper wire across the control thermostat contacts (between points **A** and **B**), and note the response of the compressor motor. The trouble is confirmed if the compressor now starts and runs normally. Replace the control thermostat assembly.

3. Compressor motor shorted or bound up—the process of elimination now leads to a defective motor/compressor assembly. The trouble can be in the start-up circuit, and if these components are accessible for servicing, they should be checked before condemning the entire compressor unit. Replace the compressor assembly only after exhausting all other possible troubles.

Compressor runs continuously; freezer overcools

The most likely cause of this trouble is a defective control thermostat. Make certain that the control knob is fastened securely to the adjustment shaft, and set the control for the least amount of cooling.

If the compressor continues running, unplug the appliance and disconnect the wiring to the thermostat control. Plug in the appliance again, and note the response. The trouble must be in the thermostat assembly if the compressor *does not* start under this test condition. If the compressor does start while the thermostat is disconnected, however, the trouble is caused by a short-circuit condition in the compressor wiring. Visually inspect the wiring between the thermostat and compressor.

Compressor and condenser fans run continuously, but unit does not cool

1. Defrost timer stuck in the DEFROST position—locate and disconnect the wire running between the defrost solenoid and defrost timer assembly (at point **E**). The trouble is in the defrost timer if the system then begins to cool.

    The freezer cabinet fan, by the way, cannot run if the defrost timer assembly is stuck in DEFROST. The trouble can thus be doubly confirmed by opening the freezer door and manually working the FC door switch open and closed. The timer is indeed defective if the symptoms persist and the fan does not run when the door switch is depressed.

2. Defrost solenoid stuck open—if the system does not begin cooling under the test conditions just described, carefully note the warmness of the evaporator coils. If the coils are warm to the touch—not room temperature, but warm—chances are good that the defrost solenoid is stuck open. Replace the defrost solenoid assembly.

3. Refrigerant system plugged or leaky—the defrost system having been checked out, inspect the refrigerant system as recommended by the manufacturer.

Frost builds up on evaporator and on the sides of the freezer compartment

1. Poor door seal—check the door seals by closing a strip of ordinary writing paper between them. If the paper can be slid around easily at any one point along the seals, the trouble is confirmed. Repair or replace the defective seal.

2. Defrost timer not receiving 120 V power—connect a voltmeter or voltage tester across the timer assembly (between points **B**

and **D**). The trouble is confirmed if no voltage appears between those two points. Check the wiring leading to the timer for loose or broken connections.

3. Defrost timer stuck in COOL—connect a temporary jumper wire across the DEFROST terminals on the defrost timer assembly (between points **D** and **E**). The trouble is confirmed if the refrigerator immediately begins a defrost cycle as noted by a warming of the evaporator coils. The actual trouble might be in the timer motor or its switch contacts, but because they are normally located in the same assembly, the entire unit should be replaced.

4. Defrost solenoid valve stuck closed—if the unit does not begin a defrosting cycle as described in the previous paragraph, the defrost solenoid is probably stuck closed. Make certain that the valve is receiving 120 V power by connecting a voltmeter across its terminals (between points **B** and **E**) while running the test condition described for trouble 3. The trouble is confirmed if this test shows 120 V across the coil, but the defrosting operation does not start. Replace the defrost solenoid valve assembly.

Ice builds up on inside of freezer door; defrosting seems otherwise normal

1. Leaky door seal on the freezer cabinet—check the door seals by closing a strip of paper between them. The seals must be repaired or replaced if the paper can be easily moved at any point along the seals.

2. Freezer door heater defective or inoperative—locate the connections to the FC door heater and make certain that they are tightly secured to a 120 V source. If the connections appear to be in good order and a voltage check shows that 120 V power is present, disconnect the wires to the FC heater and check its resistance with an ohmmeter. A reading of infinity indicates an open heater that must be replaced. Compare any other resistance reading against the figures published in the manufacturer's specifications.

Ice accumulates under evaporator

In this instance, the drain heater is most likely inoperative. Simulate a defrost cycle by connecting a temporary jumper wire across the

DEFROST terminals on the defrost timer assembly (between points **D** and **E**). Locate the drain heater wires, and connect a voltmeter across them. If the test shows 0 V, look for loose or broken wires or connections between the drain heater and its power source. If, on the other hand, the test shows full line voltage at the terminals, the drain heater is probably open. Disconnect the drain heater connections, and connect an ohmmeter across them. A reading of infinity confirms the trouble, and the drain heater must be replaced.

Provisions cabinet too warm; freezer temperatures near normal

1. Freezer cabinet (FC) fan inoperative—confirm this trouble by opening the freezer door and manually working the FC door switch. The FC fan should run whenever the switch is depressed. If the fan does not run, the trouble is either in the fan or door switch assembly.

    Locate the junction between the FC door switch and fan motor. The points will most likely be fastened by wire nuts inside the refrigerator's rear panel. Disconnect the door switch wiring from the fan motor and check the continuity of the switch assembly (between points **C** and **D**). A good fan switch shows zero resistance when it is depressed and infinite resistance when it is released. The switch is causing the trouble if it shows infinite resistance whether it is depressed or not. Replace the FC door switch assembly.

    If it turns out that the switch is in good working order, locate the wiring to the FC fan motor, and check its continuity with an ohmmeter. A reading of infinity is a sure sign of an open fan motor winding. Eliminate the possibility of a broken wire or connection to the FC fan motor before replacing it.

2. Louver mechanism sticking closed—set the provisions cabinet (PC) thermostat for maximum cooling, and close the freezer door. Open the door on the provisions cabinet, and tape the PC door switch closed with a strip of masking tape. Feel the flow of air around the air ducts leading into the provisions cabinet. If there is no cool air from the freezer entering the provisions cabinet, the trouble is confirmed.

    Remove the louver control mechanism, and note whether or not it is actually stuck closed. Replace the entire mechanism if a close visual inspection shows that a repair is not practical.

Provisions cabinet too cold; freezer temperature near normal

The most likely cause of this trouble is a badly adjusted PC thermostat or a louver control that is stuck open. Set the PC temperature control knob to the warmest setting—to OFF if that setting is available. Close the freezer door, and tape the PC door switch closed with a strip of masking tape. Feel the air around the louver mechanism. The trouble is confirmed if the moving air remains rather cool for five minutes or more.

Remove the louver control mechanism. Replace it if an on-the-spot repair is impractical.

Refrigerator blows service-line fuses after the compressor starts

See the same trouble in Sec. 13-3.2.

Cabinet lamps do not go on

See the same trouble in Sec. 13-3.2, using points **C** and **D** as switch test points.

Excessive condensation around the doors

See the same trouble in Sec. 13-3.2.

13-5 QUESTIONS

1. What do the designations PC and FC stand for?

2. How does the normal operating temperature for the freezer compartment in a refrigerator compare with the operating temperature of a freezer chest?

3. Name two types of controls that can be used to end defrosting cycles in refrigerators or freezers equipped with automatic or semiautomatic defrost systems.

4. Name five techniques for automatically starting a defrost cycle.

5. What is a mullion heater? What is it used for?

6. Why is it necessary to use a fan to circulate air inside a refrigerator or freezer equipped with an automatic defrost feature?

14

Room Air Conditioners

The primary purpose of an air-conditioning system is to lower the temperature of the air in one or more rooms in the home. Air conditioners also add to the general comfort by removing most of the moisture from the air. This dehumidifying operation is not an intentional add-on feature, however; rather, it is a convenient secondary effect caused by the cooling operation itself.

Room air-conditioning systems use the same basic refrigeration cycle described for refrigerators and freezers. Figure 14-1 displays a typical single-speed, window air conditioner unit. See Chapters 6 and 13. The fact that air conditioners must cool a much larger volume of air, however, makes it necessary to user a "stronger" and more efficient compressor and coolant.

A typical refrigerator, for instance, has a cooling capacity on the order of 750 Btu/hr, whereas a medium-size air conditioner must have a rating of about 20,000 Btu/hr. Air conditioners thus use higher evaporator pressures and temperature, and they almost always use Freon-22 (R-22) coolant.

Fig. 14-1   A single-speed room air conditioner typical of the smaller window units. (Courtesy of General Electric Major Appliance Group)

14-1   THEORY OF AIR CONDITIONERS

The basic sections of a room air conditioner include an air-circulation system, a refrigerant system, and a set of electrical controls. Figure 14-2 illustrates the basic layout of a typical room air conditioner.

14-1.1   The Air-Circulation System

As shown in Fig. 14-2, a room air conditioner contains two fans that are operated from the same motor assembly. The *evaporator fan* draws in room air, pushes it across the control thermostat and evaporator coils, and forces the resulting chilled air back into the room. The *condenser fan*, on the other hand, draws in outside air, forces it across the hot evaporator coils and compressor assembly, and directs it back outside.

The fan motor is usually a fractional-horsepower shaded-pole or induction motor. See Chapter 5 for details. The fan motor may have a two- or three-speed control that lets the user adjust the rate of air flow. The speed-control features is an important one because it actually determines the cooling rate of the air conditioning system—the higher the rate of air flow, the faster the unit can cool a room.

Figure 14-3 shows schematics for two- and three-speed shaded-pole fan motors. Note that the motor runs faster as the speed selector reduces the number of motor windings connected into the motor circuit. An induction

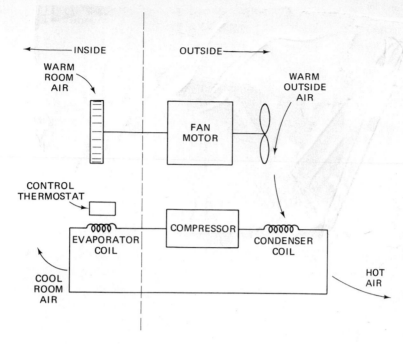

Fig. 14-2   Basic sections of a room air conditioner unit.

motor would use the same general wiring scheme for its run windings, but it would have an added start winding that would not be affected by setting the selector switch to different positions.

     Some air-conditioning systems have manual damper controls that let the user adjust the air-circulation system so that the fans either draw outside air into the room or direct room air outside. The system, in other words, can be operated as a two-way window fan. Of course the compressor (cooling system) ought to be turned off when exchanging outside and inside air.

14-1.2   The Refrigeration System

     The electrical portion of the refrigeration system consists of the motor in the compressor assembly, the motor start-up circuitry, and a thermostat control. The motor is always an integral part of the compressor assembly; therefore, unless stated otherwise, the term *compressor* applies to the motor as well as to the actual gas compression mechanism.

     Compressors for room air conditioners use heavy-duty induction motors that have horsepower ratings on the order of 1–4 hp, depending on the system's rated cooling capacity. Most compressor units are rated at 120 V, but many of them intended for commercial buildings are rated at 240 V.

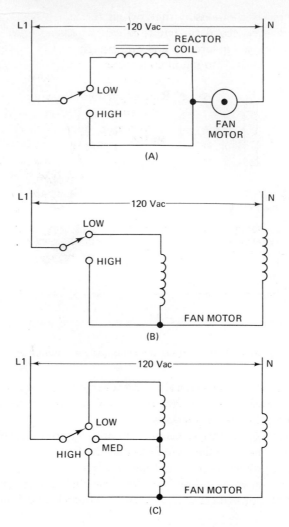

Fig. 14-3 Fan motor speed control circuits. (A) A two-speed selector using a reactor coil in the low speed circuit. (B) A two-speed selector circuit using a two-winding motor. (C) A three-speed selector circuit using a three-winding motor.

Since air conditioner compressors have relatively high horsepower ratings, most of them use a capacitor starting system of the type described in Sec. 5-2.1. The start capacitor and motor-start winding are normally cut out of the circuit once the compressor is operating above 80 percent of its normal operating speed. See Sec. 5-3.1. Some models, however, allow the capacitor and start winding to remain in the circuit at all times.

Air conditioner compressors that switch the start capacitor out of the circuit often have a second capacitor, called the *run capacitor*, connected in parallel with the start-up circuit. The run capacitor is never switched out of the circuit, and it is used to maintain a somewhat higher running torque.

Start capacitors are rated in the range of 10–100 μF, depending on the compressor's horsepower rating. Run capacitors have about one-half the rating of their start-up counterparts, running between 5 μF and 50 μF. The voltage ratings of both types of capacitors depend on the compressor's voltage rating: 200 V minimum for 120 V compressors and 400 V for 240 V air conditioners. Of course a 120 V air conditioner can use 400 V capacitors, but a 240 V system cannot use capacitors rated at 200 V.

The only motor controls for the compressor unit are an on/off switch and the main control thermostat. The on/off switch is actually part of the same switching assembly that is used to adjust the speed of the fan motor. The adjustable control thermostat regulates the room air temperature by cycling the compressor on and off.

As shown in Fig. 14-2, the thermostat sensor is located in the room-air stream, just ahead of the evaporator coils. This normally closed thermostat senses the temperature of the incoming room air; and if the air is warmer than the set-point of the thermostat control, the thermostat contacts remain closed. As the room air cools, however, the sensor detects a lower temperature and the thermostat contacts respond by opening. Opening the thermostat contacts turns off the compressor.

Figure 14-4 shows a simplified version of the compressor circuit and its controls. This particular model has no provisions for switching the start-up capacitor and motor winding out of the circuit.

The thermostat assembly is normally of the bulb type, but some use bimetal thermostats. See Chapter 4. In either case, the user adjusts the cool-

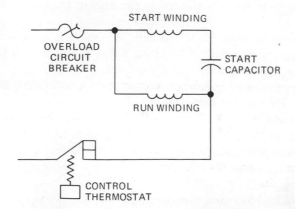

Fig. 14-4 Simplified compressor circuit.

ing temperature by rotating a control knob on the main control panel. This control is usually labeled with the terms LOW, NORMAL, and HIGH.

It is important to note at this point in the discussion that thermostat controls for room air conditioners are not scaled in degrees Fahrenheit. The reason for this is that an air conditioner cannot be expected to maintain a room temperature that is any more than 10°F below the outside temperature. Whenever the outside temperature is 95°F, for example, a properly rated air conditioner cannot cool the room efficiently to any temperature below 85°F. The actual control temperature, then, depends very much on the prevailing outside temperature, thus making a temperature-scaled thermostat control useless or misleading.

14-1.3   Electrical Controls

Figure 14-5 shows a complete schematic diagram for a rather simple room air conditioner unit. The user's controls include a mode selector switch assembly S1 and a thermostat control.

This mode selector switch allows the user to select a mode of operation by turning a rotary switch or depressing one of five different pushbuttons. The user's control actually sets a pattern of contact closures within the switch assembly.

If the user sets the selector switch for LOW FAN, for instance, contact S1-A closes to apply line voltage to the low speed winding of the fan motor. Note that the compressor circuit is not turned on. All that happens is that the fan motor runs to circulate air through the system. The user has the option of adjusting some mechanical dampers to exchange outside and inside air.

Setting the mode selector switch to HIGH FAN closes contact S1-C to increase the speed of the fan motor. The compressor motor is still not turned on.

The compressor motor is allowed to run only in the LOW COOL and HIGH COOL modes. In the LOW COOL mode power is applied to the low speed coil of the fan motor through S1-A, and full line power is applied to the compressor through contact S1-B. The blowers thus run at their low speed, but the compressor operates at its rated fixed speed.

The HIGH COOL setting differs from the LOW COOL mode only by setting the fan motor for a higher operating speed.

It is important to note that the mode selector switch has no direct bearing on the air conditioner's operating temperature. The thermostat controls the operating temperature, while the selector switch merely adjusts the rate of air flow (cooling) and determines whether or not the compressor is turned on at all.

Also note that the control thermostat has no influence upon the operation of the fan motor. The user, then, cannot expect to have the unit control

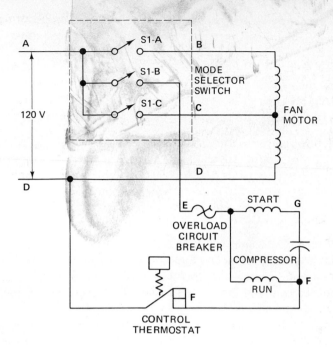

Fig. 14-5 A complete air conditioner unit using a single motor capacitor and a two-speed fan control.

MODE SELECTOR CONTACTS

	S1-A	S1-B	S1-C
OFF	O	O	O
LOW FAN	X	O	O
HIGH FAN	O	O	X
LOW COOL	X	X	O
HIGH COOL	O	X	X

O = OPEN
X = CLOSED

room temperature whenever it is operating in the LOW FAN and HIGH FAN modes.

14-2 TROUBLESHOOTING GUIDE FOR ROOM AIR CONDITIONERS

The troubleshooting notes in this section apply to 120 V room air conditioners; but the two models presented here are representative of virtually all consumer versions on the market today.

14-2.1   A Two-Speed Air Conditioner

The following troubleshooting notes apply to the air conditioner circuit in Fig. 14-5. The boldface letters indicate electrical test points commonly found in models of this type.

Unit does not run at all—seems dead

1. No power to the unit—Make certain that the air conditioner is plugged in, and check the voltage at the power input terminals (between points **A** and **D**). The trouble is confirmed if no voltage appears on the meter. Check the continuity of the power cable with an ohmmeter and make certain that 120 V power is actually available at the outlet.

2. Mode selector switch S1 defective—connect a voltmeter between the common power line and the low-speed winding on the fan motor (between points **B** and **D**). Set the mode selector switch to LOW FAN and then to LOW COOL. Note the response on the voltmeter.

    Next, connect the voltmeter between the common power line and the high-speed winding on the fan motor (between points **C** and **D**), and set the mode selector switch to HIGH FAN and HIGH COOL.

    If the voltmeter shows zero volts under both of these test conditions, the trouble is confirmed. Of course these tests assume that the line power is reaching the appliance as described in the previous trouble. Replace the mode selector switch assembly.

Compressor does not start, but fan motor runs normally

1. Compressor circuit breaker open—inspect the compressor's thermal circuit breaker, making certain that it is properly set.

2. Low line voltage—heavy-duty compressor motors cannot start if the supply voltage is more than 10–15 percent below the nameplate rating. Check the line voltage reaching the air conditioner compressor (between points **E** and **F**) *while attempting to start the motor.* The trouble is confirmed if the meter shows less than about 108 V.

    Make certain that the air conditioner is connected directly to the service outlet—there should be no extension cords in the line. If the home is an older one, the service wiring itself might be inadequate.

3. Control thermostat TH1 stuck or broken open—set the appliance to operate in either the LOW or HIGH COOL mode, and measure the voltage across the control thermostat (between points **E** and **F**). If the test shows full line voltage when the thermostat control is set for the highest cooling level, the trouble is confirmed.

    It is possible to doublecheck this diagnosis by turning off the air conditioner and "cheating" the thermostat control with a jumper wire connected across it (between points **D** and **F**). Try running the compressor with that jumper in place. There can be little doubt that the thermostat must be replaced if the compressor starts under this test condition.

4. Compressor capacitor defective—remove the capacitor from the motor circuit and check it with an ohmmeter. The capacitor is shorted or leaky if the resistance fails to rise above 100,000 Ω. It is open if the test immediately shows infinite resistance.

5. Mode selector switch S1 defective—set the air conditioner to run in either the LOW or HIGH COOL mode, and measure the voltage leaving the switch (between points **D** and **E**). The trouble is confirmed if this test shows zero volts. Replace the mode switch assembly.

6. Compressor assembly mechanically defective—the process of elimination leads to a mechanical problem in the compressor assembly if the previous five tests fail to uncover a trouble. Consult the manufacturer's servicing notes for detailed compressor tests. Replace the compressor assembly if a repair job appears impossible or impractical.

Fan does not run, but compressor runs normally

1. Fan or blower elements bent, jammed, or loose on the shaft—visually inspect the fan motor and connections to the shaft. Turn off the air conditioner, and attempt to turn the fan blades by hand. The trouble is confirmed if the fan or blower does not turn freely or if it appears to be slipping on the motor shaft.

2. Mode selector switch assembly S1 defective—apply 120 V power to the appliance, and set the mode switch to LOW FAN. Measure the voltage between the low-speed and common winding connection on the fan motor (between points **B** and **D**). The trouble is in the switch assembly if this test shows zero volts. Replace the entire switch assembly.

3. Fan motor defective—this trouble becomes apparent if the previous test shows full line voltage is reaching the fan motor, but it does not run. Doublecheck the diagnosis by removing the fan motor and checking the resistance of the windings with an ohmmeter. A reading of infinity is a clear-cut sign of an open winding. Compare any other resistance reading with the manufacturer's specifications.

Fan or compressor does not stop when switch is set to off

The mode selector switch is the most likely cause of this symptom. Replace the switch assembly.

Little or no cooling effect; fan and compressor run normally

1. Restricted air flow—visually inspect the unit, especially the air filters, for accumulated dirt and foreign objects.

2. Improper insulation around the unit—visually inspect the thermal insulation, both inside the unit and around the window.

3. Low line voltage—check the line voltage at the compressor (between points **E** and **F**) while the compressor is running. This trouble is confirmed if the test shows less than about 110 V.

4. Low refrigerant level—check the refrigerant level according to the manufacturer's servicing notes.

Evaporator accumulates excessive frost

1. Outside temperature below selected air conditioning temperature—most room air conditioners frost up whenever they are operated while the outside temperature is below 70°F. Instruct the user to avoid running the compressor during cool weather.

2. Restricted air flow—visually inspect the unit for accumulated dirt or foreign objects.

3. Control thermostat TH1 sticking closed—operate the unit at its lowest cooling setting, and spray the thermostat assembly with a bit of aerosol freon. The trouble is confirmed if the compressor continues to run. Replace the thermostat assembly.

4. Thermostat assembly bent or forced out of place—compare

the position of the thermostat sensor with the manufacturer's drawings or photos.

5. Improper refrigerant level—check the refrigerant level according to the manufacturer's specifications.

Unit blows service line fuses or circuit breaker

1. Improper fusing—check the service-line fusing for proper current and time-delay specifications.

2. Low line voltage—check the line voltage at the compressor (between points **E** and **F**) while attempting to start the unit. This trouble is confirmed if the test shows less than about 110 V. If the fuse or circuit breaker blows too quickly to get an accurate reading, take the reading across the fan motor (between points **B** and **D**) with the unit set for LOW FAN operation.

14-2.2 A Three-Speed Air Conditioner

The following troubleshooting notes apply to the air conditioner circuit in Fig. 14-6. Note that the compressor circuit in this case uses separate start and run capacitors and a relay-type start-up circuit.

The coil in the start-up relay in this machine is connected in parallel with the compressor's start winding. Whenever power is first applied to the compressor circuit, current flows through the start capacitor, the normally closed contacts of the start-up relay, and the compressor's start winding. There is very little line voltage across the start winding at first—there is not enough voltage available there to operate the start-up relay. The relay contacts thus remain closed until the compressor reaches about 80 percent of its normal operating speed.

The moment the compressor is running close to its normal operating speed, the voltage across the start winding approaches full line voltage, and the start-up relay is energized.

Energizing the start-up relay opens the relay contacts to remove the start capacitor from the circuit. The start-up relay coil and start winding of the compressor, however, continue receiving "holding" current through the run capacitor. Note that the run capacitor is never cut out of the circuit.

The resistor connected across the start capacitor is used to bleed off any electrical charge remaining on its plates after the relay contacts have opened.

Unit does not run at all—seems dead

1. No power to the unit—make certain that the air conditioner is plugged in, and check the voltage at the power input terminals

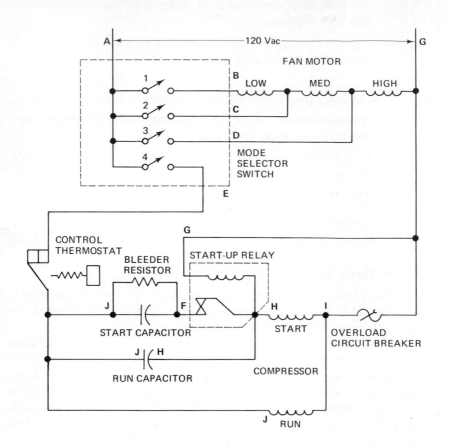

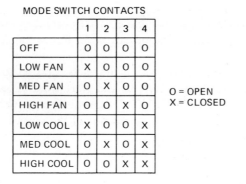

MODE SWITCH CONTACTS

	1	2	3	4
OFF	O	O	O	O
LOW FAN	X	O	O	O
MED FAN	O	X	O	O
HIGH FAN	O	O	X	O
LOW COOL	X	O	O	X
MED COOL	O	X	O	X
HIGH COOL	O	O	X	X

O = OPEN
X = CLOSED

Fig. 14-6 Schematic diagram of an air conditioner unit using start and run capacitors and a three-speed fan control.

(between points **A** and **G**). The trouble is confirmed if the meter shows no voltage. Check the continuity of the power cable with an ohmmeter or continuity tester, and make certain that 120 V power is actually available at the service outlet.

2.   Mode selector switch assembly defective—connect a voltmeter between the low-speed coil on the fan motor and the circuit's return (neutral) line (between points **B** and **G**), and attempt to start the air conditioner in the LOW COOL mode. Note the voltage; then move the voltmeter connection to the compressor circuit (between points **E** and **G**). The trouble is confirmed if both voltage tests show zero volts. This test assumes, however, that full line voltage is reaching the switch assembly as read between points **A** and **G**.

     To doublecheck this diagnosis, set the air conditioner to OFF and connect a jumper wire across contact 1 in the mode selector switch (between points **A** and **B**). There can be little doubt that the switch assembly is at fault if the fan motor begins running at its low speed. Replace the entire mode switch assembly.

Fan motor does not run at any setting; compressor runs normally

1.   Fan or blower elements bent, jammed, or loose on the motor shaft—visually inspect the fan motor and its shaft connections. Turn off the air conditioner, and attempt to turn the fan blades by hand. The trouble is confirmed if the blades do not turn freely or if they appear to be slipping on the motor shaft.

2.   Mode selector switch assembly defective—set the selector switch for LOW FAN, and connect a voltmeter across all the fan motor windings (between points **B** and **G**). The trouble is in the switch assembly if this test shows zero volts. Replace the entire switch assembly.

     It is possible to doublecheck this diagnosis by connecting a jumper wire across contact 1 in the mode switch assembly while the air conditioner is set to run in the LOW FAN mode. The switch assembly is definitely at fault if the fan motor runs under this test condition.

3.   Fan motor defective—the trouble becomes apparent if the previous test shows that full line voltage is reaching the motor windings, but the motor does not run. Disconnect the wiring to the fan motor and check the resistance of each winding with an ohmmeter. A reading of infinity between any two connec-

tions on the motor indicates an open winding. Consult the manufacturer's specifications for the correctness of any other reading.

Fan motor speed does not correspond with selector setting; compressor runs normally

The fan motor can run properly at some speed settings, but too fast, too slow, or not at all at other settings. The trouble in this case is either in the selector switch or the fan motor assembly.

1. Mode selector switch defective—disconnect the wiring between the mode selector switch and fan motor, and set the switch to its three speed ranges one at a time. Note the voltages between the output side of the selector switch and the circuit's return line:

LOW FAN	120 V	between **B** and **G**
	0 V	between **C** and **G**
	0 V	between **D** and **G**
MED FAN	0 V	between **B** and **G**
	120 V	between **C** and **G**
	0 V	between **D** and **G**
HIGH FAN	0 V	between **B** and **G**
	0 V	between **C** and **G**
	120 V	between **D** and **G**

    Any departure from this pattern of voltages indicates a defective mode selector switch. Replace the entire switch assembly.

2. Fan motor defective—the fan motor itself is most likely at fault if the switch voltages follow the pattern described in the previous test. Confirm the diagnosis by measuring the resistance of each of the windings and comparing the readings with the manufacturer's specifications. In any event, a reading of infinity indicates an open winding.

Compressor does not start, but fan runs normally

1. Compressor circuit breaker open—inspect the compressor's overload circuit breaker, making certain that it is properly set.

2. Low line voltage—heavy-duty compressor motors cannot start if the supply voltage is more than 10–15 percent below the

nameplate rating. Check the line voltage reaching the compressor circuit (between points **E** and **I**) while attempting to start the motor. The trouble is confirmed if the voltmeter shows less than about 108 V.

Make certain that the air conditioner is connected directly to a service outlet—there should be no extension cords in the line. If the home is an older one, the service wiring might have to be replaced.

3. Control thermostat TH1 stuck or broken open—set the air conditioner to operate in either the LOW or HIGH COOL mode, and measure the voltage across the control thermostat (between points **E** and **J**). If this test shows full line voltage whenever the thermostat control knob is set for the highest cooling level, the trouble is confirmed.

   It is possible to doublecheck this diagnosis before changing the thermostat control. Turn off the air conditioner and "cheat," the thermostat by connecting a jumper wire across it (between points **E** and **J**). The trouble is doubly confirmed if the compressor starts the moment the air conditioner is set to one of its COOL modes.

4. Mode selector switch assembly defective—set the air conditioner to one of its COOL modes, and check the voltage supplied to the compressor circuit (between points **E** and **G**). A reading of zero volts confirms this trouble. Replace the mode selector switch assembly.

5. Run or start capacitor shorted—remove power from the air conditioner, and disconnect the wiring to the capacitors. Discharge both capacitors by connecting a 2.2 kΩ resistor across their terminals for about fifteen seconds. Check the capacitors with an ohmmeter or capacitor tester. A low resistance or high leakage reading indicates a shorted capacitor. Replace the faulty capacitor with a new one having exactly the same specifications.

6. Start-up relay assembly defective—bypass the start-up relay by connecting a jumper wire across its contacts (between points **F** and **H**), and attempt to start the compressor by setting the mode selector switch to one of the COOL positions. The trouble is confirmed if the compressor now starts running. CAUTION: Do not allow the compressor to run more than a few moments with the jumper wire in place.

   Replace the start-up relay assembly.

7. Compressor motor defective—the logical process of elimination leads to the compressor unit itself. If the six previous tests do not indicate any other trouble, disconnect the wiring to the compressor, and check the winding resistances with an ohmmeter. Compare the results with the manufacturer's specifications.

Little or no cooling effect; fan and compressor run normally

See possible troubles and appropriate tests in Sec. 14-2.1.

Evaporator accumulates excessive frost

See possible troubles and appropriate tests in Sec. 14-2.1.

14-3 QUESTIONS

1. Describe the purpose of both motor units in a room air conditioner.
2. What is the difference between the FAN and COOL settings on the mode selector switch?
3. Why is it a poor practice to operate a room air conditioner whenever the outside temperature is below 70°F?
4. Why is it a poor practice to operate a room air conditioner through an extension cord?
5. What must be done if the outside temperature is 95°F and a room air conditioner cannot lower the inside temperature below 85°F?

Answers to Questions

ANSWERS TO QUESTIONS FOR CHAPTER 1

1. To test a lamp-type continuity tester: Touch together the ends of the test leads. If the lamp burns brightly, the tester is in good working order. Of course the lamp should not burn whenever the test leads are not touching each other.

2. The primary advantage of an ohmmeter continuity tester is that it is capable of measuring the exact resistance of circuits or load devices that have normal resistances somewhere between $0\,\Omega$ ohms and infinity. A simple continuity tester cannot distinguish a normal, moderately high resistance (a heating element, for instance) from an open-circuit fault.

3. A voltage tester is always connected in parallel with the circuit or device being tested.

4. A direct-reading ammeter must be connected directly into the circuit's path for current flow. A clamp-on meter, on the other hand, is merely clamped onto the wire carrying the current to be measured.

5. A VOM combines the functions of three separate test instruments: a voltmeter, an ohmmeter, and a milliammeter. This means that the serviceman can carry one test instrument in place of three.

ANSWERS TO QUESTIONS FOR CHAPTER 2

1. Because the 120 V power cannot be disconnected, the continuity of the coil must be checked with S1 open. Open S1, and connect a continuity tester (preferably an ohmmeter) between points **B** and **C**. The trouble is confirmed if the ohmmeter shows infinite resistance.

2. Under normal operating conditions, closing S1 applies full 120 V line voltage to the coil, and current flowing through the coil opens the hot water valve to let hot water rush into the appliance. If the coil is open, however, 120 V will appear across its terminals (between points **B** and **C**), but the water valve cannot open—water does not enter the appliance. A good test for continuity of the coil, then, is to connect a voltmeter across the coil connections (points **B** and **C**) and close S1. The trouble is confirmed if 120 V appears on the voltmeter, but the valve does not respond with a clicking sound or by allowing water to flow into the appliance.

3. The circuit in Fig. 2-8 has an on/off power switch S1 that controls the application of 120 V power to the rest of the circuit. Neon lamp L1 goes on whenever S1 is switched to ON. A second switch, S2, determines whether heater H1 or H2 is connected to the power source. A motor connected in parallel with H2 goes on whenever power is applied to H2.

    Closing S1 and setting S2 to LOW makes the lamp light and H1 heat up. Closing S1 and setting S2 to HIGH makes the lamp light and applies full line voltage to H2 and M. H2 gets hot and the motor runs. Turning off S1 completely shuts down the circuit, regardless of the setting of S2.

    The possible troubles and corresponding symptoms are as follows:

    > S1 open—the entire circuit seems "dead," regardless of the setting of the switches.
    >
    > S1 shorted—lamp L1 remains on, regardless of the settings of S1 and S2. The circuit is always ON.
    >
    > L1 open—the lamp never goes on, but the remainder of the circuit operates normally.
    >
    > L1 shorted—appliance blows a fuse or draws excessive current whenever S1 is switched to ON.

S2 open on the lamp side
(common connection)—the lamp goes on whenever S1 is set to its ON position, but the heaters and motor do not operate in any S2 position.

S2 open in the LOW branch—no heat in the LOW position, but H2 heats up, and the motor runs normally in the HIGH position.

S2 open in the HIGH branch—normal heat in the LOW position, but the motor does not run and the heater does not warm up in the HIGH position.

S2 shorted—both heaters and the motor operate whenever S1 is closed, regardless of the setting of S2.

H_1 open—no heat in the LOW setting, but normal heat and motor function in the HIGH setting. Further tests are required to distinguish this trouble from having S2 open in the LOW branch.

H1 shorted—appliance blows a fuse or draws excessive current whenever S2 is set to LOW. The HIGH position produces normal results.

H2 open—motor runs normally, but H2 does not get hot in the HIGH operating mode. The LOW mode is normal.

H2 shorted—appliance draws excessive current or blows a fuse whenever S1 is closed and S2 is set to its HIGH position. The LOW operating mode is normal.

Motor open—H2 gets hot, but the motor does not run in the HIGH mode. The LOW operating mode is normal.

Motor shorted—appliance blows a fuse or draws excessive current in the HIGH operating mode. H2 may or may not get warm, depending on the degree of motor shorting. The LOW operating mode is normal.

ANSWERS TO QUESTIONS FOR CHAPTER 3

1. Power equals voltage times current: $P = 120 \times 15 = 1800$ W.
2. Current equals power divided by voltage: $I = 1200 \div 120 = 10$ A.

3. (a) increase.

4. Total resistance equals ohms per foot times the number of feet: $R = 0.66 \times 10 = 6.6\ \Omega$.

5. Length required equals resistance desired divided by the ohms per foot: $L = 10 \div 0.5 = 20\ \text{ft}$.

6. (b) less than.

7. (a) equal to the sum of the individual power ratings.

8. (a) equal.

9. (a) greater than.

10. (a) equal to the sum of the individual power ratings.

11. (a) increase.

ANSWERS TO QUESTIONS FOR CHAPTER 4

1. A bimetal element responds to changes in temperature by bending in one direction when it is cooled and bending in the opposite direction when it is heated.

2. The distance of travel between the bimetal must be increased to increase the thermostat's trip-point temperature.

3. A warp heater control uses a small heating element that is connected in series with the appliance's main heating element. As the main heating element grows hot, so does the warp heater; and it is the warp heater that actually activates the bimetal thermostat assembly.

4. A Robertshaw control uses the expansion and contraction characteristics of fluids to operate a thermostat switch. A King Seeley control, on the other hand, uses a resistive heat sensor that changes resistance in response to temperature changes.

5. A differential thermostat is one that responds to a difference between two temperatures.

ANSWERS TO QUESTIONS FOR CHAPTER 5

1. Two north magnetic poles *repel* one another, whereas north and south magnetic poles *attract*.

2. A wire moving through a magnetic field (or a magnetic field moving around a wire) induces a current flow in that wire.

3. In a conventional induction motor, the field windings *remain stationary* while the armature windings *spin*.

4. The current drain of an induction motor is greater during start-up because the armature is not spinning fast enough to generate the required amount of back EMF in the field windings.

5. A split-phase motor uses a special start winding in the field assembly to offset the magnetic fields as required for motor start-up. A shaded-pole motor uses a single-turn shorting band (shading pole) wrapped around the field core assembly to accomplish the same offsetting effect.

6. The capacitor provides additional offset phase differences for higher starting torque

7. The centrifugal switch removes the start winding from the circuit once the motor reaches about 70 percent of its normal running speed.

8. A squirrel-cage induction motor does not have a wire-wound armature. Instead, it has a number of copper bars running lengthwise along the armature assembly.

ANSWERS TO QUESTIONS FOR CHAPTER 6

1. A Btu is the amount of heat energy that must be added or taken away from one pound of a substance to change its temperature 1°F.

2. Water, like any other liquid, cannot take on a temperature above its boiling point until all of the liquid is vaporized.

3. Increasing the vapor pressure surrounding a heated liquid raises its boiling point.

4. The natural direction of heat exchange is from the hotter to a colder body. The problem in a refrigeration system is to reverse this natural process.

5. The four basic stages or components of a mechanical refrigeration system are: (1) a compressor stage, (2) a condenser stage, (3) a reducer valve, and (4) an evaporator stage.

6. A saturated vapor is one that has a temperature above the boiling point of that substance.

ANSWERS TO QUESTIONS FOR CHAPTER 7

1. The three basic mechanical parts of a typical garbage disposer are: (a) a set of impellor blades, (b) a set of shredding blades, and (c) a motor assembly.

2. It is important to run cold water through a disposer that is in operation

in order to cool the motor assembly. Of course water is also necessary to rinse the ground-up waste material down the drain.

3. Jamming conditions caused by foreign objects are the most common causes of disposer troubles.

4. A disposer automatically applies added torque during a jamming condition because the run winding draws excessive current, which, in turn, pulls the start relay contact closed. Closing the start relay contact forces the motor to develop its peak starting power.

ANSWERS TO QUESTIONS FOR CHAPTER 8

1. The compactor drawer must be closed, the key switch must be turned on, and the START pushbutton has to be depressed before an automatic compacting cycle can begin. These actions close S1, S2, and S4 to complete the electrical circuit to the motor assembly.

2. The fact that the centrifugal switch S8 is open prevents the motor from reversing direction the moment the direction switch assembly is changed to the UP position.

3. The motor and ram drive assemblies are engineered to stall at the exact compacting pressure. When the motor stalls, it stops turning and the centrifugal switch closes to reapply power in the UP direction.

4. The START pushbutton must be held down to raise the ram until the unbalance condition clears because the START switch S4 provides the only path for current flow to the motor assembly.

ANSWERS TO QUESTIONS FOR CHAPTER 9

1. A single-cycle dishwasher has no provisions for altering the timing and sequence of operations. A multicycle dishwasher, on the other hand, can be programmed to carry out a variety of washing operations.

2. Fresh water is forced into a dishwasher by means of the home's normal water supply system.

3. A pump connected to the main drive motor is responsible for continuously recirculating the water during all wash and rinse operations.

4. Reversing the direction of the machine's water pump makes it force the used-up water out of the machine and into the home's sewerage system.

5. The run-ahead motor is responsible for advancing the timing cams so rapidly that sequence of operations is virtually eliminated.

6. The heater (1) keeps the recirculating water warm during wash and rinse operations, and (2) provides the heat for the drying operation.

7. A wetting agent breaks up beads of water on the dishes, allowing them to be dried without leaving "water spots."

ANSWERS TO QUESTIONS FOR CHAPTER 10

1. The four basic operations of any washing cycle are: fill, agitate, drain, and spin.

2. The drain and spin operations are combined into one operation in some machines.

3. A washer with a nontimed fill operation uses only enough water to fill the machine to a selected level. A machine using a timed fill operation, on the other hand, allows water to run for a certain period of time with no regard for the amount of laundry and available water pressure.

4. The water temperature is mainly determined by the temperatures of the hot and cold water available from the home's water supply system. A water temperature selector switch lets the user select a relative temperature level, but the actual temperature is determined by the water supplied.

5. A suds return system lets the user store water from a washing operation and reuse it during the next washing cycle.

6. The door interlock switch turns off the timer and main drive motors whenever the door is opened during a spin operation.

ANSWERS TO QUESTIONS FOR CHAPTER 11

1. The basic difference between gas and all-electric dryers is that the gas model uses gas flame heat as a source of heat energy, and the electric model uses electrically generated heat. Because a gas dryer has no need for an electrical heating circuit, incidentally, gas dryers are rated at 120 V instead of 240 V.

2. The term *speed control* can apply to a control that lets the user adjust the tumbling rate of the hamper; but in most instances it applies to a heat selector control that adjusts the drying speed by raising or lowering the machine's operating temperature.

3. A TIMED cycle operates with a controlled heat level applied and the hamper tumbling throughout the preset drying time. The AUTOMATIC cycle, on the other hand, runs with controlled heat applied and a tumbling

action only long enough to dry the laundry to a selected level. The AUTOMATIC drying interval is normally followed by a cool-down phase where the hamper tumbles without heat being applied.

4. The start-up latching circuit keeps the dryer operating after the user releases the START pushbutton.

5. The AUTOMATIC cycle usually operates without help from the timer motor circuit.

ANSWERS TO QUESTIONS FOR CHAPTER 12

1. A switched-heat selector is capable of operating at only three, five, or seven different heating levels, whereas an infinite heat selector can be set to operate at any heating level between full OFF and full heat.

2. An infinite heat selector system has no provisions for controlling the operating temperature of its surface unit, whereas a thermostatically controlled unit is specifically intended to control the operating temperature. The two systems are similar in that they both use a thermostat assembly—a switched-heat unit does not.

3. A surface unit that is controlled by a King Seeley system has only a pair of wires running from the sensor to the control circuit behind the user's control panel. A Robertshaw control, on the other hand, has a capillary tube running from the sensing bulb to the control unit.

4. A PREHEAT operation brings the oven temperature up to the selected level much more quickly than is possible in the normal BAKE operation.

5. The temperature range for oven self-cleaning is normally between 850°–1000°F.

6. An oven designed for self-cleaning operations has thicker heat insulation and a motor-operated door latch.

ANSWERS TO QUESTIONS FOR CHAPTER 13

1. The designations PC and FC stand for provisions cabinet and freezer cabinet, respectively. These designations are frequently used on schematic diagrams for domestic refrigerators.

2. The freezer compartments in refrigerators normally run at temperatures between 0°F and 20°F, while freezer chests can operate as low as −20°F.

3. A thermostat or timer motor can be used to end a defrosting cycle.

4. A defrosting cycle can be started by:
   a. A timer motor that closes a switch every twenty-four hours.
   b. A timer motor that runs whenever the compressor does, thus basing the defrost cycle on compressor running time.
   c. A timer motor that runs whenever the refrigerator door is open, thus basing the defrost cycle on the amount of room air that circulates through the refrigerator.
   d. A counter that keeps track of the number of times the door is opened.
   e. A scheme that starts the cycle whenever the compressor shuts off.

5. The mullion heater is a small electrical heating element that warms the mullion—the stationary space between refrigerator or freezer doors and the cabinet. The heater prevents a build-up of condensation on the outside surface.

6. A fan that runs whenever the doors are closed circulates the chilled inside air so that frost cannot build up on foods and packages in the cooling space. Such frost could not be removed by the defrost heating mechanism.

ANSWERS TO QUESTIONS FOR CHAPTER 14

1. The fan motor drives a pair of fans or blowers that (1) circulate inside air over the evaporator coil and (2) circulate outside air over the compressor and condenser coil. The compressor motor, of course, operates the compressor assembly.

2. In the FAN modes, power is applied only to the fan motor. In the COOL modes, however, power is applied to both the fan motor and the compressor.

3. The evaporator coil frosts up if the unit is operated when the outside temperature is below about 70°F. This frosting effect overheats the compressor, places a needless overload on the system, and causes an excessive accumulation of water when the frost melts.

4. Start-up current surges for a compressor motor often exceed 30 A for a second or two. An extension cord might not be able to deliver this kind of load, thus preventing the compressor from starting normally.

5. A normal room air conditioner unit cannot be expected to lower the inside temperature more than 10°F below the outside temperature. This limitation should be explained to the owner.

Index